Beginning Android Development: Create Your Own Android Apps Today

1st Edition

Contents

Introduction

Welcome! Congratulations to taking the first step to creating amazing Android applications!

The rapid rise of the Android OS offers app developers one of the largest platforms available, and this easy-to-follow book walks you through the development process step by step. This book explores everything from the simple basics to advanced aspects of Android application development.

In it, we teach you how to download the SDK, get Eclipse up and running, code Android applications, submit your app to the Google Play Store and share your finished Android apps with the world.

We walk you through all the steps in developing applications for the Android platform, including the latest Android features like scrollable widgets, enhanced UI tools and contact capabilities

Who this book is written for

This book is written for the beginning Android developer. You should ideally have some background in programming. If you are new to Java, you might want to pick up that language first. You can check out my Java programming book for beginners.

How this book is structured

In this book, we break down Android programming into smaller chunks which make individual chapters. Each chapter and its code examples are independent from those in earlier chapter so this gives you the flexibility to go directly to topics that you are interested in.

What tools do I need?

You will need a computer capable of running the Android Emulator. But having a real Android device would be useful.

Source Code

Just drop us an email at support@i-ducate.com and we will send all source code to you!

Contact

We look forward to hearing from you at support@i-ducate.com. Now wait no further and get started on your Android development learning journey!

Chapter 1: Hello Android Programming!

Welcome to the world of Android development! In this chapter, we will learn about what Android is, some of its background history of how Android has evolved and also see what the Android platform offers us from a development point of view. We will have a brief look at the Android architecture and how we can distribute Android applications to the end users through the Google Play Store. We will then setup our development environment so that we can start developing Android applications. Finally we will create our first Android application and will learn about the anatomy of an Android application. So let's get started!

What is Android?

If you are interested in developing applications for Android platform, you might already have some idea about what Android is. Android is an operating system based on a modified version of Linux, which powers devices of different hardware configurations. The most common class of Android powered devices are smart phones but they aren't limited to smart phones only. Broad ranges of other devices are powered by Android operating system as well, like – tabLet's, ebook readers, smart televisions and many other embedded devices run on the Android OS.

But Android is more than just an operating system. You can have a look at how Google's Andy Rubin description of Android -

> "The first truly open and comprehensive platform for mobile devices. It includes an operating system, user-interface and applications — all of the software to run a mobile phone but without the proprietary obstacles that have hindered mobile innovation."

In other words, Android is actually an ecosystem, made up of several components -

- A free and open source operating system for embedded devices, which is

based on the Linux kernel
- An open source software development platform for writing applications which runs on Android OS
- and devices that run the Android OS

Brief History and Motivation

Android was originally created by a startup, named **Android Inc**, which was later (in 2005) acquired by Google. In November 2007, a consortium called **Open Handset Alliance** (OHA) was formed with 34 companies to develop Android in an aim to deliver better mobile experience for consumers by driving innovation in mobile technology and reducing cost by removing license fees for both handset manufacturers and software developers. The OHA as per this point of writing has more than 80 members, including hardware manufacturers, software developers, mobile carriers, commercialization companies etc.

The Android framework is distributed under the Apache Software License (ASL/ Apache2) which enables the distribution of both open source and close source derivation of source code. This allows the device manufacturers to make improvements to the Android platform without having to provide these improvements back to the open source community. Thus vendors can make their own proprietary extension and differentiate their products from their competitors.

While device manufacturers can add their proprietary extensions, they at the same time follow a Compatibility Definition Document (CDD) and Compatibility Test Suite (CTS) which describes the capabilities required for a Android device to support the software stack. As a result, an application developed for an Android device will run on a wide variety of Android devices from different manufacturers and hardware configurations. Thus the Android platform offers a unified approach of application development. That's why the Android platform attracts large number of developers and the number of applications developed for android devices have been ever increasing.

Over one billion Android smart phones and tables are already in use, and more than 1.5 million Android devices are being activated daily. These statistics suggest that there are huge opportunities for Android application developers. As more and more Android devices are being activated, the app downloads have been growing at an exponential rate.

As an Android application developer, you get many benefits, some of them are -

- Unlike some other platforms, you don't need any certification to become a Android developer.
- Your application can reach millions of target audience via the Play Store application which is pre-installed on most Android devices.
- The application approval process for distribution over the Google Play Store is minimal unlike the Apple app store.

Android platform is made free and open by Google. With huge number of Android devices out there and distribution of application through Play Store, Android application developers have the opportunity to reach millions of users with their apps.

Android Versions

Since the release of the first commercial version of Android 1.0 on 23 September 2008, a number of versions were released over time. Each release corresponds to an API level number. The below table lists different versions with release date, API level and the code names associated with that release -

Android Version	API Level	Codename	Release Date
1.0	1	-	23 September, 2008
1.1	2	-	9 February, 2009
1.5	3	Cupcake	27 April, 2009
1.6	4	Donut	15 September, 2009
2.0	5	Eclair	26 October, 2009
2.0.1	6	Eclair	3 December, 2009
2.1	7	Eclair	12 January, 2010
2.2 – 2.2.3	8	Froyo	20 May, 2010
2.3 – 2.3.3	9	Gingerbread	6 December, 2010
2.3.3 – 2.3.7	10	Gingerbread	9 February, 2011
3.0	11	Honeycomb	22 February, 2011
3.1	12	Honeycomb	10 May, 2011
3.2	13	Honeycomb	15 July, 2011
4.0 – 4.02	14	Ice Cream Sandwich	19 October, 2011

4.03 – 4.04	15	Ice Cream Sandwich	16 December, 2011
4.1	16	Jelly Bean	9 July, 2012
4.2	17	Jelly Bean	13 November, 2012
4.3	18	Jelly Bean	24 July, 2013
4.4	19	Kit Kat	31 October, 2013

Table 1.1 : Android Versions

Android versions 3.x were tablet-only releases which included support for large screen devices. They were optimized for tabLet's and a few other improvements. Later those features were included in version 4.0 and there was again a unified OS for all platforms including smart phones, tabLet's and even large screen smart televisions. At the time of writing (March 2014) the latest version of Android is 4.4 (Kit Kat).

Features of Android

Android provides a rich set of features. As Android is open source and proprietary extensions are so often included by different manufacturers, you can't expect a fixed software or hardware configurations for all Android devices. However, the following list highlights some of the noteworthy features you can expect on most Android devices -

- **Cellular Network**: Supports GSM, EDGE, 3G, UMTS, 4G, LTE, CDMA, EVDO for telephony or data transfer, which enables you to make or receive calls or SMS/MMS messages and transfer data across mobile networks.
- **Media Support**: Wide ranges of media support are provided, which includes, but not limited to – H.263, H.264 (in 3GP or MP4 container), MPEG4, ACC, AMR, MP3, MIDI, Ogg Vorbis, WAV, JPEG, PNG, GIF , BMP etc.
- **P2P Connectivity**: Supports pear-to-pear connection via Wi-Fi, Bluetooth, NFC.
- **Hardware Support**: Camera, GPS, Compass, Accelerometer Sensor, Proximity Sensor etc.
- **Web Browsing**: Support for integrated open-source HTML5 WebKit-based browser.
- **Storage**: Supports SQLite for data storage, which is a lightweight, server-less relational database.

- **Multi-tasking**: Provides support for multi-tasking applications.
- **Multi-touch Screens**: Supports multi-touch screens.

Architecture of Android

The components of the Android platform are laid in four layers as shown in figure 1.1. Those components can be divided into five sections. Let's briefly talk about them -

- **Linux Kernel**: The Linux kernel is at the bottom of the four layer architecture stack. Android is based on a modified version of the Linux kernel, which is optimized for embedded devices and hand held systems. This layer contains the device driver for various hardware components that are shipped with Android devices. Other core services like process and memory management, security, network and power management etc are handled by the Linux kernel as well.

- **Libraries**: Various C/C++ core libraries are included in the Android software stack, which runs on top of the kernel layer. These includes -
  - Surface Manager to provide display management
  - OpenGL for 2D and 3D graphics
  - SSL and Webkit for integrated web browser and Internet security
  - SQLite for providing database support
  - Media Library for audio and video playback etc.

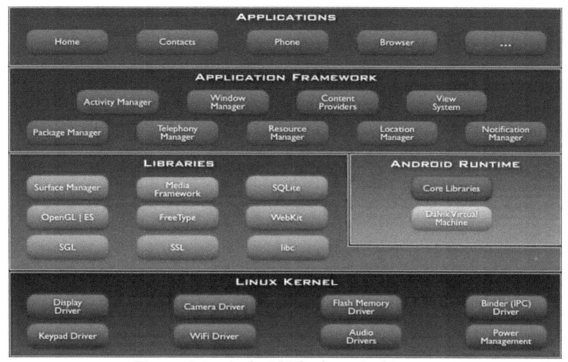
Figure 1.1 : Android Platform Architecture

- **Android Runtime**: The Android runtime belongs to the same layer as the Libraries. It includes Core Libraries and the Dalvik Virtual Machine. The Android run time is the engine which powers the applications running on Android devices and along with the libraries it form the basis for Application Framework.

  - **Core Libraries**: The Android core libraries provide you most of the functionality of core Java libraries. In addition to those Java libraries, it also includes Android specific libraries as well.

  - **Dalvik VM**: The Dalvik VM is the Android's version of the Java Virtual Machine (VM) optimized for embedded devices. A device can run multiple instances of this Dalvik VM efficiently. Threading and low level memory management are handled by the Linux Kernel.

- **Application Framework**: All the classes you use to create Android applications are provided by this Application Framework. As a application developer, you use this layer as an abstraction to access hardware and other resources.
- **Application Layer**: Application layer contains all the applications shipped with Android devices and the applications developed by third party developers. This application layer runs within the Android runtime.

13

Android Devices in the Market

A wide variety of devices are powered by the Android Platform, including -

- Smart Phones
- TabLet's
- Netbooks
- Internet Televisions
- Media Players
- E-Book Readers
- Smart Watches
- Smart Refrigerators
- and many other devices

We have previously seen that different versions of Android are available. When a new Android version is released, not all the existing Android devices are upgraded to the latest version. That's why it is important for us developers to know which Android versions are currently in use and their market share. Table 1.2 shows different Android versions in use (as of March 3, 2014) -

Version	Codename	API	Distribution
2.2	Froyo	8	1.2%
2.3.3 - 2.3.7	Gingerbread	10	19.0%
3.2	Honeycomb	13	0.1%
4.0.3 - 4.0.4	Ice Cream Sandwich	15	15.2%
4.1.x	Jelly Bean	16	35.3%
4.2.x		17	17.1%
4.3		18	9.6%
4.4	KitKat	19	2.5%

Table 1.2: Different Android Versions in Use

The Google Play Store

In order to make the third party applications accessible to users, Android devices

14

come with a pre-installed application named the "Google Play Store" (formerly known as Android Market). This enables third party application developers to develop their Android application and deliver them through the Play Store. In order to publish applications through the Play Store, you simply need to create a developer account with a one time fee of just $25.

The Play Store allows developers to publish their apps as either free or paid. Developers can also integrate in-app purchases and other features provided by the Play Store in order to monetize their apps.

Further details of app publishing to the Play Store and other distribution channels will be discussed in detail later in Chapter 12.

Getting Help From the Developer Community

In this section, I will refer to some of the resources that you can consult whenever you need help regarding issues with Android development. There are many developer communities around to help you, a few of them are -

- **Stack Overflow** (http://www.stackoverflow.com/) – As a programmer, you might be already familiar with this excellent resource. If you aren't familiar with stack overflow yet, it is a great question and answer resource website, which is collaboratively edited by developers. You will find this site useful for not only Android development, but also for other programming languages. The Android questions can be accessed at http://stackoverflow.com/questions/tagged/android

- **Android Developer Site** (http://developer.android.com/) - This website has a section which contains training lessons for beginner developers. It also has other useful resources, like design guidelines, API documentation, references, tools, information about publishing etc.

- **Android Developers Blog** (http://android-developers.blogspot.com/) - The official Android developers blog. It contains updates about new features, information about future releases and other useful information.

- **Android Discuss Group** (http://groups.google.com/group/android-discuss) - The Google group which has discussions related to Android programming. The core Android developers often monitor this group.

Obtaining The Required Tools

You can develop Android applications on either Windows, Linux or Mac OS X. In order to setup your development environment for Android application development, you will need the following software -

* Java Development Kit (JDK) version 6 or 7
* Android SDK/ADT Bundle

Installing Java Development Kit (JDK)

Android requires Java Development Kit (JDK) version 6 or 7. To download the JDK specific to your operating system, visit -

http://www.oracle.com/technetwork/java/javase/downloads/index.html

You will find both 32-bit and 64-bit version of JDK. choose the version based on your computer hardware configuration and operating system. Installation of JDK should be quite straight forward for you, however you can consult the official installation instructions available at -

http://docs.oracle.com/javase/7/docs/webnotes/install/index.html

Installing the Android SDK/ADT Bundle

The Android SDK/ADT bundle comes with a version of Eclipse IDE which is pre-configured with the latest Android Software Development Kit (SDK) and the Android Development Tools (ADT) plugin. The ADT bundle greatly simplifies the process of setting up the development environment for Android development. You can download the ADT bundle for your operating system at -

http://developer.android.com/sdk/index.html

After you download the ADT bundle, extract the ZIP archive to your system. You will find two subfolders inside the extracted folder -

* 'eclipse' folder – this contains a version of Eclipse IDE
* 'sdk' folder – contains the Android SDK

If we have properly setup JDK for your OS and extracted the ADT bundle, then we have the necessary softwares to start developing Android applications. But how do we test our Android applications? We have two ways to run and test our Android applications -

- Testing them on real Android Phones or
- Using an Emulator to create an Android Virtual Device (AVD) and test our apps on it

We will first see how to create an AVD. Next, if you have an Android device, we will see what are the steps necessary to test our Android apps on it.

Creating an Android Virtual Device (AVD)

The Android Emulator which is included in the Android SDK allows you to test your Android applications on your computer rather than just on actual Android devices. Using the Emulator, you can create Android Virtual Devices (AVDs) which lets you emulate actual Android devices by specifying it's hardware and software configurations. You can specify different characteristics of emulated devices, like screen size, pixel density, SD card size, RAM, Android OS version etc. The AVD Manager let's you create and manage different virtual devices for you. We access the AVD Manager from within Eclipse. Follow the steps below to start Eclipse and access the AVD Manager -

- The 'eclipse' subfolder which was created by extracting the ADT bundle contains the Eclipse executable. Run Eclipse and you will see a prompt to specify your workspace (Figure 1.2). The workspace is a directory which will store all the projects files you create. Specify your desired directory or alternatively you can accept the suggested location.

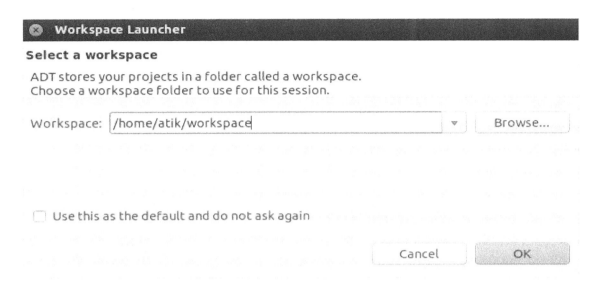

Figure 1.2: Workspace select prompt

- Once you select the workspace, you will see the default welcome screen of Eclipse (Figure 1.3). This screen will show some welcome information and links to tutorials, as well as a button to create a new application. For now, close this welcome screen.

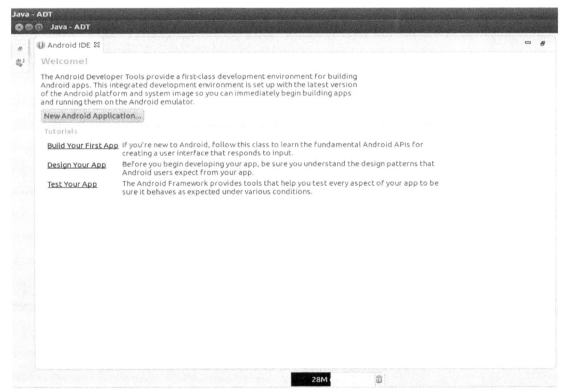

Figure 1.3: Eclipse welcome screen

- After you close the Eclipse welcome screen, you will see a screen with a number of empty windows (in Eclipse, they are called views). You will also see a tool bar which has a number of icons at the top of the Eclipse screen,. One of them looks like a small phone (marked with red circle, figure 1.4). Clicking that icon will open the AVD Manager (figure 1.5). Alternatively, you can access AVD Manager from - *Window → Android Virtual Device Manager*

Figure 1.4: AVD Manager tool bar icon

Figure 1.5: AVD Manager

- We create a new AVD by clicking the "New..." option which lets us choose the configurations of our emulated device (figure 1.6).

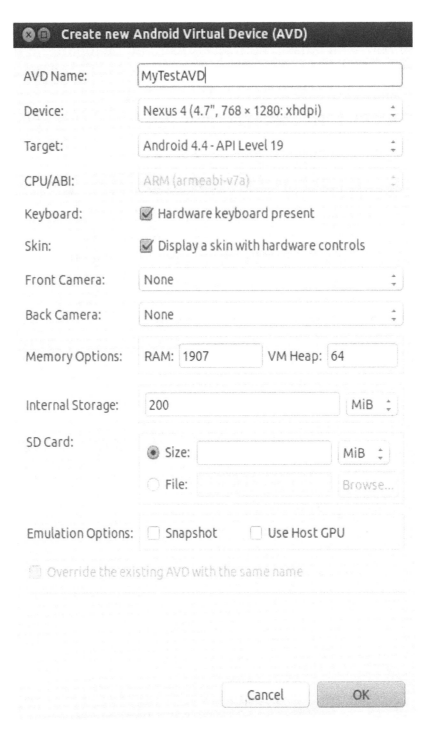

Figure 1.6: Create New AVD options

- Instead of using "New..." option to create AVD, we will create a AVD of a preconfigured device. A list of preconfigured devices can be found by accessing the device definition tab (figure 1.7).

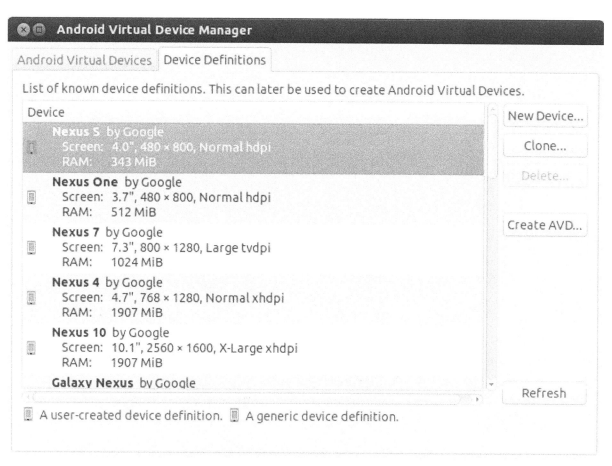

Figure 1.7: A list of known device definitions

- From the Device Definitions tab, you can create a AVD by selecting a device name and then choose the "Create AVD..." option. For now, let's create a AVD for the Nexus S by Google (figure 1.8). Accept all the default values and provide a SD card size of 100 MiB.

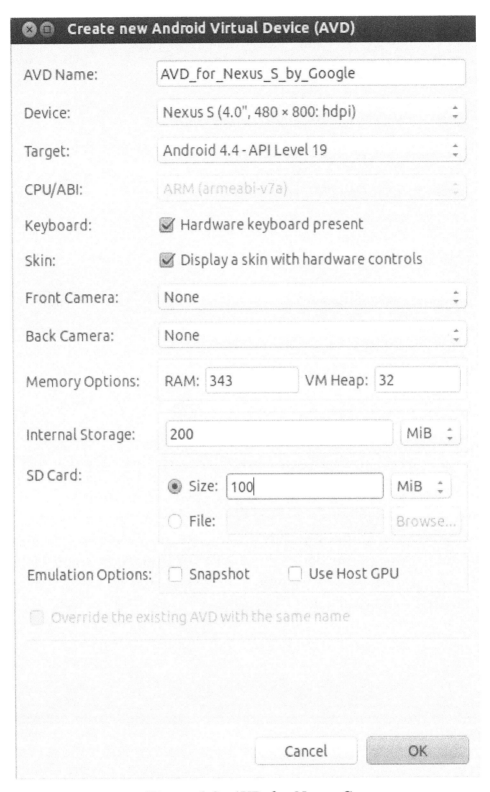

Figure 1.8: AVD for Nexus S

With this, you would have created your first AVD successfully. It is recommended to create a few AVDs corresponding to different API levels and hardware configurations. This way you can test your application on different versions of Android OS.

Now let's start running the AVD. From the AVD Manager, select the AVD and click "Start..." button (figure 1.9). This will open a new window to launch your AVD.

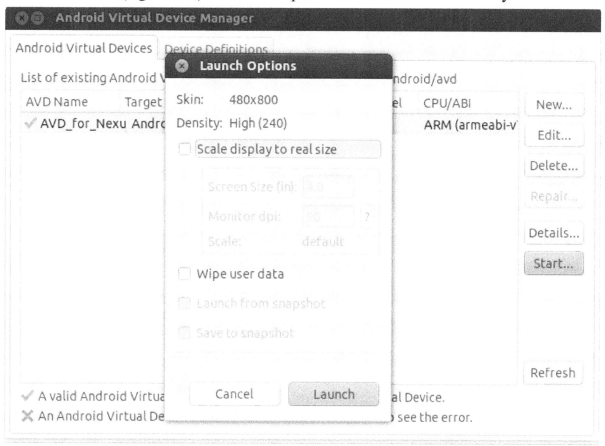

Figure 1.9: Launch AVD

If you have a small monitor, then you can check the "Scale display to real size" option and provide the screen size yourself. Now click the "Launch" option to start the AVD. It will start the AVD (figure 1.10).

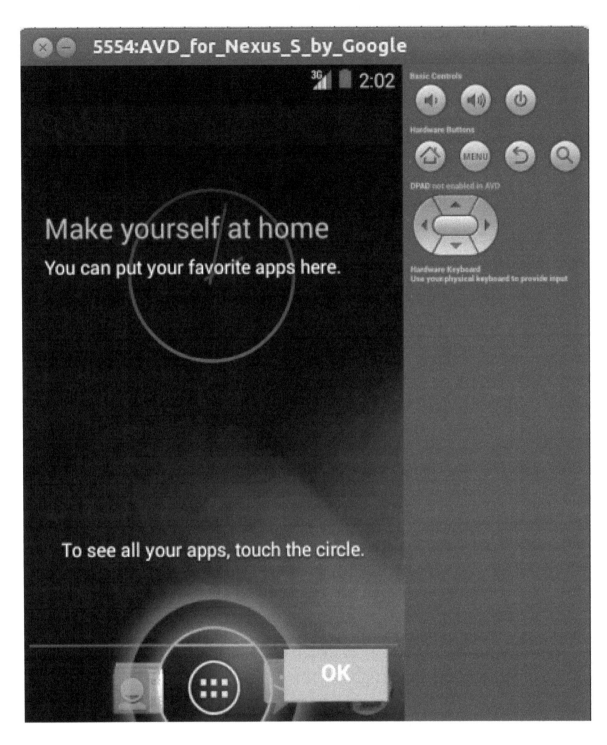

Figure 1.10: Running AVD

It can take a while to launch an emulator, so it is recommended that you don't close an emulator very often. The usual practice is to launch an emulator at the start of your development and keep it open till you are done for that session.

Setting Up Android Devices for Testing

AVDs can be very convenient if you don't have an Android device, but it can be a bit slow to test apps on a AVD. So if you have an Android device, you should use that for your development purpose. To test your apps on actual devices, follow these instructions at http://developer.android.com/tools/device.html

If you are developing on the Windows platform, you will need the USB driver for Android devices and in some cases, device specific drivers will be needed as well. For a list of available USB driver sites, you can check this link -

http://developer.android.com/tools/extras/oem-usb.html

Creating Your First Android Application

Now that we have setup our development environment, we will create our first Android application. This will be a simple "Hello World" application, but the goal is to give you an idea about the steps required in order to create an Android application using the ADT bundle. The later section will show you the project structure and various components of an Android application. Follow the steps below -

1. First, run the eclipse IDE and then create a new "Android Application Project" by selecting File → New → Android Application Project (figure 1.11).

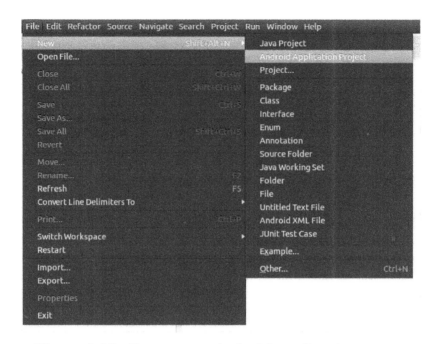

Figure 1.11: Create new Android application project

2. This will open the new application creation wizard (figure 1.12) -

Figure 1.12: Create new application wizard

3. Fill this wizard with the following information -

- **Application Name**: Name of the application which will appear in application launch menu and other places. Let's name our application as "Hello World".

- **Project Name**: Project name is the name of the eclipse project. Once you provide the value of the application name, the project name field is auto filled with the same name of the application (by removing the space characters). So this field should have the value of "HelloWorld".

- **Package Name**: This is the Java package name for your application's source code. Android and the Google Play store uses package name as the application's unique identifier. To make your package name unique, the general practice is to use the reverse domain name of your organization as the prefix of package name. For example, our domain name is iducate.com and we will use 'com.iducate' as the prefix for our application's package name. So we choose the full package name as "com.iducate.helloworld".

- **Minimum Required SDK**: The minimum Android API level required to run your application. Android devices running version below this API level will not be able to run your application. Set the minimum required SDK as API level 8.

- **Target SDK**: This is the preferred API level which our application is targeting. We should generally target the latest API level. So let's choose target SDK as API level 19 (which is the latest at the time of writing this book).

- **Compile With**: The API level used while compiling the application. Typically, we choose latest the API level to compile our apps. Choose the latest API level for this field as well.

- **Theme**: The application's default theme. Keep the default value.

After filling the wizard, it should look like figure 1.13. Click the "Next" button to move to the next step.

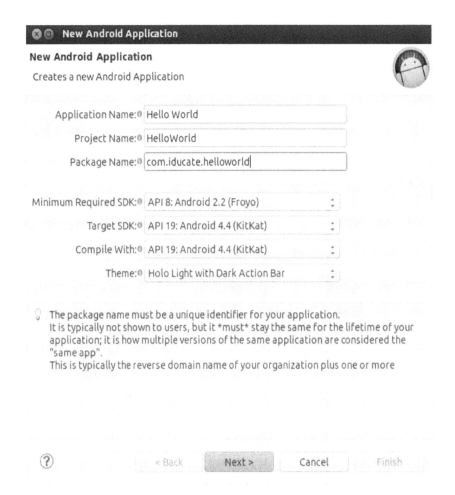

Figure 1.13: Filled wizard for Hello World application

4. The next screen will show you the project configuration options (figure 1.14) -

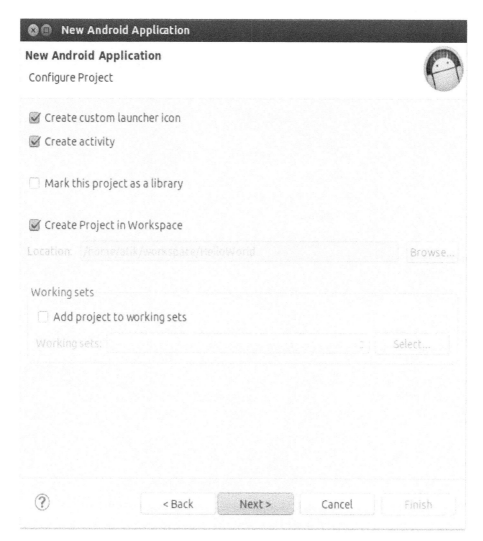

Figure 1.14: Configure Project

This screen's options will affect your subsequent steps where you will be able to choose the custom launcher icon and configure Activity for your application. Just use the default settings and click the "Next" button.

5. In the next screen, you will have the option to configure the launcher icon for your application (figure 1.15). The launcher icon will be shown on your device's home screen. Since there are Android devices of varying screen sizes and densities, you will most likely want to provide different versions of launcher icons. We will learn how to do that in a later chapter. For now, use the default settings and click the "Next" button.

Figure 1.15: Configure launcher icon

6. The next step will let you select the template for your application's Activity (figure 1.16). Templates provide you a starting point for your Activity. We will discuss about Activities in detail in a later chapter. For now, select 'blank Activity' and click "Next". The next step will let you choose the name of the Activity and a layout associated with that activity (figure 1.17). Use the default options and click the "Finish" button.

Figure 1.16: Create Activity

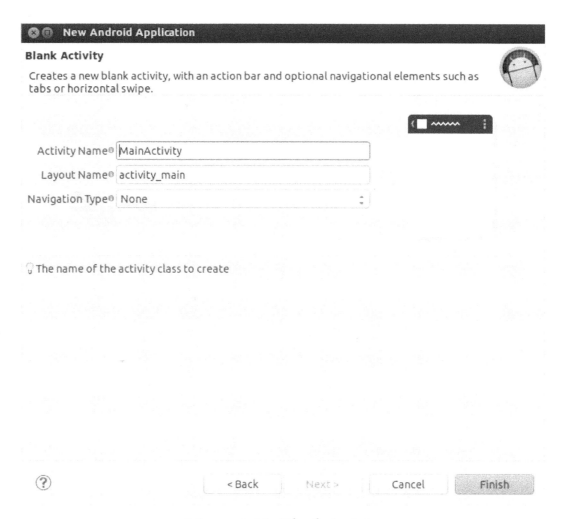

Figure 1.17: Blank Activity

With these steps, you will create a new Android application project. Once the project is created, the Eclipse IDE should look like figure 1.18.

Figure 1.18: Eclipse IDE after creating the project

7. Now open the activity_main.xml file under the res/layout directory and replace that file's code with following code -

```
<LinearLayout xmlns:android="http://schemas.android.com/apk/res/android"
   xmlns:tools="http://schemas.android.com/tools"
   android:id="@+id/LinearLayout1"
   android:layout_width="match_parent"
   android:layout_height="match_parent"
   android:orientation="vertical" >

   <Button
      android:id="@+id/btnHello"
      android:layout_width="wrap_content"
      android:layout_height="wrap_content"
      android:layout_gravity="center"
      android:onClick="sayHello"
      android:text="Say Hello" />

</LinearLayout>
```

8. Update the MainActivity.java file (which is located in the 'src' directory and under the package name) with following code -

33

```java
package com.iducate.helloworld;

import android.os.Bundle;
import android.view.View;
import android.widget.TextView;
import android.app.Activity;
import android.app.Dialog;

public class MainActivity extends Activity {

    @Override
    protected void onCreate(Bundle savedInstanceState) {
        super.onCreate(savedInstanceState);
        setContentView(R.layout.activity_main);
    }

    public void sayHello(View view) {

        Dialog dialog = new Dialog(this);

        dialog.setTitle("Greetings");

        TextView textView = new TextView(this);
        textView.setText("Hello World");
        textView.setPadding(20, 20, 20, 20);

        dialog.setContentView(textView);

        dialog.show();
    }

}
```

Running The HelloWorld Project

Now we will run our HelloWorld project. From your Project Explorer view, right click on the project name, from the context menu, select Run As → Android Application (figure 1.19).

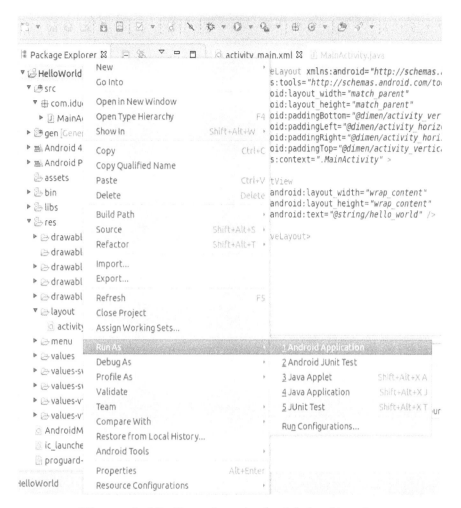

Figure 1.19: Running Android Application

Now if you are running a AVD (or real device attached), you will see the HelloWorld application running. It has a single button labeled "Say Hello". Click that button and you will see the "Hello World" message as a dialog window (figure 1.20).

Figure 1.20: Running HelloWorld Application

If you have a single AVD (or real device) running which is compatible with the target platform of the application, then Eclipse will run the application in that AVD. In the case where none of the AVD is running, Eclipse will check against the list of created AVDs and will launch the first one which is compatible with the target platform. However, if you have multiple compatible AVD (or real device) running, then Eclipse will let you pick one by prompting you a dialog (figure 1.21).

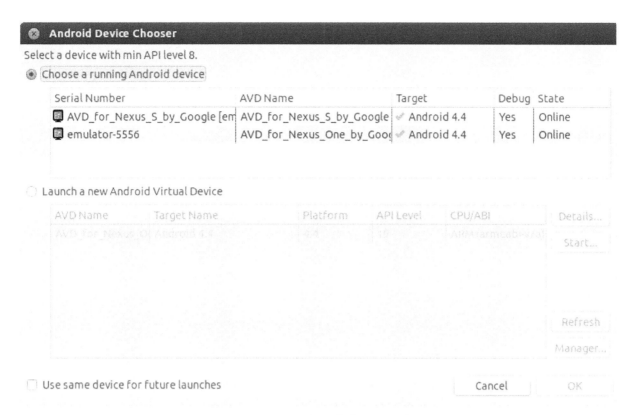

Figure 1.21: Android device chooser

How does it work?

A screen of Android application corresponds to an Activity. Remember step 6 of in the application creation process? We had specified to create a new blank Activity (figure 1.16) and then we were prompted to provide a name for that Activity and layout file (figure 1.17) which we left as default name "MainActivity" and layout as "activity_main". As a result, the new Activity class named "MainActivity.java" was created under the 'src/' directory of our project structure (figure 1.22) and under the 'res/layout/' directory, a layout file named "activity_main.xml" was created (figure 1.23).

Figure 1.22: MainActivity.java file

Figure 1.23: activity_main.xml file

The layout file 'activity_main.xml' contains a single element, a button with the text label "Say Hello".

```
<Button
    android:id="@+id/btnHello"
    android:layout_width="wrap_content"
    android:layout_height="wrap_content"
    android:layout_gravity="center"
    android:onClick="sayHello"
    android:text="Say Hello" />
```

You will see along with other properties, it has a property "android:onClick" with the value "sayHello". This indicates that, the button click will be handled by a method named "sayHello()" of MainActivity.java class.

```
public void sayHello(View view) {

    Dialog dialog = new Dialog(this);

    dialog.setTitle("Greetings");

    TextView textView = new TextView(this);
    textView.setText("Hello World");
    textView.setPadding(20, 20, 20, 20);

    dialog.setContentView(textView);

    dialog.show();
}
```

The sayHello() method creates a dialog window with a TextView element and then calls the show() method of dialog object to show the dialog window.

A Brief Tour of Eclipse Views

We now go through the several panels in the Eclipse window.

Project Explorer View

All of your projects in the current workspace will be shown under the 'Project Explorer 'View. Currently, the project explorer view is showing the HelloWorld project we have created earlier. You can see that the root directory of our HelloWorld project is "HelloWorld", under which there are many other files and directories which have been created automatically for us as part of the Eclipse's

"New Android Application Project" creation process. We will discuss more about the project structure later.

Editor View

The Editor View is shown right to the Project Explorer View. It allows us to edit code files.

Outline View

The Outline View, which is at the right side of figure 1.18, shows a tree structure of different elements of currently opened files within the Editor View.

Other Views

In figure 1.18, below the Editor View, you will see some other views like - "Problems", "Javadoc", "Declaration" etc. You will get useful debug information, documentation etc in these windows. There are many other views available within Eclipse, you can remove any existing view or add other views as you wish. You can access the views from Window → Show View option and then selecting the desired view. One particularly useful view is Logcat View. Add the Logcat View by Window → Show View → Other → Android → Logcat . The Logcat view will appear at the bottom section, grouped with existing views.

Anatomy of an Android Application

We have created our first Hello World application and have talked briefly about how it is showing the message "Hello World" as a dialog window. In this section, we will go a bit deeper and look inside some of the files. But first we will see the file structure of the HelloWorld project (figure 1.24).

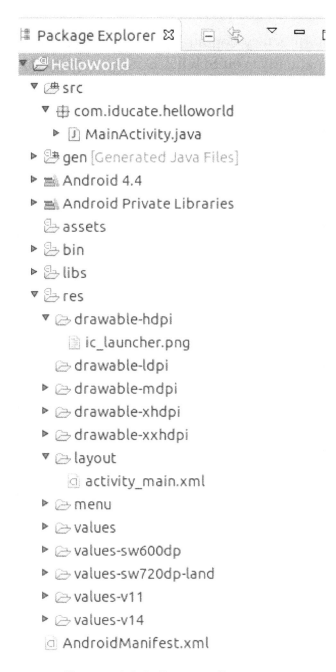

Figure 1.24: Project Structure

Let's briefly discuss the various files and folder that are created with our HelloWorld project -

- **src** : This folder contains Java source files for our project. The Java files are organized under the package name. We have a single Java file named "MainActivity.java", which is under the package 'com.iducate.helloworld'. You will put all your Java source files under this directory.

- **gen** : The 'gen' directory contains the R.java file, which is generated by the compiler automatically. You SHOULD NOT modify this R.java file.

- **Android 4.4** : This directory contains the android.jar file, which contains all the Android class libraries.

- **assets** : This directory will typically contain asset files, like database, text files etc.

- **bin** : This directory will contain the files produced by the ADT tool during the build process. Along with some other files, you will find the '.apk' file for your application which is the application binary of the Android application.

- **libs** : The 'libs' directory will typically contain third party jar libraries which will be used for your Android applications.

- **res** : The res directory contains resources of your Android application. It includes different sub-directories for different types of resources, like -

  - **drawable directories** – You will find drawable sub-directories which contain images and other XML drawable resources. To provide images of different pixel densities for devices of various screen sizes, you will need to put the images in corresponding sub-directories i.e. 'ldpi' for low pixel density devices, 'mdpi' for medium density devices etc). We will talk about this later in detail. Initially you will find the drawable folders having the application launcher icon, ic_launcher.png.

  - **layout** – The layout directory contains XML layout files used by Activities (and fragments).

  - **menu** – This directory contains XML files which define menu items.

  - **values** – This directory contains XML files for string resources, dimensions, styles etc.

- **AndroidManifest.xml** – This is the manifest file for your Android application, which contains information about your application components, permissions required, version information and other things.

Next, we will see contents of some of the important files of our HelloWorld project. Let's start with the Activity file, "MainActivity.java" -

```java
package com.iducate.helloworld;

import android.os.Bundle;
import android.view.View;
import android.widget.TextView;
import android.app.Activity;
import android.app.Dialog;

public class MainActivity extends Activity {

    @Override
    protected void onCreate(Bundle savedInstanceState) {
        super.onCreate(savedInstanceState);
        setContentView(R.layout.activity_main);
    }

    public void sayHello(View view) {

        Dialog dialog = new Dialog(this);

        dialog.setTitle("Greetings");

        TextView textView = new TextView(this);
        textView.setText("Hello World");
        textView.setPadding(20, 20, 20, 20);

        dialog.setContentView(textView);

        dialog.show();
    }

}
```

Figure 1.25: MainActivity.java file

We can see that MainActivity class is a subclass of Activity class. We will talk more about Activities in chapter 2. For now, take a look at the below line -

```java
setContentView(R.layout.activity_main);
```

We have called a method setContentView(), which sets the layout file "activity_main.xml" referenced by 'R.layout.activity_main'. The layout file is a resource. The R.java file has reference to all the resources of our project. For each resource type, R.java file has an inner class and for each resource of that type, the R.java file will have a static field which represents that resource id. From within our Java source file, we simply reference a resource using those ids. That's why we have referenced the activity_main.xml layout resource as R.layout.activity_main.

Next let's see the code of activity_main.xml file under the 'res/layout' directory.

```
<LinearLayout xmlns:android="http://schemas.android.com/apk/res/android"
    xmlns:tools="http://schemas.android.com/tools"
    android:id="@+id/LinearLayout1"
    android:layout_width="match_parent"
    android:layout_height="match_parent"
    android:orientation="vertical" >

  <Button
      android:id="@+id/btnHello"
      android:layout_width="wrap_content"
      android:layout_height="wrap_content"
      android:layout_gravity="center"
      android:onClick="sayHello"
      android:text="Say Hello" />

</LinearLayout>
```

We will not go into the details of this file right now. Instead, let's have a look at the contents of one last file, AndroidManifest.xml -

```
1  <?xml version="1.0" encoding="utf-8"?>
2  <manifest xmlns:android="http://schemas.android.com/apk/res/android"
3      package="com.iducate.helloworld"
4      android:versionCode="1"
5      android:versionName="1.0" >
6
7      <uses-sdk
8          android:minSdkVersion="8"
9          android:targetSdkVersion="19" />
10
11     <application
12         android:allowBackup="true"
13         android:icon="@drawable/ic_launcher"
14         android:label="@string/app_name"
15         android:theme="@style/AppTheme" >
16         <activity
17             android:name="com.iducate.helloworld.MainActivity"
18             android:label="@string/app_name" >
19             <intent-filter>
20                 <action android:name="android.intent.action.MAIN" />
21
22                 <category android:name="android.intent.category.LAUNCHER" />
23             </intent-filter>
24         </activity>
25     </application>
26
27 </manifest>
```

The AndroidManifest.xml file contains important information about the application -

- **Application Package** : Defines the application's default package name. (Line 3)

- **Version Code** : The version code is an integer value which represents your application's version number. With each new update release of your application, the version number must increase from the previous version number. This version code is used by Play Store to determine if the application is updated. (Line 4)

- **Version Name** : Version name is displayed to the user. You can follow whether version naming convention you like (for example 1.0.1 to represent a minor release). (Line 5)

- **SDK information** : Specifies the minimum required SDK and target SDK. (Lines 7-9)

- **App Icon, Label and Theme** : Specifies the icon, label and theme of the

45

application. (Lines 12-14)

- **Activity** : Each Activity (and other components) of the application must be specified within the manifest file. We have a single Activity named "MainActivity" and we have an <activity> tag to represent that Activity. (Lines 16-24)

  - **Activity Name** : Name of the Activity. If the Activity is within the application's default package, we use the class name only without specifying the package name prefix. (Line 17)

  - **Activity Label** : Label of the Activity. (Line 18)

  - **<intent-filter>** : We specify that this Activity is the main activity of the application which serves as a entry point of the application. This will appear in the launcher area. (Lines 19-23)

Summary

This chapter starts with an overview of developing an app using the Android platform. We have gone through setting up of our development environment with the Android Development Tools Bundle. Next, we have created a Hello World Android application and finally we discussed about the anatomy of an Android application.

By now you should have at least some sort of idea about what Android is and feel comfortable using Eclipse's new application creation wizard to create a very simple Android application. In later chapters, we will start learning about fundamental concepts of Android platform starting with Activities and Intents which will be covered in the next chapter.

Chapter 2: Activities, Fragments and Intents

In this chapter, you will learn about one of the fundamental building blocks of Android – the activity. We will discuss about details of activities and understand their life cycles. Next, we will discuss about Intents which enables different components of applications to talk to each other. Intents enables different applications to work together seamlessly. We will also learn about fragments which can be thought of as miniature activities that can be grouped together to form an activity.

Understanding Activities

Activities represent the user interface of your Android applications. Though it is entirely possible to have an application without a single activity, if you want users to interact with your application, your application will most likely have one or more activities.

An activity is represented by a Java class which extends the Activity base class. Let's have a look at a simple activity class -

```java
package com.iducate.helloworld;

import android.os.Bundle;
import android.widget.TextView;
import android.app.Activity;
import android.app.Dialog;

public class MainActivity extends Activity {

    @Override
    protected void onCreate(Bundle savedInstanceState) {
        super.onCreate(savedInstanceState);
        setContentView(R.layout.activity_main);
    }
```

}

Here we see an activity named "MainActivity" which extends the base Activity class. Our "MainActivity" class starts with a package declaration and next follows some import statements. The above example activity class has a single method, "onCreate()" which is an overwritten method of the base Activity class. Within that method, we first call the superclass's onCreate() method and then set the layout resource to be used for that activity.

The setContentView() method is defined within the Activity base class and we can call this method from our activity classes to load the layout file -

```
setContentView(R.layout.activity_main);
```

This will load the layout file named "activity_main.xml" which is located under the res/layout directory.

Each activity of your Android application should be declared in the AndroidManifest.xml file -

```xml
<?xml version="1.0" encoding="utf-8"?>
<manifest xmlns:android="http://schemas.android.com/apk/res/android"
    package="com.iducate.helloworld"
    android:versionCode="1"
    android:versionName="1.0" >

    <uses-sdk
        android:minSdkVersion="8"
        android:targetSdkVersion="19" />

    <application
        android:allowBackup="true"
        android:icon="@drawable/ic_launcher"
        android:label="@string/app_name"
        android:theme="@style/AppTheme" >
        <activity
            android:name="com.iducate.helloworld.MainActivity"
            android:label="@string/app_name" >
            <intent-filter>
                <action android:name="android.intent.action.MAIN" />
```

```
        <category
android:name="android.intent.category.LAUNCHER" />
        </intent-filter>
    </activity>
  </application>

</manifest>
```

In the highlighted lines, we define an <activity> node under the <application> node. For each of your activity, you should define a separate <activity> node with that activity's information.

Activity Life Cycle Methods

At any point in time, an activity is in one of four possible states -

- **Active**: The activity is running in the foreground and users can interact with it.
- **Paused**: The activity is running but another activity is overlaying part of the screen. In this case, the current activity might be partially visible. Because the first activity is in a paused state, users can't interact with that activity. This is not a very common situation because most of the activities are set to fill the screen.
- **Stopped**: The activity is running but hidden by some other activity.
- **Dead**: The activity is destroyed either by pressing the Back button or destroyed by the system.

The Activity base class defines a series of methods which are called as the activity transits between the above mentioned states. These methods are known as activity life cycle methods -

- onCreate() - this method is called when the activity is first created
- onStart() - called when the activity becomes visible to the user
- onResume() - called when the activity starts interacting with the user
- onPause() - called when the current activity is being paused. This happens when some other activity starts overlaying the current activity
- onStop() - called when the activity is no longer visible
- onDestroy() - called before the activity is destroyed either by pressing the Back button or by the system to conserve memory

- onRestart() - called when a previously stopped activity restarts and comes to the foreground again

When implementing the above methods in your own activity, you should chain upward and invoke the parent class's edition of the method.

Figure 2.1 illustrates the life cycle of an activity and the various stages it goes through. (Image courtesy - http://developer.android.com/reference/android/app/Activity.html).

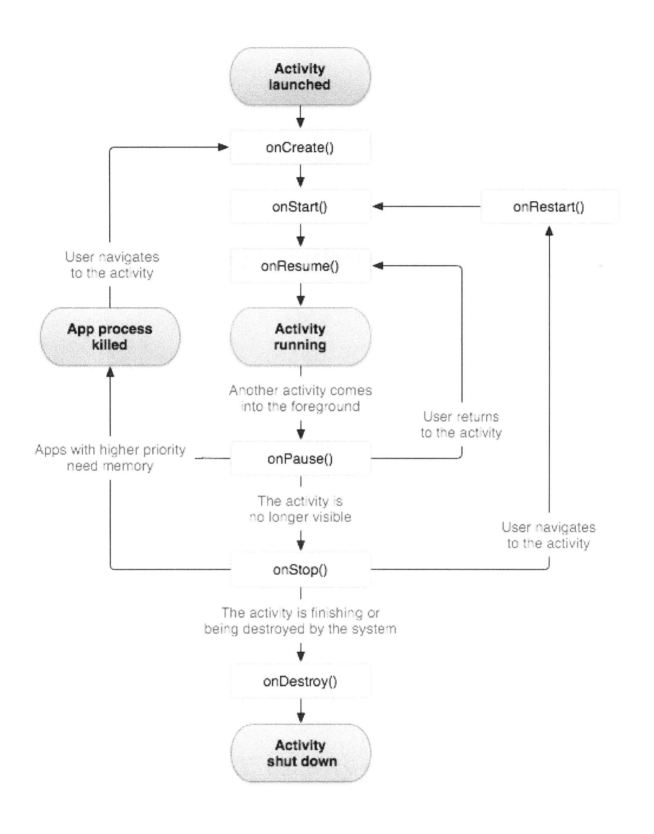

Figure 2.1: Activity life cycle

In order to better understand the life cycle methods of an activity, we will create a new project and implement these life cycle methods to our own activity. Then we will check the behaviors by trying out different user interactions. Follow the steps below -

1. Create a new Android application project using Eclipse with the configurations shown in figure 2.2 -

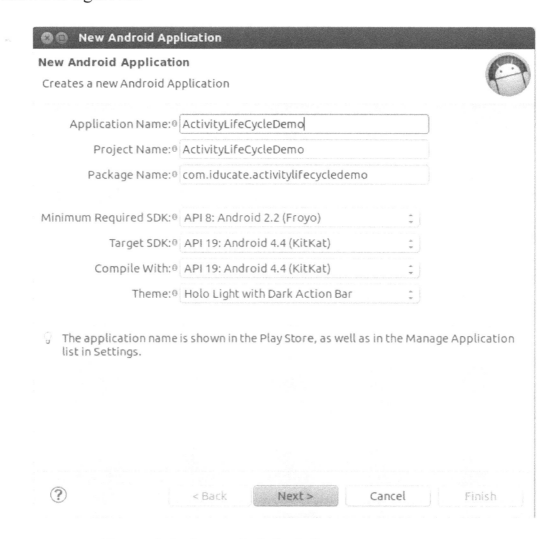

Figure 2.2: ActivityLifeCycleDemo project creation

As you can see, we have named our application "ActivityLifeCycleDemo". For other steps of application creation, leave the default values and finish creating the application.

2. Once the application is created successfully, replace the code for MainActivity.java file with the following code -

```java
package com.iducate.activitylifecycledemo;

import android.os.Bundle;
import android.util.Log;
import android.app.Activity;

public class MainActivity extends Activity {

    private final String TAG = "ActivityLifeCycle";

    @Override
    protected void onCreate(Bundle savedInstanceState) {
        super.onCreate(savedInstanceState);
        setContentView(R.layout.activity_main);
        Log.d(TAG, "onCreate() called");
    }

    @Override
    protected void onStart() {
        super.onStart();
        Log.d(TAG, "onStart() called");
    }

    @Override
    protected void onRestart() {
        super.onRestart();
        Log.d(TAG, "onRestart() called");
    }

    @Override
    protected void onResume() {
        super.onResume();
        Log.d(TAG, "onResume() called");
    }


    @Override
    protected void onPause() {
```

```
        super.onPause();
        Log.d(TAG, "onPause() called");
    }


    @Override
    protected void onStop() {
        super.onStop();
        Log.d(TAG, "onStop() called");
    }



    @Override
    protected void onDestroy() {
        super.onDestroy();
        Log.d(TAG, "onDestroy() called");
    }

}
```

As you can see, we have implemented all the activity life cycle methods and added a log message with each method name. These log messages are shown in the LogCat View. Note that the LogCat View logs other system messages as well. In the previous chapter, we have added the LogCat View. If you haven't done that yet, from within Eclipse IDE, select Window → Show View → Other... → Android → LogCat. This will add LogCat view to Eclipse (generally at the bottom section grouped with existing views).

When you run your application, the LogCat view will be cluttered with a bunch of system generated log messages. For now, we are only interested in the log messages that the activity life cycle methods generate. Thus, we add a filter to LogCat so that only the log messages with tag "ActivityLifeCycle" will be shown (figure 2.3).

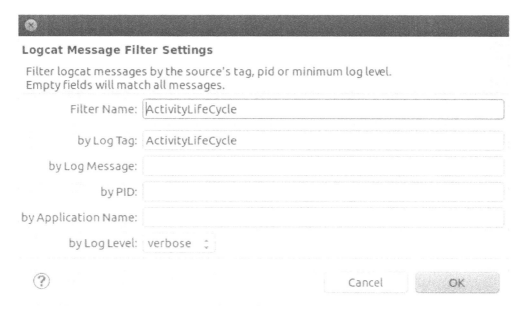

Figure 2.3: Adding filter to LogCat

3. Now run your application in an emulator or in an actual Android phone and maximize the LogCat view. If you look at the LogCat view, you will see similar messages as in figure 2.4 -

Level	Time	PID	TID	Application	Tag	Text
D	03-28 15:25:37.290	14851	14851	com.iducate.activitylifecycledemo	ActivityLifeCycle	onCreate() called
D	03-28 15:25:37.291	14851	14851	com.iducate.activitylifecycledemo	ActivityLifeCycle	onStart() called
D	03-28 15:25:37.292	14851	14851	com.iducate.activitylifecycledemo	ActivityLifeCycle	onResume() called

Figure 2.4: LogCat view

You will see three log messages which are generated by the three life cycle methods of our activity. Those life cycle methods were called when we run the application. From the log messages, we can tell which methods were called. We can see the first message called is onCreate(), then onStart() and finally the onResume() method. At this stage, our application is running in the foreground and can interact with user.

4. Now we click the BACK button (either soft BACK button or hardware button - which one available depends on your device or emulator). Then we will see few more log messages corresponding to a few other life cycle methods of our activity (figure 2.5) -

Level	Time	PID	TID	Application	Tag	Text
D	03-28 15:25:37.290	14851	14851	com.iducate.activitylifecycledemo	ActivityLifeCycle	onCreate() called
D	03-28 15:25:37.291	14851	14851	com.iducate.activitylifecycledemo	ActivityLifeCycle	onStart() called
D	03-28 15:25:37.292	14851	14851	com.iducate.activitylifecycledemo	ActivityLifeCycle	onResume() called
D	03-28 15:25:43.783	14851	14851	com.iducate.activitylifecycledemo	ActivityLifeCycle	onPause() called
D	03-28 15:25:44.410	14851	14851	com.iducate.activitylifecycledemo	ActivityLifeCycle	onStop() called
D	03-28 15:25:44.410	14851	14851	com.iducate.activitylifecycledemo	ActivityLifeCycle	onDestroy() called

Figure 2.5: LogCat view

We can see that pressing the BACK button resulted in three more life cycle methods, onPause(), onStop() and then onDestroy() being called sequentially.

5. From the application launcher area, launch our ActivityLifeCycleDemo application again. This time our LogCat view will have three more log messages corresponding to three life cycle methods of our activity (figure 2.6). Those three log messages suggest that onCreate(), onStart() and onResume() methods were called.

Level	Time	PID	TID	Application	Tag	Text
D	03-28 15:25:37.290	14851	14851	com.iducate.activitylifecycledemo	ActivityLifeCycle	onCreate() called
D	03-28 15:25:37.291	14851	14851	com.iducate.activitylifecycledemo	ActivityLifeCycle	onStart() called
D	03-28 15:25:37.292	14851	14851	com.iducate.activitylifecycledemo	ActivityLifeCycle	onResume() called
D	03-28 15:25:43.783	14851	14851	com.iducate.activitylifecycledemo	ActivityLifeCycle	onPause() called
D	03-28 15:25:44.410	14851	14851	com.iducate.activitylifecycledemo	ActivityLifeCycle	onStop() called
D	03-28 15:25:44.410	14851	14851	com.iducate.activitylifecycledemo	ActivityLifeCycle	onDestroy() called
D	03-28 15:25:49.537	14851	14851	com.iducate.activitylifecycledemo	ActivityLifeCycle	onCreate() called
D	03-28 15:25:49.538	14851	14851	com.iducate.activitylifecycledemo	ActivityLifeCycle	onStart() called
D	03-28 15:25:49.541	14851	14851	com.iducate.activitylifecycledemo	ActivityLifeCycle	onResume() called

Figure 2.6: LogCat view

6. Now click the HOME button of the emulator or phone to bring up the home screen of your emulator or device. This time, from the new log message (figure 2.7) that corresponds to the interaction of clicking the HOME button, notice that only onPause() and onStop() methods were called. Unlike the previous time, when we clicked the BACK button and onDestroy() was called, clicking the HOME button will not call the onDestroy() method.

Level	Time	PID	TID	Application	Tag	Text
D	03-28 15:25:37.290	14851	14851	com.iducate.activitylifecycledemo	ActivityLifeCycle	onCreate() called
D	03-28 15:25:37.291	14851	14851	com.iducate.activitylifecycledemo	ActivityLifeCycle	onStart() called
D	03-28 15:25:37.292	14851	14851	com.iducate.activitylifecycledemo	ActivityLifeCycle	onResume() called
D	03-28 15:25:43.783	14851	14851	com.iducate.activitylifecycledemo	ActivityLifeCycle	onPause() called
D	03-28 15:25:44.410	14851	14851	com.iducate.activitylifecycledemo	ActivityLifeCycle	onStop() called
D	03-28 15:25:44.410	14851	14851	com.iducate.activitylifecycledemo	ActivityLifeCycle	onDestroy() called
D	03-28 15:25:49.537	14851	14851	com.iducate.activitylifecycledemo	ActivityLifeCycle	onCreate() called
D	03-28 15:25:49.538	14851	14851	com.iducate.activitylifecycledemo	ActivityLifeCycle	onStart() called
D	03-28 15:25:49.541	14851	14851	com.iducate.activitylifecycledemo	ActivityLifeCycle	onResume() called
D	03-28 15:25:54.427	14851	14851	com.iducate.activitylifecycledemo	ActivityLifeCycle	onPause() called
D	03-28 15:25:55.015	14851	14851	com.iducate.activitylifecycledemo	ActivityLifeCycle	onStop() called

Figure 2.7: LogCat view

7. Now once again, start the ActivityLifeCycleDemo application either from the launcher or from recent apps and you will see three new log messages (figure 2.8) -

Level	Time	PID	TID	Application	Tag	Text
D	03-28 15:25:37.290	14851	14851	com.iducate.activitylifecycledemo	ActivityLifeCycle	onCreate() called
D	03-28 15:25:37.291	14851	14851	com.iducate.activitylifecycledemo	ActivityLifeCycle	onStart() called
D	03-28 15:25:37.292	14851	14851	com.iducate.activitylifecycledemo	ActivityLifeCycle	onResume() called
D	03-28 15:25:43.783	14851	14851	com.iducate.activitylifecycledemo	ActivityLifeCycle	onPause() called
D	03-28 15:25:44.410	14851	14851	com.iducate.activitylifecycledemo	ActivityLifeCycle	onStop() called
D	03-28 15:25:44.410	14851	14851	com.iducate.activitylifecycledemo	ActivityLifeCycle	onDestroy() called
D	03-28 15:25:49.537	14851	14851	com.iducate.activitylifecycledemo	ActivityLifeCycle	onCreate() called
D	03-28 15:25:49.538	14851	14851	com.iducate.activitylifecycledemo	ActivityLifeCycle	onStart() called
D	03-28 15:25:49.541	14851	14851	com.iducate.activitylifecycledemo	ActivityLifeCycle	onResume() called
D	03-28 15:25:54.427	14851	14851	com.iducate.activitylifecycledemo	ActivityLifeCycle	onPause() called
D	03-28 15:25:55.015	14851	14851	com.iducate.activitylifecycledemo	ActivityLifeCycle	onStop() called
D	03-28 15:26:01.405	14851	14851	com.iducate.activitylifecycledemo	ActivityLifeCycle	onRestart() called
D	03-28 15:26:01.406	14851	14851	com.iducate.activitylifecycledemo	ActivityLifeCycle	onStart() called
D	03-28 15:26:01.406	14851	14851	com.iducate.activitylifecycledemo	ActivityLifeCycle	onResume() called

Figure 2.8: LogCat View

This time, we can see that onRestart(), onStart() and onResume() methods were called, but onCreate() wasn't called.

How It Works?

As you can see from the preceding example, when an activity is created for the first time, the onCreate() method is called, followed by onStart() and then onResume(). At that state, the activity becomes active and can interact with user events. The onCreate() method is called only when an activity is newly created, not when the activity is restored from a paused state (paused state of an activity happens when some other activity comes to foreground and the previous activity becomes invisible). But onStart() and onResume() will always be called when the activity becomes visible, regardless of that activity is created or restored.

On the other hand, onPause() and onStop() methods are called when the current activity is sent to the background. In addition to these two method calls, when the user presses the BACK button, the onDestroy() method call is followed.

You don't need to overwrite all these life cycle methods in every activity, rather you will likely to overwrite some of them based on your requirements.

- You will most likely overwrite onCreate() method often. Since this method is called only when an activity is created, you will instantiate objects that you will be using in your application and also inflate the layout.
- Because onResume() is called every time an activity comes to the foreground, you will want to start any service or anything that you want to run while your activity is in the foreground.
- The onPause() method should stop any service or other things that you don't want to run when your activity isn't in the foreground. You will also want to save the current state of your activity in this method as well.
- The onDestroy() method can be used to free up resources before your activity is destroyed.

Android Activity Classes

In addition to the Activity base class, Android SDK provides some other subclasses of Activity that wrap up the use of common UI widgets such as displaying lists or maps. Some of the subclasses of Activity are -

- **ListActivity** – The ListActivity is useful for displaying a ListView widget. If you want your entire activity to show a ListView, this class can be helpful by providing you a ListView widget and some helpful methods to bound data sources to your ListView widget, event handlers etc.

- **ExpandableListActivity** – This provides a similar facility like ListActivity, but supports ExpandableListView.

- **FragmentActivity** – This subclass enables you to use Fragments from the support library.

The Intent Object

An Intent encapsulates a request made to Android to perform some task for an activity or another component. You can view an Intent as a message-passing mechanism that works between the components of your application and also between applications. Using Intents, you can interact between two activities, like moving from one activity to another, passing data to another activity, fetching results from another activity etc. Intents also allow you to start particular services and broadcast events as well.

Linking Activities Using Intent

One of the common uses of Intents is to communicate between components of your application. Using Intents, you can start activities which allows you to create a workflow consisting of different screens. In this section, we will create an application with two activities and see how we can launch the second activity from the first activity. Follow the steps bellow -

1. Create a new application named "IntentDemo", with the configuration options shown in figure 2.9 -

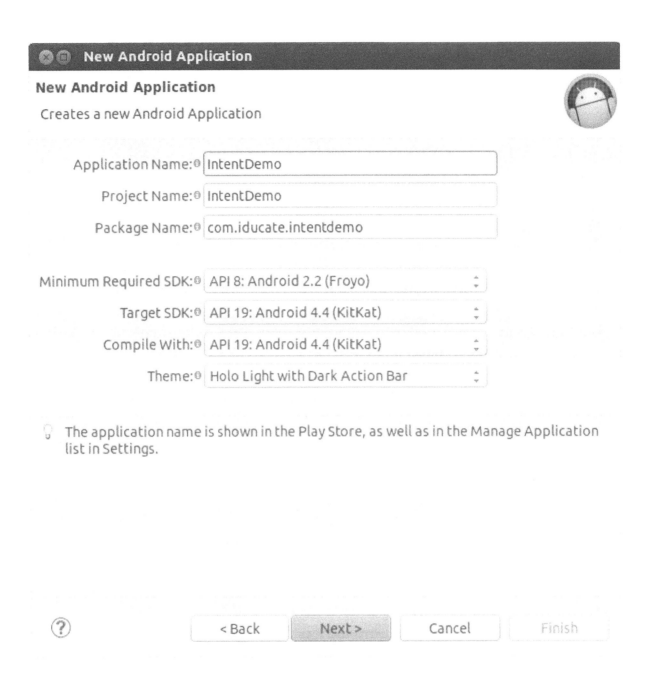

Figure 2.9: New application creation

Leave the default values for the other options and finish the application creation process.

2. We want to have a button on our first activity so that we can start a new activity by clicking that button. Replace the code for activity_main.xml file with the following code -

<LinearLayout xmlns:android="http://schemas.android.com/apk/res/android"

```xml
    xmlns:tools="http://schemas.android.com/tools"
    android:id="@+id/LinearLayout1"
    android:layout_width="match_parent"
    android:layout_height="match_parent"
    android:orientation="vertical" >

    <Button
        android:id="@+id/btnLaunch"
        android:layout_width="wrap_content"
        android:layout_height="wrap_content"
        android:layout_gravity="center"
        android:layout_marginTop="30dp"
        android:onClick="launchActivity"
        android:text="Launch Activity" />

</LinearLayout>
```

3. Next, update the code of MainActivity.java to handle the button click event -

```java
package com.iducate.intentdemo;

import android.app.Activity;
import android.content.Intent;
import android.os.Bundle;
import android.view.View;

public class MainActivity extends Activity {

    @Override
    protected void onCreate(Bundle savedInstanceState) {
        super.onCreate(savedInstanceState);
        setContentView(R.layout.activity_main);
    }

    public void launchActivity(View view) {
        Intent intent = new Intent(this, SecondActivity.class);
        startActivity(intent);
    }
}
```

4. Now we need to create our second activity. If you remember from the previous section, creating a new activity typically involves the creation of an activity class

file, a XML layout file to be used by that activity and finally registering that activity in our AndroidManifest.xml file. Let's create a new activity class named "SecondActivity.java" under the src/ directory and under our package name with the following code -

```java
package com.iducate.intentdemo;

import android.app.Activity;
import android.os.Bundle;

public class SecondActivity extends Activity {

        @Override
        protected void onCreate(Bundle savedInstanceState) {
                super.onCreate(savedInstanceState);
                setContentView(R.layout.activity_second);
        }
}
```

Next, create a new layout file "activity_second.xml" under res/layout directory with the following code -

```xml
<?xml version="1.0" encoding="utf-8"?>
<LinearLayout xmlns:android="http://schemas.android.com/apk/res/android"
   android:layout_width="match_parent"
   android:layout_height="match_parent"
   android:orientation="vertical" >

   <TextView
      android:id="@+id/textView1"
      android:layout_width="wrap_content"
      android:layout_height="wrap_content"
      android:layout_gravity="center"
      android:layout_marginTop="30dp"
      android:text="This is second activity" />

</LinearLayout>
```

Finally, we need to register our new activity. Open the AndroidManifest.xml file and include the code below under the <application> node -

```xml
<activity android:name="com.iducate.intentdemo.SecondActivity" />
```

The AndroidManifest.xml file will look like this -

```xml
<?xml version="1.0" encoding="utf-8"?>
<manifest xmlns:android="http://schemas.android.com/apk/res/android"
  package="com.iducate.intentdemo"
  android:versionCode="1"
  android:versionName="1.0" >

  <uses-sdk
    android:minSdkVersion="8"
    android:targetSdkVersion="19" />

  <application
    android:allowBackup="true"
    android:icon="@drawable/ic_launcher"
    android:label="@string/app_name"
    android:theme="@style/AppTheme" >
    <activity
      android:name="com.iducate.intentdemo.MainActivity"
      android:label="@string/app_name" >
      <intent-filter>
        <action android:name="android.intent.action.MAIN" />

        <category android:name="android.intent.category.LAUNCHER" />
      </intent-filter>
    </activity>
    <activity android:name="com.iducate.intentdemo.SecondActivity" />
  </application>

</manifest>
```

5. Run the application and you will see a button like in figure 2.10 -

Figure 2.10: Running IntentDemo application

6. If you click the "Launch Activity" button, the second activity will appear (figure 2.11) -

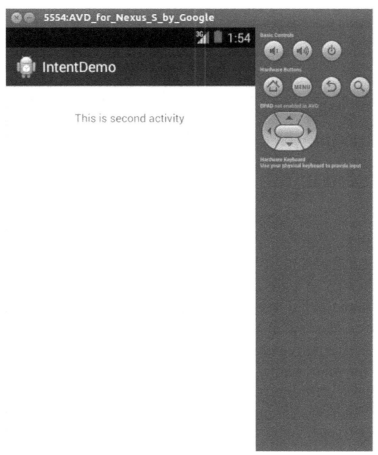

Figure 2.11: New activity launched

How It Works?

The first activity, "MainActivity.java" sets the "activity_main.xml" file as it's layout -

setContentView(R.layout.activity_main);

The activity_main.xml file has a single button element. This button element has some visual attributes - a text label "Launch Activity" and another important attribute "onClick" with the value of "launchActivity".

```
<Button
    android:id="@+id/btnLaunch"
    android:layout_width="wrap_content"
    android:layout_height="wrap_content"
    android:layout_gravity="center"
    android:layout_marginTop="30dp"
```

```
android:onClick="launchActivity"
android:text="Launch Activity" />
```

By setting this onClick attribute of button element, we can handle the button click event from our MainActivity.java file by defining a method launchActivity() -

```
public void launchActivity(View view) {
    Intent intent = new Intent(this, SecondActivity.class);
    startActivity(intent);
}
```

Within this launchActivity() method, we create a new Intent object by passing the Context object and the Activity class to be invoked as parameter. Activity class itself is a subclass of Context, so we can use this as Context. The second parameter is the name of the second Activity class. Then we call the startActivity() method of Activity class with the intent object as parameter to start the second activity. There are alternative constructs for creating a new instance of Intent class. Instead of using the class name, we can use something called "intent filter" which is convenient if we wish to invoke the activity of another application. We will learn more about that later. Invoking activities from within the same application is usually done using class names. This is known as explicit intent.

While working with Android, you will often encounter the Context object. The Context object represents the current state of the application. It is actually an interface to global information of an application environment. The activity and service classes are subclasses of the context class. You can use getApplicationContext(), getContext() or getBaseContext() methods to get the context.

Passing Data Using Intent Object

While starting a new activity using Intent, we can optionally pass data to our new activity. The Intent object can optionally bundle some data with it and can pass that data to the target activity. This enables us to pass data between activities. The next example shows us how we can use an EditText widget to take user input from our first activity and then pass that user input text to the second activity. We will use the same IntentDemo project that we created in the previous section. Follow the steps below -

1. First, update the layout of our first activity. We will add an EditText widget to

take in user input. Update the activity_main.xml file with the following code -

```xml
<LinearLayout xmlns:android="http://schemas.android.com/apk/res/android"
    xmlns:tools="http://schemas.android.com/tools"
    android:id="@+id/LinearLayout1"
    android:layout_width="match_parent"
    android:layout_height="match_parent"
    android:orientation="vertical" >

    <EditText
        android:id="@+id/etMessage"
        android:layout_width="match_parent"
        android:layout_height="wrap_content"
        android:ems="10"
        android:hint="Enter your message here..." >

        <requestFocus />
    </EditText>

    <Button
        android:id="@+id/btnLaunch"
        android:layout_width="wrap_content"
        android:layout_height="wrap_content"
        android:layout_gravity="center"
        android:onClick="launchActivity"
        android:text="Launch Activity" />

</LinearLayout>
```

2. Now update the MainActivity.java file with the following code -

```java
package com.iducate.intentdemo;

import android.app.Activity;
import android.content.Intent;
import android.os.Bundle;
import android.view.View;
import android.widget.EditText;

public class MainActivity extends Activity {

    private EditText etMessage;
```

```
        @Override
        protected void onCreate(Bundle savedInstanceState) {
                super.onCreate(savedInstanceState);
                setContentView(R.layout.activity_main);

                etMessage = (EditText) findViewById(R.id.etMessage);
        }

        public void launchActivity(View view) {
                String message = etMessage.getText().toString();

                Intent intent = new Intent(this, SecondActivity.class);
                intent.putExtra("message", message);
                startActivity(intent);
        }
}
```

3. Our activity_second.xml layout file should contain the following code -

```xml
<?xml version="1.0" encoding="utf-8"?>
<LinearLayout xmlns:android="http://schemas.android.com/apk/res/android"
   android:layout_width="match_parent"
   android:layout_height="match_parent"
   android:orientation="vertical" >

   <TextView
      android:id="@+id/tvMessage"
      android:layout_width="wrap_content"
      android:layout_height="wrap_content"
      android:layout_gravity="center" />

</LinearLayout>
```

This layout file contains only a single TextView widget which initially has no text label. We will update this text label from our SecondActivity.java file using the message that user enters in to the EditText.

4. Now update the SecondActivity.java file with the following code -

```
package com.iducate.intentdemo;
```

```
import android.app.Activity;
import android.os.Bundle;
import android.widget.TextView;

public class SecondActivity extends Activity {

    @Override
    protected void onCreate(Bundle savedInstanceState) {
        super.onCreate(savedInstanceState);
        setContentView(R.layout.activity_second);

        TextView tvMessage = (TextView) findViewById(R.id.tvMessage);

        tvMessage.setText(getIntent().getStringExtra("message"));
    }
}
```

5. Now run the application. We will see a screen with a text field and button as shown in figure 2.12 -

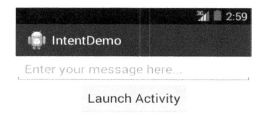

Figure 2.12: Running IntentDemo application

6. Now enter some text and press the "Launch Activity" button which will launch our second activity (figure 2.13) with the text entered in the previous screen -

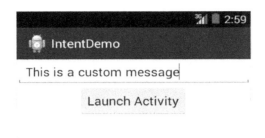

Figure 2.13: New activity launched

How It Works?

The activity_main.xml file contains an EditText widget which provides an input area -

70

```
<EditText
    android:id="@+id/etMessage"
    android:layout_width="match_parent"
    android:layout_height="wrap_content"
    android:ems="10"
    android:hint="Enter your message here..." >

    <requestFocus />
</EditText>
```

We have set an ID for this EditText element and some other attributes. From our MainActivity.java class, we will access EditText element using this ID. We will learn more about EditText and other widgets in later chapters.

In our MainActivity.java class, we have declared an EditText instance -

```
    private EditText etMessage;
```

And then within the onCreate() method, we initialize that instance of EditText -

```
    TextView tvMessage = (TextView) findViewById(R.id.tvMessage);
```

Again, the button press event is handled by the launchActivity() method of the MainActivity.java class -

```
    public void launchActivity(View view) {
        String message = etMessage.getText().toString();

        Intent intent = new Intent(this, SecondActivity.class);
        intent.putExtra("message", message);
        startActivity(intent);
    }
```

The launchActivity() method gets the text entered to the EditText element as a string using the getText() method. We then pass that string to the second activity using putExtra() method of Intent class and start the second activity using the startActivity() method call.

When the second activity is launched, we get that string from the Intent object.

```
@Override
protected void onCreate(Bundle savedInstanceState) {
    super.onCreate(savedInstanceState);
    setContentView(R.layout.activity_second);

    TextView tvMessage = (TextView) findViewById(R.id.tvMessage);

    tvMessage.setText(getIntent().getStringExtra("message"));
}
```

You can see that the onCreate() method of SecondActivity.java class first initializes the TextView and then sets the string value that we have passed from the previous activity. We can get the Intent object which is called by our activity by using the method getIntent(). To retrieve the passed data, we use the getStringExtra() method of Intent object.

Returning Results From Intent

We have previously seen how we can start a new activity and also how to pass data to the newly started activity from our current activity. But it is also possible to start a new activity which return results to the current activity. In that case, instead of using startActivity() method, we will use the startActivityForResult() method. Let's see an example of how to do that.

We will create a new application with two activities. The first activity will have a TextView widget and a Button. When user clicks the Button, a new activity will be started with a button and a EditText widget to enter some text. Once user enters some text to that EditText area and presses the button, it will close that activity and return to the first activity. The TextView of first activity will also be updated with the text returned from the second activity.

1. Create a new application named "ActivityForResults".

2. Update the activity_main.xml file with the code below where we have a TextView element and a button element. In addition to setting some other attributes of these elements, we have set id attributes for them and for the button element, we have set the android:onClick attribute to handle the button click.

```
<LinearLayout xmlns:android="http://schemas.android.com/apk/res/android"
    xmlns:tools="http://schemas.android.com/tools"
    android:id="@+id/LinearLayout1"
```

```xml
    android:layout_width="match_parent"
    android:layout_height="match_parent"
    android:orientation="vertical"
    android:paddingBottom="@dimen/activity_vertical_margin"
    android:paddingLeft="@dimen/activity_horizontal_margin"
    android:paddingRight="@dimen/activity_horizontal_margin"
    android:paddingTop="@dimen/activity_vertical_margin"
    tools:context=".MainActivity" >

    <TextView
        android:id="@+id/tvOutput"
        android:layout_width="wrap_content"
        android:layout_height="wrap_content"
        android:layout_gravity="center"
        android:text="Welcome Guest!" />

    <Button
        android:id="@+id/btnSetName"
        android:layout_width="wrap_content"
        android:layout_height="wrap_content"
        android:layout_gravity="center"
        android:onClick="setName"
        android:text="Set Name" />

</LinearLayout>
```

3. Now update the code for MainActivity.java file with the following code -

```java
package com.iducate.activityforresults;

import android.os.Bundle;
import android.view.View;
import android.widget.TextView;
import android.app.Activity;
import android.content.Intent;

public class MainActivity extends Activity {

    private static final int REQUEST_CODE_NAME = 0;
    private TextView tvOutput;

    @Override
    protected void onCreate(Bundle savedInstanceState) {
```

```java
        super.onCreate(savedInstanceState);
        setContentView(R.layout.activity_main);

        tvOutput = (TextView) findViewById(R.id.tvOutput);
    }

    public void setName(View view) {
        Intent intent = new Intent(this, SecondActivity.class);
        startActivityForResult(intent, REQUEST_CODE_NAME);
    }

    @Override
    protected void onActivityResult(int requestCode, int resultCode,
            Intent data) {
        super.onActivityResult(requestCode, resultCode, data);

        if (requestCode == REQUEST_CODE_NAME) {
            if (resultCode == RESULT_OK) {
                String name = data.getStringExtra("name");
                tvOutput.setText("Welcome back "+name);
            }
        }
    }
}
```

We will go through the details of the code later.

3. We will need to create a second activity for our application. Let's first create a layout file activity_second.xml under the res/layout directory. We will use this layout file for our activity. Put in the following code -

```xml
<?xml version="1.0" encoding="utf-8"?>
<LinearLayout xmlns:android="http://schemas.android.com/apk/res/android"
    android:layout_width="match_parent"
    android:layout_height="match_parent"
    android:orientation="vertical" >

    <EditText
        android:id="@+id/etName"
        android:layout_width="match_parent"
        android:layout_height="wrap_content"
        android:ems="10"
```

```
      android:hint="Enter your name..." >

    <requestFocus />
  </EditText>

  <Button
    android:id="@+id/btnSubmit"
    android:layout_width="wrap_content"
    android:layout_height="wrap_content"
    android:layout_gravity="center"
    android:onClick="submitName"
    android:text="Submit" />

</LinearLayout>
```

4. Now create a Activity class SecondActivity.java in the src directory and put the file under our package name. This file should contain the following code -

```java
package com.iducate.activityforresults;

import android.app.Activity;
import android.content.Intent;
import android.os.Bundle;
import android.view.View;
import android.widget.EditText;

public class SecondActivity extends Activity {

    @Override
    protected void onCreate(Bundle savedInstanceState) {
        super.onCreate(savedInstanceState);
        setContentView(R.layout.activity_second);
    }

    public void submitName(View view) {
        EditText etName = (EditText) findViewById(R.id.etName);
        String name = etName.getText().toString();

        Intent intent = new Intent();
        intent.putExtra("name", name);
        setResult(RESULT_OK, intent);

        //closes current activity
```

```
            finish();
        }
}
```

5. Finally we need to register this new activity to our AndroidManifest.xml file -

```xml
<?xml version="1.0" encoding="utf-8"?>
<manifest xmlns:android="http://schemas.android.com/apk/res/android"
    package="com.iducate.activityforresults"
    android:versionCode="1"
    android:versionName="1.0" >

    <uses-sdk
        android:minSdkVersion="8"
        android:targetSdkVersion="19" />

    <application
        android:allowBackup="true"
        android:icon="@drawable/ic_launcher"
        android:label="@string/app_name"
        android:theme="@style/AppTheme" >
        <activity
            android:name="com.iducate.activityforresults.MainActivity"
            android:label="@string/app_name" >
            <intent-filter>
                <action android:name="android.intent.action.MAIN" />

                <category android:name="android.intent.category.LAUNCHER" />
            </intent-filter>
        </activity>
        <activity
android:name="com.iducate.activityforresults.SecondActivity" />
    </application>

</manifest>
```

6. Now run the application and you will see a screen similar to figure 2.14 -

76

Figure 2.14: Running ActivityForResults application

7. If you click the "Set Name" button, you will be presented with a screen to enter your name (figure 2.15) -

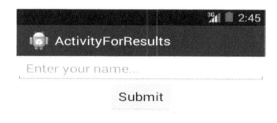

Figure 2.15: SecondActivity

8. Once you enter your name and press the "Submit" button, you will be taken to the first activity again. This time, the TextView will be updated with your name (figure 2.16) that you entered in the previous step -

Figure 2.16: TextView updated with result from second activity

How It Works?

The layout file for our MainActivity.java file contains a TextView widget and a button widget. When we initially launch the application, we will see that activity because in our AndroidManifest.xml file, we set intent-filter for that activity to make it the entry point of our application -

```
<activity
      android:name="com.iducate.activityforresults.MainActivity"
   android:label="@string/app_name" >
   <intent-filter>
      <action android:name="android.intent.action.MAIN" />
      <category android:name="android.intent.category.LAUNCHER" />
   </intent-filter>
</activity>
```

At this point, the TextView element will show a preset message. The Button widget's android:onClick property specifies the method name which will be called when someone clicks that button -

```
<Button
   android:id="@+id/btnSetName"
   android:layout_width="wrap_content"
   android:layout_height="wrap_content"
   android:layout_gravity="center"
   android:onClick="setName"
   android:text="Set Name" />
```

The setName() method is defined in our MainActivity.java file -

```
public void setName(View view) {
      Intent intent = new Intent(this, SecondActivity.class);
      startActivityForResult(intent, REQUEST_CODE_NAME);
}
```

This method creates a new instance of Intent class and call the startActivityForResult() method which will launch the second activity "SecondActivity.java" and return some result from that activity. The

79

startActivityForResult() method takes two parameters. The first one is the instance of Intent class and the second one is the request code. The request code is just an integer which we defined as constant -

private static final int REQUEST_CODE_NAME = 0;

We will use this request code later to verify the returned result. This is necessary because our activity can call startActivityForResult() method several times with distinct intent object and request code. When the result is returned from some other activity, we will use the request code to identify the request for which that result was returned.

Now when the second activity is launched by the startActivityForResult() method call due to button click from the first activity, we will see a layout with one EditText widget to take in user input and a button.

```
<Button
  android:id="@+id/btnSubmit"
  android:layout_width="wrap_content"
  android:layout_height="wrap_content"
  android:layout_gravity="center"
  android:onClick="submitName"
  android:text="Submit" />
```

The button click will be handled by the submitName() method of SecondActivity.java class.

```
public void submitName(View view) {
        EditText etName = (EditText) findViewById(R.id.etName);
        String name = etName.getText().toString();

        Intent intent = new Intent();
        intent.putExtra("name", name);
        setResult(RESULT_OK, intent);

        //closes current activity
        finish();
    }
```

This method simply retrieves the text content of EditText widget and instantiates a new instance of Intent class. We pass the text content as an extra value to intent object and call the setResult() method with that intent. We also pass the result type RESULT_OK to indicate that the result is returned successfully. Finally, we call finish() method to close the second activity.

Now as soon as the above piece of code is executed and the second activity is closed, the result returned from the second activity will call the onActivityResult() method of MainActivity.java with three parameters. The parameters are request code, result code and the intent object. Request code will be an integer value of the same code that is passed in while making the request. For successful return of result, the result code should be RESULT_OK.

```java
@Override
protected void onActivityResult(int requestCode, int resultCode,
        Intent data) {
    super.onActivityResult(requestCode, resultCode, data);

    if (requestCode == REQUEST_CODE_NAME) {
        if (resultCode == RESULT_OK) {
            String name = data.getStringExtra("name");
            tvOutput.setText("Welcome back "+name);
        }
    }
}
```

The onActivityResult() method is a callback method which will be called every time a result is returned as a response to our startActivityForResult() method call. That's why we need to check the request code to make sure we are dealing with the appropriate result. Finally, after checking if the result code indicates success, we update the TextView widget of MainActivity.java with the result returned from the intent object.

Calling Built-in Applications Using Intents

We have already seen how we can call activities of our own application using Intents. But we can also call activities of other applications using intents from our own application. This enables application developers to take advantage of using the functionality of other applications from their own application. To consider an example, suppose you are building an application that needs to load a web page. Now instead of writing code to build your own web browser, you can use Intent to

81

call the existing web browsers to display that web page.

We will see an example application that invokes some of the built-in applications in Android. Follow the steps below -

1. Create a new application named IntentsExample.

2. Update the layout file, activity_main.xml with the following code -

```
<LinearLayout xmlns:android="http://schemas.android.com/apk/res/android"
    xmlns:tools="http://schemas.android.com/tools"
    android:id="@+id/LinearLayout1"
    android:layout_width="match_parent"
    android:layout_height="match_parent"
    android:orientation="vertical" >

    <Button
        android:id="@+id/btnBrowseWeb"
        android:layout_width="match_parent"
        android:layout_height="wrap_content"
        android:onClick="browseWeb"
        android:text="Web Browser" />

    <Button
        android:id="@+id/btnShowMap"
        android:layout_width="match_parent"
        android:layout_height="wrap_content"
        android:onClick="showMap"
        android:text="Show Map" />

    <Button
        android:id="@+id/btnMakeCall"
        android:layout_width="match_parent"
        android:layout_height="wrap_content"
        android:onClick="makeCall"
        android:text="Make Call" />

</LinearLayout>
```

3. Now update the activity file MainActivity.java with the following code -

```
package com.iducate.intentsexample;
```

```java
import android.net.Uri;
import android.os.Bundle;
import android.view.View;
import android.app.Activity;
import android.content.Intent;

public class MainActivity extends Activity {

    @Override
    protected void onCreate(Bundle savedInstanceState) {
      super.onCreate(savedInstanceState);
      setContentView(R.layout.activity_main);
    }

    public void browseWeb(View view) {
      Intent intent = new Intent(android.content.Intent.ACTION_VIEW,
                      Uri.parse("http://www.google.com"));
      startActivity(intent);
    }

    public void showMap(View view) {
      Intent intent = new Intent(android.content.Intent.ACTION_VIEW,
                      Uri.parse("geo:26.934,-80.106"));
      startActivity(intent);
    }

    public void makeCall(View view) {
      Intent intent = new Intent(android.content.Intent.ACTION_DIAL,
                      Uri.parse("tel:+82345623"));
      startActivity(intent);
    }
}
```

3. Now run the application and you will see a screen similar to figure 2.17 -

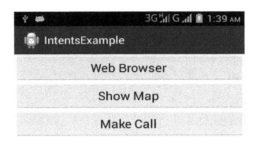

Figure 2.17: Running IntentsExample application

4. You will see three buttons. Clicking each of them will invoke the built-in application to perform different tasks. First, click the "Web Browser" button which will prompt us to open the URL in our preferred web browser as shown in figure 2.18 -

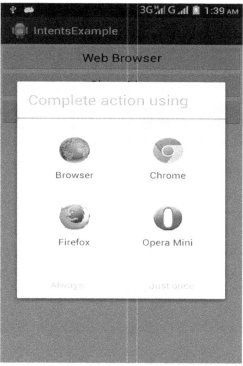

Figure 2.18: Web browser chooser prompt

Once we select the preferred browser, it will load the specified URL (figure 2.19). Note that if your device has only a single web browser, you will not see the browser pick option. Instead the URL will directly load to your default browser.

Figure 2.19: URL loaded to web browser

5. If we click the second button ("Show Map"), it will invoke the map application (figure 2.10) -

Figure 2.20: Invoking Map application

6. Finally if we click the "Make Call" button, we will see the dialer application as shown in figure 2.21 -

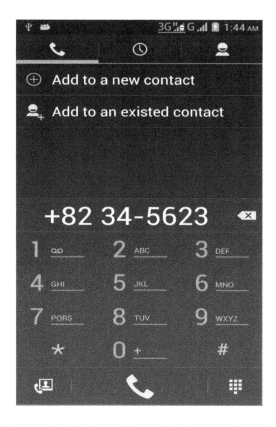

Figure 2.21: Invoking dialer application

How It Works?

This example application shows us how to use implicit intents to perform some tasks. Unlike explicit intents, where we had to tell the activity class name, using implicit intent, we tell the action we would like to perform and specify the data associated with that action. For example, we might say we want to load the web page of www.google.com. The action will be to browse website and the data is the URL of the website we want to visit. Depending upon the action we want to perform, we will need to provide associated data. This data is specified as an Uri object.

Some actions are -

* ACTION_VIEW
* ACTION_DIAL
* ACTION_SEND
* ACTION_PICK
* ACTION_EDIT
* ACTION_DELETE

and some example data -

- http://www.google.com
- geo:26.934, -80.106
- tel:+82345623

We use the parse() method of Uri class to create an Uri object from our data. Then using the action and Uri object, we instantiate a new instance of Intent class -

```
Intent intent = new Intent(android.content.Intent.ACTION_VIEW,
                    Uri.parse("http://www.google.com"));
```

Here we created an Uri object from a URL string and using the action android.content.Intent.ACTION_VIEW, we have created a new Intent object. Then we simply call the startActivity() method by passing that Intent object as parameter -

```
startActivity(intent);
```

As soon as the startActivity() method is executed, the Android system will launch your phone's default web browser (in case multiple browsers are installed, it will let you pick one) and load the requested web page defined by the Uri object.

Similarly this will launch a map application with your provided location coordinates -

```
Intent intent = new Intent(android.content.Intent.ACTION_VIEW,
                Uri.parse("geo:26.934,-80.106"));
startActivity(intent);
```

Finally, a third example will launch dialer application with a phone number you have provided as parameter of parse() method or Uri class -

```
Intent intent = new Intent(android.content.Intent.ACTION_DIAL,
                Uri.parse("tel:+82345623"));
    startActivity(intent);
```

Note that, you aren't required to provide data as that part is optional -

```
Intent intent = new Intent(android.content.Intent.ACTION_DIAL);
```

```
startActivity(intent);
```

In that case, the dialer application will be launched but without any phone number.

The Intent class has a number of setter methods which enables you to set different fields. You can create an Intent object without passing any parameters to the constructor -

```
Intent intent = new Intent();
```

You can then call different setter methods to set action, data etc -

```
intent.setData(Uri.parse("tel:+82345623"));
intent.setAction(android.content.Intent.ACTION_DIAL);
```

Intent Fields

The Intent object can have a number of fields -

- Action
- Data
- Category
- Type
- Component
- Extras
- Flags

We have talked about action and data fields in our previous section. We have also used Extras to pass data from one activity to another. Let's talk about other fields.

Category

The category field can provide additional information about the components that can handle the intent. For example –

CATEGORY_BROWSABLE – can be invoked by a browser to display data specified by a Uri.

We will understand this better when we talk about intent filters.

Type

The type field specifies the MIME type of the Intent data. We can use setType() method of Intent object to explicitly specify the MIME type. For example -

```
intent.setType("IMAGE/JPG");
```

If the type is unspecified, Android will infer the type.

Component

With the component field, you can specify the component that should receive that Intent. We use this when we want to explicitly specify the class name that should receive that intent. We have seen a few examples of that already. We can set the component field either to the constructor of Intent object or by calling methods.

```
Intent intent = new Intent(this, SecondActivity.class);
```

Here we have specified the component field. This intent will be received only by SecondActivity.java class.

Alternatively, you can set component by calling any of the setComponent(), setClass() or setClassName() methods.

Flags

Flags specify how Intent should be handled. For example – we can use the flag FLAG_ACTIVITY_NO_HISTORY to specify not to put that activity in the history stack. Use the setFlags() method to set the flags.

Using Intent Filters

In a previous section, we have seen how we can use an Intent to call other applications. Now we will see how we can enable other activities to invoke our own activity, which is accomplished by using something called Intent Filters. Using intent filters, we declare that our application is capable of doing a specific task. We will see an example of using intent filter to create an application that is capable of loading web pages.

1. Create a new application called MyWebBrowser.

2. Add a WebView widget to activity_main.xml file -

```xml
<?xml version="1.0" encoding="utf-8"?>
<WebView xmlns:android="http://schemas.android.com/apk/res/android"
  android:id="@+id/webkit"
  android:layout_width="match_parent"
  android:layout_height="match_parent" />
```

3. Now update your MainActivity.java file with the following code -

```java
package com.iducate.mywebbrowser;

import android.os.Bundle;
import android.webkit.WebView;
import android.app.Activity;

public class MainActivity extends Activity {

        @Override
        protected void onCreate(Bundle savedInstanceState) {
                super.onCreate(savedInstanceState);
                setContentView(R.layout.activity_main);

                WebView browser=(WebView)findViewById(R.id.webkit);
                browser.loadUrl(getIntent().getDataString());
        }

}
```

3. Finally, update your AndroidMainfest.xml file so that it has the following code -

```xml
<?xml version="1.0" encoding="utf-8"?>
<manifest xmlns:android="http://schemas.android.com/apk/res/android"
  package="com.iducate.mywebbrowser"
  android:versionCode="1"
  android:versionName="1.0" >

  <uses-sdk
    android:minSdkVersion="8"
    android:targetSdkVersion="19" />
```

```
<uses-permission android:name="android.permission.INTERNET" />

<application
    android:allowBackup="true"
    android:icon="@drawable/ic_launcher"
    android:label="@string/app_name"
    android:theme="@style/AppTheme" >
    <activity
        android:name="com.iducate.mywebbrowser.MainActivity"
        android:label="@string/app_name" >
        <intent-filter>
            <action android:name="android.intent.action.VIEW" />

            <category android:name="android.intent.category.DEFAULT" />

            <data android:pathPattern=".*" />
            <data android:scheme="http" />
        </intent-filter>
    </activity>
</application>

</manifest>
```

4. When you run this application, you will find that the application is only installed, not running. That's fine because we will not directly run this application from the launcher. We will instead use this application with the help of another application.

5. Run the IntentsExample application which we have created in a previous section. You will see three buttons (figure 2.17). Click the "Web Browser" button which will let you choose a browser. This time, in addition to the available web browsers, the list will contain the "MyWebBrowser" application (figure 2.22).

Figure 2.22: MyWebBrowser

6. If you select MyWebBrowser from the list of browsers, you will see the web page will load on our MyWebBrowser application -

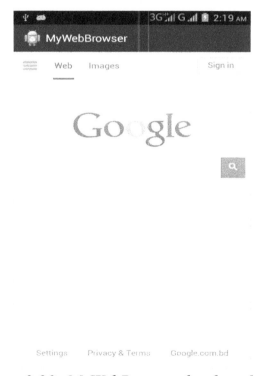

Figure 2.23: MyWebBrowser loads web page

How It Works?

The MyWebBrowser application has a single activity, MainActivity.java. Within our AndroidManifest.xml file under the <activity> node for our activity, we have added intent filters -

```
<intent-filter>
<action android:name="android.intent.action.VIEW" />

<category android:name="android.intent.category.DEFAULT" />

<data android:pathPattern=".*" />
  <data android:scheme="http" />
</intent-filter>
```

These intent filters tell the Android system that this activity is capable of loading web pages. Thus when another application requests to load a web page, this application will be included within the application chooser prompt as a browser client. Any application can invoke our activity by specifying the action android.intent.action.VIEW .

We need to add a permission in order to use Internet connection in our manifest file-

```
<uses-permission android:name="android.permission.INTERNET" />
```

So when another application wants to load a web page, they will have the option to use our application. Within the MainActivity.java class, we get the URL of the requested web page using the intent object.

```
WebView browser=(WebView)findViewById(R.id.webkit);
browser.loadUrl(getIntent().getDataString());
```

The getIntent() method of activity class enables us to get the intent which has started our activity. The getDataString() method of the intent object gives us the URL of the web page. We then load the URL within the WebView widget.

Resolving Intent Filter Collision

By now you can guess several activities (in either the same or different application) That have the same intent filter name. In that case, Android will let the user choose their preferred activity for performing that task by showing them a selection of choices (similar to figure 2.22).

From a list of options, users can choose an option and make that as default. In that case, that choice will be remembered and any future request will be automatically handled by that activity.

Fragments

Using fragments, you can define reusable UI components which enables you to create dynamic and flexible UI designs that can be adopted to suite a wide range of screen sizes. Each fragment is an independent module and is tightly bound to the Activity into which it is attached. You can use a fragment across multiple activities. Fragments can be added or removed dynamically.

You can combine multiple fragments in a single activity and build a multi-pane UI. This approach is particularly useful if you want to utilize the larger screen space of tablet devices.

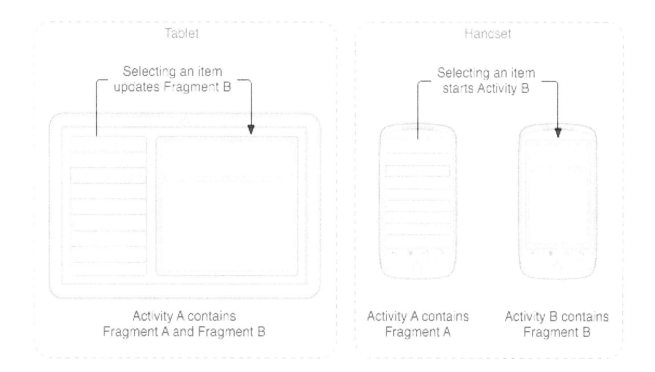

Figure 2.24: Using Fragments (Image Courtesy: http://developer.android.com/*)*

The above figure illustrates an example of using fragments to create separate layouts for phone and tablet devices. Let's say we have a list of items and selecting any of those items will show the details view of that item. We can define two separate fragments. The first fragment will display a list of items, while the second fragment will display the details of that selected item. For smart phone devices, we can use two separate activities for these two fragments. The first activity will contain the first fragment and the second activity will contain the second fragment. This way, if someone selects an item from the first activity, it will start a new activity. For tablet devices, those two fragments can be added to a single activity. In that case, selecting an item from the first fragment will update the second fragment.

Fragments were added with the release of Android 3.0, (API level 11), so you can use fragments on platforms from Android 3.0 onward. But by using the support library, it is possible to use fragments on older versions of Android. In that case, your activity should extend FragmentActivity class. This will support fragments on platforms from Android 1.6 onward.

Working with Fragments

The example below will show you how you can use fragments in your application. Follow the steps below -

1. Create a new Android application project called "FragmentsDemo".

2. In the res/layout folder, create a new layout file and name it my_frag.xml with the following code -

```xml
<?xml version="1.0" encoding="utf-8"?>
<LinearLayout xmlns:android="http://schemas.android.com/apk/res/android"
    android:layout_width="match_parent"
    android:layout_height="match_parent"
    android:orientation="vertical" >

    <TextView
        android:id="@+id/textView1"
        android:layout_width="wrap_content"
        android:layout_height="wrap_content"
```

```
    android:text="Hello World from Fragment!"
    android:textAppearance="?android:attr/textAppearanceLarge" />
```

```
</LinearLayout>
```

3. Now in src directory under the package name, create a new Java class "MyFragment.java". This is our fragment class, put in the following code -

```
package com.iducate.fragmentsdemo;

import android.app.Fragment;
import android.os.Bundle;
import android.view.LayoutInflater;
import android.view.View;
import android.view.ViewGroup;

public class MyFragment extends Fragment {

    @Override
    public View onCreateView(LayoutInflater inflater, ViewGroup
                        container,Bundle savedInstanceState) {

        View view = inflater.inflate(R.layout.my_frag, null, false);
        return view;
    }
}
```

4. Update your activity_main.xml file with the following content -

```
<RelativeLayout xmlns:android="http://schemas.android.com/apk/res/android"
    xmlns:tools="http://schemas.android.com/tools"
    android:layout_width="match_parent"
    android:layout_height="match_parent"
    tools:context=".MainActivity" >

    <fragment
        android:id="@+id/fragment1"
        android:name="com.iducate.fragmentsdemo.MyFragment"
        android:layout_width="wrap_content"
        android:layout_height="wrap_content"
        android:layout_alignParentTop="true"
```

```
android:layout_centerHorizontal="true"
tools:layout="@layout/my_frag" />
```

```
</RelativeLayout>
```

5. Now if you run the application, you will see a similar result as in figure 2.25 -

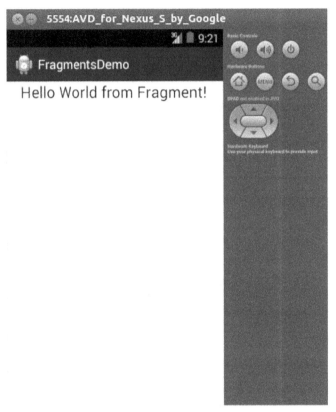

Figure 2.25: Running FragmentsDemo application

How It Works?

We have created a new fragment called "MyFragment", which is a subclass of "Fragment" class. The MyFragment class overwrites the onCreateView() method of Fragment class.

```
@Override
public View onCreateView(LayoutInflater inflater, ViewGroup
      container,Bundle savedInstanceState) {

   View view = inflater.inflate(R.layout.my_frag, null, false);
   return view;
}
```

Within the onCreateView() method, we first inflate a layout file named "my_frag.xml" file. This XML file contains the layout for our fragment. We then return this inflated layout.

The my_frag.xml layout file simply contains a TextView which shows a text message -

```
<TextView
    android:id="@+id/textView1"
    android:layout_width="wrap_content"
    android:layout_height="wrap_content"
    android:text="Hello World from Fragment!"
    android:textAppearance="?android:attr/textAppearanceLarge" />
```

Next, within the layout file of our activity, "activity_main.xml" file, we have used <fragment> element to set our fragment -

```
<fragment
    android:id="@+id/fragment1"
    android:name="com.iducate.fragmentsdemo.MyFragment"
    android:layout_width="wrap_content"
    android:layout_height="wrap_content"
    android:layout_alignParentTop="true"
    android:layout_centerHorizontal="true"
    tools:layout="@layout/my_frag" />
```

The android:name attribute of <fragment> defines the class name of fragment. This is how our activity class knows which fragment to load in this particular activity. This example shows how we can add a static fragment to our activity. But fragments can be added dynamically as well. We will see how we can add fragments dynamically in the next section.

Adding Fragments Dynamically

The real power of fragments comes into play when we add them dynamically to an activity at runtime. This enables us to use logic to dynamically add/remove fragments depending upon the device screen or other factors. For example, if our application is running on a smart phone, we can add a single fragment while we can add multiple fragments when the application is running on tablet device.

The example below will show how we can dynamically load different fragments based on screen orientation. We will use the previous example (FragmentsDemo) and modify it to dynamically load fragments. Follow the steps below -

1. We will create two new fragment classes and two corresponding layout files to be used by those fragments. Let's first create a new layout file, called fragment_a.xml under res/layout directory with the following code -

```xml
<?xml version="1.0" encoding="utf-8"?>
<LinearLayout xmlns:android="http://schemas.android.com/apk/res/android"
    android:layout_width="match_parent"
    android:layout_height="match_parent"
    android:orientation="vertical" >

    <TextView
        android:id="@+id/textView1"
        android:layout_width="wrap_content"
        android:layout_height="wrap_content"
        android:text="Fragment A"
        android:textAppearance="?android:attr/textAppearanceLarge" />

</LinearLayout>
```

2. Create another layout file fragment_b.xml under res/layout directory with the following code -

```xml
<?xml version="1.0" encoding="utf-8"?>
<LinearLayout xmlns:android="http://schemas.android.com/apk/res/android"
    android:layout_width="match_parent"
    android:layout_height="match_parent"
    android:orientation="vertical" >

    <TextView
        android:id="@+id/textView1"
        android:layout_width="wrap_content"
        android:layout_height="wrap_content"
        android:text="Fragment B"
        android:textAppearance="?android:attr/textAppearanceLarge" />

</LinearLayout>
```

3. Now we will create a new Fragment class, FragmentA.java with the following

100

code in src directory under our package -

```java
package com.iducate.fragmentsdemo;

import android.app.Fragment;
import android.os.Bundle;
import android.view.LayoutInflater;
import android.view.View;
import android.view.ViewGroup;

public class FragmentA extends Fragment {
    @Override
    public View onCreateView(LayoutInflater inflater, ViewGroup
        container,Bundle savedInstanceState) {
         View view = inflater.inflate(R.layout.fragment_a, null, false);
         return view;
    }
}
```

4. Next, create another Fragment class FragmentB.java in the src directory under our package with the following code -

```java
package com.iducate.fragmentsdemo;

import android.app.Fragment;
import android.os.Bundle;
import android.view.LayoutInflater;
import android.view.View;
import android.view.ViewGroup;

public class FragmentB extends Fragment {

    @Override
    public View onCreateView(LayoutInflater inflater, ViewGroup
        container,Bundle savedInstanceState) {
        View view = inflater.inflate(R.layout.fragment_b, null, false);
        return view;
    }
}
```

5. Finally update your MainActivity.java activity class with the following code -

```
package com.iducate.fragmentsdemo;

import android.app.Activity;
import android.app.FragmentManager;
import android.app.FragmentTransaction;
import android.content.res.Configuration;
import android.os.Bundle;

public class MainActivity extends Activity {

    @Override
    protected void onCreate(Bundle savedInstanceState) {
        super.onCreate(savedInstanceState);

        FragmentManager fragmentManager = getFragmentManager();
        FragmentTransaction ft =fragmentManager.beginTransaction();

        //detect orientation
        if(getResources().getConfiguration().orientation ==
                            Configuration.ORIENTATION_LANDSCAPE) {
            //landscape mode
            FragmentA fragmentA = new FragmentA();
            ft.replace(android.R.id.content, fragmentA);
        }
        else {
            //portrait mode
            FragmentB fragmentB = new FragmentB();
            ft.replace(android.R.id.content, fragmentB);
        }

        ft.commit();
    }

}
```

6. Now if your run the application, you will see FragmentB loaded when the device in portrait mode and once you change the orientation to landscape mode (for emulator, press Ctrl + F11) you will see FragmentA loaded (figure 2.26) -

Fragment A

Fragment B

Figure 2.26: Dynamically loaded fragments

How It Works?

We have created two separate fragment classes, FragmentA.java and FragmentB.java with two corresponding layout files fragment_a.xml and fragment_b.xml. We have overwritten the onCreateView() method of both fragment classes to inflate the corresponding layout files. That process is similar to our previous example. Both layout files contain a single TextView element so we can identify which fragment is loaded at runtime.

Now in our MainActivity.java file, we will dynamically add fragments. In order to work with fragments, we first instantiate a FragmentManager instance -

```
FragmentManager fragmentManager = getFragmentManager();
```

We also need the FragmentTransaction class to perform transaction on fragments (like add, remove or replace etc) -

```
FragmentTransaction ft =fragmentManager.beginTransaction();
```

We then detect the screen orientation and based on portrait or landscape mode, we add separate fragments to our activity dynamically -

```
//detect orientation
if(getResources().getConfiguration().orientation ==
                                Configuration.ORIENTATION_LANDSCAPE) {
        //landscape mode
        FragmentA fragmentA = new FragmentA();
        ft.replace(android.R.id.content, fragmentA);
}
else {
        //portrait mode
        FragmentB fragmentB = new FragmentB();
        ft.replace(android.R.id.content, fragmentB);
}
```

We have used the replace() method of FragmentTransaction which essentially first removes the existing fragment and then adds the new fragment. We have passed two parameters to the replace() method. The first one is the android.R.id.content which refers to the content view of activity. This content view comes with Android. We could instead use our own view if we wanted. The second parameter is the instance of fragment class we want to add.

Finally to make the transaction happen, we call the commit() method -

```
ft.commit();
```

Life Cycle of a Fragment

Like activities, fragments have their own life cycle as well. A series of event handlers are available for fragments which are triggered as the fragments are created, started, resumed, paused, stopped or destroyed. Figure 2.27 summarizes the fragment life cycle -

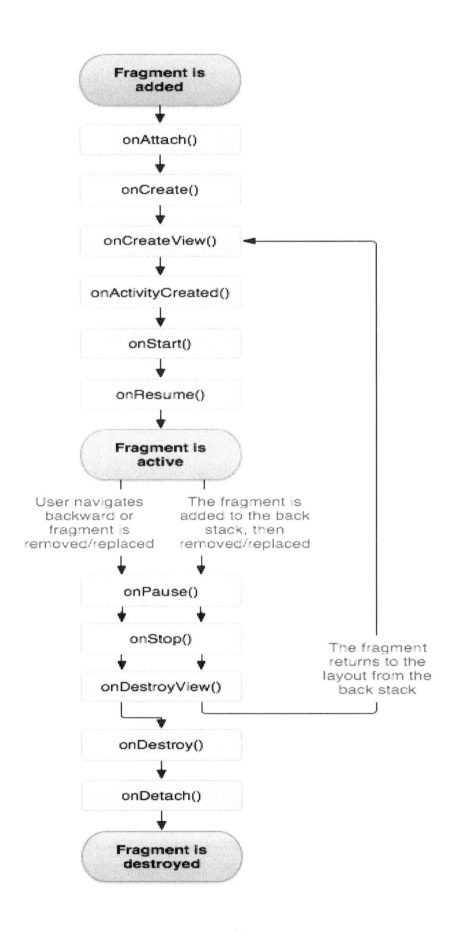

Figure 2.27: Fragment life cycle (Image Courtesy: http://developer.android.com/)

In order to better under the various life cycle methods of fragment, we will modify the previous project and add all the life cycle methods to our fragment -

1. We will use our same FragmentDemo project. First, open the MainActivity.java file and update that file with the following code -

```java
package com.iducate.fragmentsdemo;

import android.app.Activity;
import android.app.FragmentManager;
import android.app.FragmentTransaction;
import android.os.Bundle;

public class MainActivity extends Activity {

    @Override
    protected void onCreate(Bundle savedInstanceState) {
        super.onCreate(savedInstanceState);

        FragmentManager fragmentManager = getFragmentManager();
        FragmentTransaction ft= fragmentManager.beginTransaction();

        FragmentA fragmentA = new FragmentA();
        ft.add(android.R.id.content, fragmentA);
        ft.commit();
    }

}
```

We have dynamically added a single fragment, FragmentA. That fragment will have all the life cycle methods of a fragment.

2. Update the FragmentA.java file with the following code -

```java
package com.iducate.fragmentsdemo;

import android.app.Activity;
```

```java
import android.app.Fragment;
import android.os.Bundle;
import android.util.Log;
import android.view.LayoutInflater;
import android.view.View;
import android.view.ViewGroup;

public class FragmentA extends Fragment {

    private static final String TAG = "FragmentLifeCycle";

    @Override
    public void onAttach(Activity activity) {
        super.onAttach(activity);
        Log.d(TAG, "onAttach() called");
    }

    @Override
    public void onCreate(Bundle savedInstanceState) {
        super.onCreate(savedInstanceState);
        Log.d(TAG, "onCreate() called");
    }

    @Override
    public View onCreateView(LayoutInflater inflater, ViewGroup
    container,Bundle savedInstanceState) {
        Log.d(TAG, "onCreateView() called");

        View view = inflater.inflate(R.layout.fragment_a, null,
                                            false);
        return view;
    }

    @Override
    public void onActivityCreated(Bundle savedInstanceState) {
        super.onActivityCreated(savedInstanceState);
        Log.d(TAG, "onActivityCreated() called");
    }

    @Override
    public void onStart() {
        super.onStart();
        Log.d(TAG, "onStart() called");
```

```java
    }

    @Override
    public void onResume() {
        super.onResume();
        Log.d(TAG, "onResume() called");
    }

    @Override
    public void onPause() {
        super.onPause();
        Log.d(TAG, "onPause() called");
    }

    @Override
    public void onStop() {
        super.onStop();
        Log.d(TAG, "onStop() called");
    }

    @Override
    public void onDestroyView() {
        super.onDestroyView();
        Log.d(TAG, "onDestroyView() called");
    }

    @Override
    public void onDestroy() {
        super.onDestroy();
        Log.d(TAG, "onDestroy() called");
    }

    @Override
    public void onDetach() {
        super.onDetach();
        Log.d(TAG, "onDetach() called");
    }
}
```

3. Now run the application and open the LogCat view. If you filter the LogCat messages with tag "FragmentLifeCycle", your LogCat view will have the following messages -

Level	Time	PID	TID	Application	Tag	Text
D	04-01 23:36:28.573	13177	13177	com.iducate.fragmentsdemo	FragmentLifeCycle	onAttach() called
D	04-01 23:36:28.573	13177	13177	com.iducate.fragmentsdemo	FragmentLifeCycle	onCreate() called
D	04-01 23:36:28.611	13177	13177	com.iducate.fragmentsdemo	FragmentLifeCycle	onCreateView() called
D	04-01 23:36:28.612	13177	13177	com.iducate.fragmentsdemo	FragmentLifeCycle	onActivityCreated() called
D	04-01 23:36:28.612	13177	13177	com.iducate.fragmentsdemo	FragmentLifeCycle	onStart() called
D	04-01 23:36:28.613	13177	13177	com.iducate.fragmentsdemo	FragmentLifeCycle	onResume() called

Figure 2.28: LogCat View

From the above log messages, you can see that when we start the application, onAttach() method is first called followed by onCreate(), onCreateView(), onActivityCreated(), onStart() and onResume().

4. Now press the HOME button of your emulator or phone. This will output the following log messages -

Level	Time	PID	TID	Application	Tag	Text
D	04-01 23:36:28.573	13177	13177	com.iducate.fragmentsdemo	FragmentLifeCycle	onAttach() called
D	04-01 23:36:28.573	13177	13177	com.iducate.fragmentsdemo	FragmentLifeCycle	onCreate() called
D	04-01 23:36:28.611	13177	13177	com.iducate.fragmentsdemo	FragmentLifeCycle	onCreateView() called
D	04-01 23:36:28.612	13177	13177	com.iducate.fragmentsdemo	FragmentLifeCycle	onActivityCreated() called
D	04-01 23:36:28.612	13177	13177	com.iducate.fragmentsdemo	FragmentLifeCycle	onStart() called
D	04-01 23:36:28.613	13177	13177	com.iducate.fragmentsdemo	FragmentLifeCycle	onResume() called
D	04-01 23:37:03.347	13177	13177	com.iducate.fragmentsdemo	FragmentLifeCycle	onPause() called
D	04-01 23:37:03.982	13177	13177	com.iducate.fragmentsdemo	FragmentLifeCycle	onStop() called

Figure 2.29: LogCat view

We can see that pressing the HOME button resulted in two new life cycle method calls, onPause() and onStop().

5. Now launch the application again either from the launcher menu or from recent apps options (pressing and holding HOME button will show the recent apps). This will result in other life cycle method calls -

Level	Time	PID	TID	Application	Tag	Text
D	04-01 23:36:28.573	13177	13177	com.iducate.fragmentsdemo	FragmentLifeCycle	onAttach() called
D	04-01 23:36:28.573	13177	13177	com.iducate.fragmentsdemo	FragmentLifeCycle	onCreate() called
D	04-01 23:36:28.611	13177	13177	com.iducate.fragmentsdemo	FragmentLifeCycle	onCreateView() called
D	04-01 23:36:28.612	13177	13177	com.iducate.fragmentsdemo	FragmentLifeCycle	onActivityCreated() called
D	04-01 23:36:28.612	13177	13177	com.iducate.fragmentsdemo	FragmentLifeCycle	onStart() called
D	04-01 23:36:28.613	13177	13177	com.iducate.fragmentsdemo	FragmentLifeCycle	onResume() called
D	04-01 23:37:03.347	13177	13177	com.iducate.fragmentsdemo	FragmentLifeCycle	onPause() called
D	04-01 23:37:03.982	13177	13177	com.iducate.fragmentsdemo	FragmentLifeCycle	onStop() called
D	04-01 23:37:12.067	13177	13177	com.iducate.fragmentsdemo	FragmentLifeCycle	onStart() called
D	04-01 23:37:12.067	13177	13177	com.iducate.fragmentsdemo	FragmentLifeCycle	onResume() called

Figure 2.30: LogCat view

6. Finally, click the BACK button and you will get the following LogCat view -

Level	Time	PID	TID	Application	Tag	Text
D	04-01 23:36:28.573	13177	13177	com.iducate.fragmentsdemo	FragmentLifeCycle	onAttach() called
D	04-01 23:36:28.573	13177	13177	com.iducate.fragmentsdemo	FragmentLifeCycle	onCreate() called
D	04-01 23:36:28.611	13177	13177	com.iducate.fragmentsdemo	FragmentLifeCycle	onCreateView() called
D	04-01 23:36:28.612	13177	13177	com.iducate.fragmentsdemo	FragmentLifeCycle	onActivityCreated() called
D	04-01 23:36:28.612	13177	13177	com.iducate.fragmentsdemo	FragmentLifeCycle	onStart() called
D	04-01 23:36:28.613	13177	13177	com.iducate.fragmentsdemo	FragmentLifeCycle	onResume() called
D	04-01 23:37:03.347	13177	13177	com.iducate.fragmentsdemo	FragmentLifeCycle	onPause() called
D	04-01 23:37:03.982	13177	13177	com.iducate.fragmentsdemo	FragmentLifeCycle	onStop() called
D	04-01 23:37:12.067	13177	13177	com.iducate.fragmentsdemo	FragmentLifeCycle	onStart() called
D	04-01 23:37:12.067	13177	13177	com.iducate.fragmentsdemo	FragmentLifeCycle	onResume() called
D	04-01 23:37:17.061	13177	13177	com.iducate.fragmentsdemo	FragmentLifeCycle	onPause() called
D	04-01 23:37:17.716	13177	13177	com.iducate.fragmentsdemo	FragmentLifeCycle	onStop() called
D	04-01 23:37:17.716	13177	13177	com.iducate.fragmentsdemo	FragmentLifeCycle	onDestroyView() called
D	04-01 23:37:17.718	13177	13177	com.iducate.fragmentsdemo	FragmentLifeCycle	onDestroy() called
D	04-01 23:37:17.718	13177	13177	com.iducate.fragmentsdemo	FragmentLifeCycle	onDetach() called

Figure 2.31: LogCat view

How It Works?

As we can see, fragments goes through different states which are associated with different life cycle methods. When a fragment is created, the following life cycle methods are called -

- onAttach()
- onCreate()
- onCreateView()
- onActivityCreated()

Next a couple more methods are called before fragments become visible -

- onStart()
- onResume()

At this stage, the fragment is running on it's host activity. Now when the fragment is invisible, two methods are called -

- onPause()
- onStop()

When a fragment is destroyed (which means the hosting activity is destroyed), the following methods are called -

- onPause()
- onStop()
- onDestroyView()
- onDestroy()
- onDetach()

Among the above methods, some of them have Bundle object as their parameter so you can restore the state of fragments -

- onCreate()
- onCreateView()
- onActivityCreated()

You can save the state of a fragment within the onSaveInstanceState() method. We will learn more about that in a later chapter.

Whenever a fragment is attached to an activity, its life cycle states are closely associated to the hosting activity. In addition to those states, there are some other fragment specific states -

- onAttached() - called when the fragment is attached to it's host activity
- onCreateView() - this method will return a view of the fragment
- onActivityCreated() - called when an activity's onCreate() method is called
- onDestroyView() - this method is called when the fragment's view is removed
- onDetach() - called when the fragment is detached from the hosting activity

Interactions between Fragments

In many cases, your activity will contain more than one fragment. In that case, you will need to interact between those fragments. That's why it is important to know how we can access a view of one fragment from another fragment. The next example will demonstrate that.

We will use the FragmentsDemo project. Follow the steps below -

1. Update the layout file fragment_a.xml with the code below -

```xml
<?xml version="1.0" encoding="utf-8"?>
<LinearLayout xmlns:android="http://schemas.android.com/apk/res/android"
    android:layout_width="match_parent"
    android:layout_height="match_parent"
    android:orientation="vertical" >

    <TextView
        android:id="@+id/fragmentATextView"
        android:layout_width="wrap_content"
        android:layout_height="wrap_content"
        android:text="Fragment A"
        android:textAppearance="?android:attr/textAppearanceLarge" />

</LinearLayout>
```

2. Next, update the FragmentA.java class with the following code -

```java
package com.iducate.fragmentsdemo;

import android.app.Fragment;
import android.os.Bundle;
import android.view.LayoutInflater;
import android.view.View;
import android.view.ViewGroup;

public class FragmentA extends Fragment {

    @Override
    public View onCreateView(LayoutInflater inflater, ViewGroup
    container,Bundle savedInstanceState) {
        View view = inflater.inflate(R.layout.fragment_a, null,
                        false);
        return view;
    }
}
```

3. We will then update fragment_b.xml file to include a button element -

```xml
<?xml version="1.0" encoding="utf-8"?>
```

```xml
<LinearLayout xmlns:android="http://schemas.android.com/apk/res/android"
    android:layout_width="match_parent"
    android:layout_height="match_parent"
    android:orientation="vertical" >

    <TextView
        android:id="@+id/fragmentBTextView"
        android:layout_width="wrap_content"
        android:layout_height="wrap_content"
        android:text="Fragment B"
        android:textAppearance="?android:attr/textAppearanceLarge" />

    <Button
        android:id="@+id/btnGetText"
        android:layout_width="wrap_content"
        android:layout_height="wrap_content"
        android:text="Get Text" />

</LinearLayout>
```

4. Update FragmentB.java file as follows -

```java
package com.iducate.fragmentsdemo;

import android.app.Fragment;
import android.os.Bundle;
import android.view.LayoutInflater;
import android.view.View;
import android.view.View.OnClickListener;
import android.view.ViewGroup;
import android.widget.Button;
import android.widget.TextView;
import android.widget.Toast;

public class FragmentB extends Fragment {

    @Override
    public View onCreateView(LayoutInflater inflater, ViewGroup
                container,Bundle savedInstanceState) {
        View view = inflater.inflate(R.layout.fragment_b, null,
                                false);
        return view;
    }
```

```java
    @Override
    public void onStart() {
        super.onStart();

        Button btnGetText = (Button) getActivity()
                    .findViewById(R.id.btnGetText);

        btnGetText.setOnClickListener(new OnClickListener() {

            @Override
            public void onClick(View v) {
                TextView fragmentATextView = (TextView) getActivity()
                            .findViewById(R.id.fragmentATextView);
                Toast.makeText(getActivity(),
                            fragmentATextView.getText().toString(),
                            Toast.LENGTH_SHORT).show();
            }
        });
    }
}
```

5. Next, we will update the layout file for our activity file to include both fragments. Update the activity_main.xml file -

```xml
<LinearLayout xmlns:android="http://schemas.android.com/apk/res/android"
    xmlns:tools="http://schemas.android.com/tools"
    android:layout_width="fill_parent"
    android:layout_height="fill_parent"
    android:orientation="horizontal" >

    <fragment
        android:id="@+id/fragment1"
        android:name="com.iducate.fragmentsdemo.FragmentA"
        android:layout_width="0dp"
        android:layout_height="wrap_content"
        android:layout_weight="1"
        tools:layout="@layout/fragment_a" />

    <fragment
        android:id="@+id/fragment2"
        android:name="com.iducate.fragmentsdemo.FragmentB"
        android:layout_width="0dp"
```

```
        android:layout_height="wrap_content"
        android:layout_weight="1"
        tools:layout="@layout/fragment_b" />
```

```
</LinearLayout>
```

6. Finally, we will update our MainActivity.java file -

```
package com.iducate.fragmentsdemo;

import android.app.Activity;
import android.os.Bundle;

public class MainActivity extends Activity {

        @Override
        protected void onCreate(Bundle savedInstanceState) {
                super.onCreate(savedInstanceState);
                setContentView(R.layout.activity_main);
        }
}
```

7. Now if you run the application, you will see two fragments loaded. Click the button of FragmentB and you will see a toast message containing the text of FragmentA TextView widget (figure 2.32) -

Figure 2.32: Running FragmentsDemo application

How It Works?

Because fragments are hosted to activities, the getActivity() method can be used to get the activity in which the fragment is currently attached to. Then, we use the findViewById() method of activity class to get the view widgets (TextView, Button etc). This is how we get the button widget from FragmentB class -

```
Button btnGetText = (Button) getActivity()
                            .findViewById(R.id.btnGetText);
```

We then attach an OnClickListener to listen to the button click event -

```
btnGetText.setOnClickListener(new OnClickListener() {

        @Override
        public void onClick(View v) {
                TextView fragmentATextView = (TextView) getActivity()
                        .findViewById(R.id.fragmentATextView);
                Toast.makeText(getActivity(),
                        fragmentATextView.getText().toString(),
                        Toast.LENGTH_SHORT).show();
```

```
                    }
            });
```

Within the onClick() method of OnClickListener class, we get the TextView of FragmentA and then show that text as a Toast notification. Toast notifications are created using the makeText() method of Toast class which takes three parameters - the Context object, a string to display as notification and the duration. We then finally use the show() method of Toast class to display the message. Toast messages are non-persistent. They flash on the screen for a few seconds and then disappears. Toasts are a convenient way to notify users about general events.

Displaying Notifications

While Toast notifications are good for some cases, it is not so good for displaying important messages. Due to the non-persistent nature of Toast notifications, users might miss notifications if they aren't looking at their screen. So we need a better way to display notifications.

The NotificationManager let's us display persistent messages in the status bar of the device. The next example will show us how to do that.

1. Create a new project NotificationDemo.

2. Now, update the activity_main.xml layout file to add a button so that we can trigger a notification upon clicking that button -

```
<LinearLayout xmlns:android="http://schemas.android.com/apk/res/android"
    android:layout_width="fill_parent"
    android:layout_height="fill_parent"
    android:orientation="vertical" >

    <Button
        android:id="@+id/btnNotify"
        android:layout_width="wrap_content"
        android:layout_height="wrap_content"
        android:layout_gravity="center"
        android:onClick="notifyMe"
        android:text="Notify Me" />

</LinearLayout>
```

3. We will create a new layout file notification.xml with a text message under res/layout directory with the following code -

```xml
<?xml version="1.0" encoding="utf-8"?>
<LinearLayout xmlns:android="http://schemas.android.com/apk/res/android"
    android:layout_width="match_parent"
    android:layout_height="match_parent"
    android:orientation="vertical" >

    <TextView
        android:id="@+id/textView1"
        android:layout_width="wrap_content"
        android:layout_height="wrap_content"
        android:text="Are you ready for the challenge?" />

</LinearLayout>
```

4. Create a new activity class NotificationRecieverActivity.java which will be invoked when users click the notification message from the status bar -

```java
package com.iducate.notificationdemo;

import android.app.Activity;
import android.os.Bundle;

public class NotificationReceiverActivity extends Activity {

    @Override
    protected void onCreate(Bundle savedInstanceState) {
        super.onCreate(savedInstanceState);
        setContentView(R.layout.notification);
    }
}
```

As you can see, this activity file simply inflates the layout file notification.xml.

5. We need to register this new activity in our AndroidManifest.xml file -

```xml
<?xml version="1.0" encoding="utf-8"?>
<manifest xmlns:android="http://schemas.android.com/apk/res/android"
    package="com.iducate.notificationdemo"
    android:versionCode="1"
```

```
android:versionName="1.0" >

<uses-sdk
    android:minSdkVersion="8"
    android:targetSdkVersion="19" />

<application
    android:allowBackup="true"
    android:icon="@drawable/ic_launcher"
    android:label="@string/app_name"
    android:theme="@style/AppTheme" >
    <activity
        android:name="com.iducate.notificationdemo.MainActivity"
        android:label="@string/app_name" >
        <intent-filter>
            <action android:name="android.intent.action.MAIN" />

            <category android:name="android.intent.category.LAUNCHER" />
        </intent-filter>
    </activity>
    <activity
android:name="com.iducate.notificationdemo.NotificationReceiverActivity"
>
    </activity>
</application>

</manifest>
```

6. Finally, update the MainActivity.java file with the following code -

```
package com.iducate.notificationdemo;

import android.app.Activity;
import android.app.NotificationManager;
import android.app.PendingIntent;
import android.content.Context;
import android.content.Intent;
import android.os.Bundle;
import android.support.v4.app.NotificationCompat;
import android.view.View;

public class MainActivity extends Activity {
```

```java
@Override
protected void onCreate(Bundle savedInstanceState) {
        super.onCreate(savedInstanceState);
        setContentView(R.layout.activity_main);
}

public void notifyMe(View view) {
        Intent intent = new Intent(this,

NotificationReceiverActivity.class);
        PendingIntent pendingIntent =

PendingIntent.getActivity(this, 0,intent, 0);

        // build the notification
        NotificationCompat.Builder notificationBuilder = new
                        NotificationCompat.Builder(
            getApplicationContext()).setTicker("Ready for the
                                                challenge?")
                .setSmallIcon(android.R.drawable.stat_sys_warnin
                                                g)
                .setAutoCancel(true).setContentTitle("Challenge
                                                Reminder")

                .setContentText("This is a reminder about
                upcoming
challenge.").setContentIntent(pendingIntent);

        NotificationManager notificationManager = (NotificationManager)
getSystemService(Context.NOTIFICATION_SERVICE);

        notificationManager.notify(0, notificationBuilder.build());
    }
}
```

We will go through the details of the above file later. First, let's run the application.

7. If you run the application, you will see a screen with a single button "Notify Me". Clicking that button will generate a notification at the status bar (figure 2.33) -

121

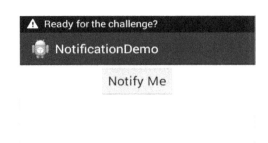

Figure 2.33: Status bar notification

8. Expanding the status bar will show the detail view of the notification -

Figure 2.34: Notification details view

9. Clicking that notification will start a new activity -

Figure 2.35: New activity started from notification

How It Works?

We have created a new activity NotificationRecieverActivity.java with a layout file notification.xml which we want to launch when user clicks the notification message from the status bar.

Our activity_main.xml layout contains a button element with android:onClick attribute set to "notifiyMe". The notifyMe() method of MainActivity will handle the button click event. These steps should be familiar to you.

Within the notifyMe() method, we create a new instance of Intent class -

```
Intent intent = new Intent(this,NotificationReceiverActivity.class);
```

We then create an instance of PendingIntent class -

123

```
PendingIntent pendingIntent = PendingIntent.getActivity(this, 0,intent, 0);
```

With PendingIntent, you specify the actions to be taken in the future. By giving a PendingIntent to another application, you give permission to that application to perform the specified operations on behalf of you. We have created a new pending intent by calling getActivity() method with parameters like context, request code, intent object and a flag code. You can learn more about PendingIntent at -

http://developer.android.com/reference/android/app/PendingIntent.html

Next, we build a Notification builder with the information like notification text, subject, ticker text, intent, icon etc -

```
NotificationCompat.Builder notificationBuilder = new
    NotificationCompat.Builder(getApplicationContext())
          .setTicker("Ready for the challenge?")
          .setSmallIcon(android.R.drawable.stat_sys_warning)
          .setAutoCancel(true).setContentTitle("Challenge Reminder")
          .setContentText("This is a reminder about upcoming
                           challenge.")
          .setContentIntent(pendingIntent);
```

Then we get the NotificationManger using getSystemService() method call from our activity -

```
NotificationManager notificationManager = (NotificationManager)
          getSystemService(Context.NOTIFICATION_SERVICE);

notificationManager.notify(0, notificationBuilder.build());
```

Finally we call the notify() method of notification manager object to trigger the notification.

Notification builder is available from API level 11. But using the support library's NotificationCompat.Builder class, we can provide support from API level 4. If you don't need to support older platforms, you can use the Notification.Builder class.

Summary

In this chapter, we have learned about the Activity class, a building block of Android application. Activities have a number of life cycle methods. We have examined those methods by triggering various events. Next, we have learned about Intent objects which serves as a message-passing mechanism for the Android platform and help us to communicate between different components of same (or other) application. We have seen a number of examples that demonstrate usages of intents to start activities, send data, return result from other activities and also how to call other applications from our application. We learned about the concept of intent filers. We have then learned about fragments which enables us to build flexible multi-pane UI to adopt different screen sizes. Finally, we have seen how we can notify users using Toast notifications and more persistent notifications using the NotificationManger class. The next chapter will explore user interface design of an Android application.

Chapter 3: Understanding the Android User Interface

In this chapter, we will learn about ViewGroups. ViewGroups help lay out different view widgets to create the user interface of an Android app. The Android platform offers a number of ViewGroups. We will look at each of their characteristics and learn how they arrange view widgets. We will also see how to manage screen orientation changes, learn how we can listen to and handle different UI events.

Understanding the Components of a Screen

We have learnt in the previous chapter that the screen of an Android application is represented by an activity class. We have learned about activity classes in chapter 2, but we didn't spend too much time on the graphical user interface (GUI) design. The user interface of an Android application usually contains different view widgets like text input boxes, buttons, text labels, images and so on. Your UI is defined in a XML file. Let's look at an example layout file which is automatically generated as part of Eclipse's project creation process. This file is the 'activity_main.xml' file located under the 'res/layout' directory.

```xml
<RelativeLayout        xmlns:android="http://schemas.android.com/apk/res/android"
    xmlns:tools="http://schemas.android.com/tools"
    android:layout_width="match_parent"
    android:layout_height="match_parent"
    android:paddingBottom="@dimen/activity_vertical_margin"
    android:paddingLeft="@dimen/activity_horizontal_margin"
    android:paddingRight="@dimen/activity_horizontal_margin"
    android:paddingTop="@dimen/activity_vertical_margin"
    tools:context=".MainActivity" >

    <TextView
        android:layout_width="wrap_content"
        android:layout_height="wrap_content"
        android:text="@string/hello_world" />
```

```
</RelativeLayout>
```

You can see that the XML layout file starts with the root node `<RelativeLayout>` , which is one of the available Android ViewGroup. This ViewGroup contains a single `<TextView>` element. Now let's see how this layout file is used by the activity class to create the UI -

```
protected void onCreate(Bundle savedInstanceState) {
    super.onCreate(savedInstanceState);
    setContentView(R.layout.activity_main);
}
```

In the onCreate() method of the activity class, we refer to the layout file by calling the setContentView() method. We call such a reference to the layout as *inflating* it. When a layout file is inflated, all the widgets in the layout file are instantiated as defined by it's attributes. Once this is done, Android will create the UI for your application.

It is possible to create a UI without using XML files by using code. But using XML files for defining layout and then inflating those layout files from activity classes is the standard practice among the developer community. An exception is when you will need to generate the UI dynamically during runtime. A later section of this chapter will show you how you can create a UI dynamically.

Views and ViewGroups

An Android UI consists of Views and ViewGroups. A View is a widget that appears on the screen, like a text label, text input area, image or button. The android.view.View class represents the basic building block for user interface components and all Views are derived from that class.

A ViewGroup is a special View that contains one or more other Views. The base class for ViewGroup is the android.view.ViewGroup which is a subclass of the android.view.View class. Different ViewGroups let's you arrange Views differently for example, arranging them in horizontal or vertical order, tabular format or arranging them relatively to other Views etc. A ViewGroup can contain other ViewGroups as well (figure 3.1, image courtesy http://

127

developer.android.com) -

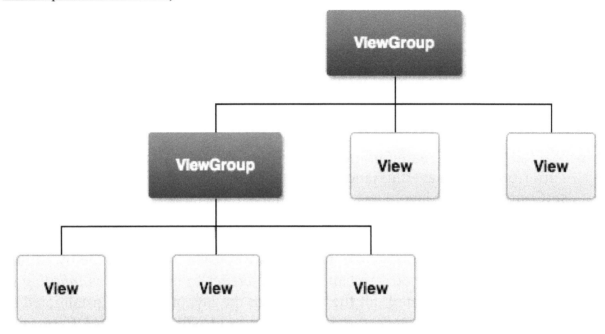

Figure 3.1: ViewGroup hierarchy

Android supports a number of ViewGroups -

- LinearLayout
- RelativeLayout
- TableLayout
- FrameLayout
- ScrollView

Your Android application's user interface will be built using a hierarchy of View and ViewGroup objects. The following sections will introduce you to different ViewGroups.

More will be discussed about Views in Chapter 4 and Chapter 5.

LinearLayout

LinearLayout arranges widgets or child containers in columns or rows, placing them one after the next. Thus, you can get a layout where child elements are arranged either vertically or horizontally. There are four main areas to configure for a LinearLayout – orientation, fill model, weight and gravity.

Orientation

The `android:orientation` property of a LinearLayout determines the orientation of child elements. It can take one of two values -

- vertical – which arranges child elements vertically
- horizontal – which arranges child elements horizontally

For example, the below code snippet sets the vertical orientation -

```
<LinearLayout xmlns:android="http://schemas.android.com/apk/res/android"
    android:layout_width="match_parent"
    android:layout_height="match_parent"
    android:gravity="center"
    android:orientation="vertical" >
```

Fill Model

The fill model of a LinearLayout (or any other layout type) determines how much space each child widget gets. While allocating space, LinearLayout prioritize the widgets on the basis of order in which they were added. For example, if a LinearLayout has two child widgets and its first child requests all the available spaces, then LinearLayout will allocate all the spaces to the first child. However as a result, the second child will not get any space.

All child widgets inside a LinearLayout must explicitly specify the width and height by defining the attributes `android:layout_width` and `android:layout_height`. You could provide the values of these two attributes in several ways -

- Providing specific dimensions, like 200 dp (density independent pixels)
- You can provide as much space the widget needs to accommodate it's contents, using the value **wrap_content**
- Another option is to allocate all available spaces of it's parent container, using the value **match_parent** (prior to API level 8, it was known as fill_parent)

Weight

There will be times when you will need to split the available spaces of your UI layout among two (or more) widgets in some proportion. For example, say you have two buttons contained within a horizontal LinearLayout and you want to allocate each of the buttons equal width based on available spaces. You can use the android:layout_weight property and set equal weight to accomplish this -

```xml
<?xml version="1.0" encoding="utf-8"?>
<LinearLayout xmlns:android="http://schemas.android.com/apk/res/android"
   android:layout_width="match_parent"
   android:layout_height="match_parent"
   android:orientation="horizontal" >

   <Button
      android:id="@+id/button1"
      android:layout_width="0dp"
      android:layout_height="wrap_content"
      android:layout_weight="1"
      android:text="Button 1" />

   <Button
      android:id="@+id/button2"
      android:layout_width="0dp"
      android:layout_height="wrap_content"
      android:layout_weight="1"
      android:text="Button 2" />

</LinearLayout>
```

When we set weight for widgets, we usually set the android:layout_width property for those widgets to "0dp". The layout for above XML code will look like figure 3.2 -

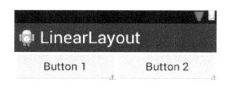

Figure 3.2: LinearLayout with android:layout_weight property

Gravity

When you add widgets to your LinearLayout, you will notice that everything is left and top-aligned. For LinearLayout with horizontal orientation, the widgets will start filling the space from left to right, while for vertical orientation, the widgets will appear from top to bottom. If you want to align the widgets otherwise, you can do so using the android:layout_gravity property.

If your LinearLayout is set to vertical orientation, you can use the android:layout_gravity property to set the horizontal alignment of the widgets within that container -

```
<?xml version="1.0" encoding="utf-8"?>
<LinearLayout xmlns:android="http://schemas.android.com/apk/res/android"
   android:layout_width="match_parent"
   android:layout_height="match_parent"
   android:orientation="vertical" >

   <Button
      android:id="@+id/button1"
      android:layout_width="wrap_content"
      android:layout_height="wrap_content"
      android:layout_gravity="center"
```

131

```
  android:text="Button 1" />

</LinearLayout>
```

This will make your button widget center-aligned horizontally -

Figure 3.3: Widget aligned center

On the other hand, if the LinearLayout is horizontally orientated, you can use the android:layout_gravity property to align the widgets vertically -

```
<?xml version="1.0" encoding="utf-8"?>
<LinearLayout xmlns:android="http://schemas.android.com/apk/res/android"
   android:layout_width="match_parent"
   android:layout_height="match_parent"
   android:orientation="horizontal" >

   <Button
      android:id="@+id/button1"
      android:layout_width="wrap_content"
      android:layout_height="wrap_content"
      android:layout_gravity="bottom"
      android:text="Button 1" />

</LinearLayout>
```

We have set the android:layout_gravity property of button widget to "bottom", which will push the button at the bottom of the screen -

Figure 3.4: Widget aligned bottom

Density Independent Pixel

Android devices have varying screen densities. You will find Android devices with densities ranging from 120 dpi to 320 dpi. Based on screen density, devices can generally be categorized into the following four groups -

- Low density (ldpi) – 120 dpi
- Medium density (mdpi) – 160 dpi
- High density (hdpi) – 240 dpi
- Extra High Density (xhdpi) – 320 dpi

Because the pixel density of device screen varies, when you specify dimensions in terms of pixels, you will notice that the views are rendered differently in devices of different pixel density. To overcome this problem, the density independent pixels, "dp" or "dip" unit is used. Using the dp unit ensures that the views of your layout will be scaled automatically depending upon the screen density and hence, always get the views in the right proportion.

1 dp is equivalent to one pixel on a 160 dpi screen. So if you have a widget that has an width of 160dp, then -

- Running on 320 dpi screen will take 320 pixels
- Running on 240 dpi screen will take 240 pixels
- Running on 160 dpi screen will take 160 pixels

This is how Android scales the view automatically based on the screen density of the device.

An Example LinearLayout

In this section, we will create a simple project to demonstrate the concepts we have learned about LinearLayout and will design a LinearLayout with some widgets. We will be creating a simple user login screen.

1. Create a new project called 'LinearLayoutDemo'.

2. Update the layout file activity_main.xml with the following code -

```
<LinearLayout xmlns:android="http://schemas.android.com/apk/res/android"
    android:layout_width="match_parent"
    android:layout_height="match_parent"
    android:orientation="vertical" >

    <LinearLayout
        android:layout_width="match_parent"
        android:layout_height="wrap_content"
        android:orientation="horizontal"
        android:padding="10dp" >

        <TextView
            android:layout_width="0dp"
            android:layout_height="wrap_content"
            android:layout_weight="1"
            android:text="Username" />

        <EditText
            android:layout_width="0dp"
            android:layout_height="wrap_content"
            android:layout_weight="2" />
    </LinearLayout>

    <LinearLayout
```

```
    android:layout_width="match_parent"
    android:layout_height="wrap_content"
    android:orientation="horizontal"
    android:padding="10dp" >

    <TextView
        android:layout_width="0dp"
        android:layout_height="wrap_content"
        android:layout_weight="1"
        android:text="Password" />

    <EditText
        android:layout_width="0dp"
        android:layout_height="wrap_content"
        android:layout_weight="2" />
</LinearLayout>

<Button
    android:layout_width="wrap_content"
    android:layout_height="wrap_content"
    android:layout_gravity="center"
    android:text="Login" />

</LinearLayout>
```

3. If you run the application, you will see a screen similar to figure 3.5 -

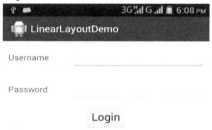

How It Works?

This example demonstrates how we can use several LinearLayout containers to create a UI. The root container for our activity_main.xml file is a LinearLayout with vertical orientation -

```
<LinearLayout       xmlns:android="http://schemas.android.com/apk/res/
android"
    android:layout_width="match_parent"
    android:layout_height="match_parent"
    android:orientation="vertical" >
...
</LinearLayout>
```

This root LinearLayout container holds three child elements - two LinearLayouts and a button widget. Each child LinearLayout contains a TextView and a EditText widget in horizontal orientation.

```
<LinearLayout
android:layout_width="match_parent"
android:layout_height="wrap_content"
android:orientation="horizontal"
android:padding="10dp" >
...
</LinearLayout>
```

We have also set padding to each child LinearLayout container which applies a padding of 10 dp around the content.

Within each child LinearLayout container, the TextView and EditText widgets share the available width by setting the weight property - the TextView takes one third of the available space and EditText takes the rest of the two thirds.

Finally after the two inner LinearLayouts, we have a button widget within the root LinearLayout -

```
<Button
android:layout_width="wrap_content"
```

```
    android:layout_height="wrap_content"
    android:layout_gravity="center"
    android:text="Login" />
```

Note that we have aligned the button element to center. Since the root LinearLayout is vertically oriented, the button will be centered horizontally.

RelativeLayout

While LinearLayout gives you a simple container where you can arrange widgets in a row or in a column, for more complex UIs, you will might need to nest multiple LinearLayouts. This is especially when your UI gets more complicated and you want more flexibility to arrange widgets within your container. The RelativeLayout is a powerful container type which can help you achieve this. It enables you to arrange widgets within your container *relative* to one another.

Let's see an example UI design using RelativeLayout.

1. Create a new project called 'RelativeLayoutDemo'.

2. Update the activity_main.xml file with following code -

```
<RelativeLayout            xmlns:android="http://schemas.android.com/apk/res/
android"
    xmlns:tools="http://schemas.android.com/tools"
    android:layout_width="match_parent"
    android:layout_height="match_parent" >

    <EditText
        android:id="@+id/editText1"
        android:layout_width="match_parent"
        android:layout_height="wrap_content"
        android:layout_alignParentLeft="true"
        android:layout_alignParentTop="true" />

    <Button
        android:id="@+id/button1"
        android:layout_width="wrap_content"
        android:layout_height="wrap_content"
        android:layout_alignParentRight="true"
        android:layout_below="@+id/editText1"
```

```
    android:text="Submit" />

<Button
    android:id="@+id/button2"
    android:layout_width="wrap_content"
    android:layout_height="wrap_content"
    android:layout_alignParentLeft="true"
    android:layout_below="@+id/editText1"
    android:text="Cancel" />

</RelativeLayout>
```

3. Now if you run the application, you should get a screen similar to figure 3.6 -

Figure 3.6: Running RelativeLayoutDemo application

How it works?

Our UI contains an EditText widget and couple of Button widgets below. We have used a single RelativeLayout container to hold all three child views. Within our RelativeLayout container, the view widgets are arranged relative to one another and relative to the parent container.

First we have the EditText widget. We have aligned that widget at the top left corner of our container -

```
<EditText
android:id="@+id/editText1"
android:layout_width="match_parent"
android:layout_height="wrap_content"
android:layout_alignParentLeft="true"
android:layout_alignParentTop="true" />
```

The android:layout_alignParentTop and android:layout_alignParentLeft attributes are used to place our EditText widget aligned with the container's top and left edge.

Next, we have two Button widgets below EditText. The button labeled "Submit" is aligned right -

```
<Button
android:id="@+id/button1"
android:layout_width="wrap_content"
android:layout_height="wrap_content"
android:layout_alignParentRight="true"
android:layout_below="@+id/editText1"
android:text="Submit" />
```

We have specified two properties to place the widget below our EditText widget and at right side of the screen.

Similarly, we have placed another button at the below of EditText and left aligned it with container's edge -

```
<Button
android:id="@+id/button2"
android:layout_width="wrap_content"
android:layout_height="wrap_content"
android:layout_alignParentLeft="true"
android:layout_below="@+id/editText1"
android:text="Cancel" />
```

So this is how you arrange your widgets within a RelativeLayout container by referencing them relative to either container or other widgets.

TableLayout

With TableLayout, you can arrange your views in rows and columns. Each row in a TableLayout is designated by the <TableRow> element. Within each row, you can put one or more views. Each view within your row will take at least one column. However, if you want any view widget to span across multiple columns, you can do that by explicitly specifying the number of columns. The number of columns of your TableLayout will be the maximum of available columns among all the rows.

Let's see an example of how we can use TableLayout.

1. Create a new project 'TableLayoutDemo'.

2. Update the activity_main.xml file with the following code -

```xml
<TableLayout xmlns:android="http://schemas.android.com/apk/res/android"
    android:layout_width="match_parent"
    android:layout_height="match_parent" >

  <TableRow
    android:layout_width="match_parent"
    android:layout_height="wrap_content" >

    <TextView
      android:layout_width="wrap_content"
          android:layout_height="wrap_content"
      android:layout_marginLeft="20dip"
      android:text="Username" >
    </TextView>

    <EditText
      android:layout_width="0dp"
      android:layout_height="wrap_content"
      android:layout_marginLeft="20dip"
      android:layout_marginRight="20dip"
      android:layout_weight="1" >
    </EditText>
  </TableRow>

  <TableRow
    android:layout_width="match_parent"
    android:layout_height="wrap_content" >
```

```
<TextView
    android:layout_width="wrap_content"
    android:layout_height="wrap_content"
    android:layout_marginLeft="20dip"
    android:text="Password" >
</TextView>

<EditText
    android:layout_width="0dp"
    android:layout_height="wrap_content"
    android:layout_marginLeft="20dip"
    android:layout_marginRight="20dip"
    android:layout_weight="1" >
</EditText>
</TableRow>

<TableRow
    android:layout_width="match_parent"
    android:layout_height="wrap_content"
    android:gravity="center" >

    <Button
        android:layout_width="wrap_content"
        android:layout_height="wrap_content"
        android:layout_span="2"
        android:text="Login" >
    </Button>
</TableRow>

</TableLayout>
```

3. Running this application will show a screen similar to figure 3.7

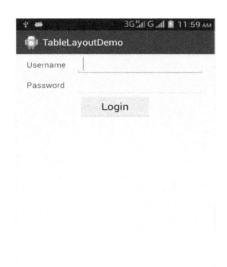

Figure 3.7: Running TableLayoutDemo application

How does it work?

Our TableLayout has three <TableRow> elements which define three rows. The first two rows contain two elements and the third row contains a single element. Our TableLayout will have two columns. The width of any column is determined by the maximum width taken by any view of that column. For the first column, we have TextView widgets. The width of those TextView widgets are set to 'wrap_content'. For the EditText widgets, we have weight property set to 1, which means all the remaining spaces for the <TableRow> will be allocated to those elements. Since <TableRow> element's width is set to 'match_parent', it will allocate the rest of the available space of that row to the EditText widgets.

The third row contains only a single element, a button widget -

```
<Button
  android:layout_width="wrap_content"
  android:layout_height="wrap_content"
  android:layout_span="2"
  android:text="Login" >
```

We have set the android:layout_span attribute of button widget to specify that it should span across both columns. This is because we want it to be center aligned, which is done by setting android:gravity property of parent <TableRow> to center -

```
    <TableRow
    android:layout_width="match_parent"
    android:layout_height="wrap_content"
    android:gravity="center" >
```

FrameLayout

The FrameLayout container arranges all the child widgets on top of each other. That means that within a single FrameLayout, you can display only one element. If you add a new element to your FrameLayout, that element will be placed on top of the previous element.

1. Let's create a new project called 'FrameLayoutDemo'.

2. Update the activity_main.xml layout file with the following code -

```
<FrameLayout xmlns:android="http://schemas.android.com/apk/res/android"
    android:layout_width="fill_parent"
    android:layout_height="fill_parent" >

    <Button
        android:id="@+id/button1"
        android:layout_width="204dp"
        android:layout_height="128dp"
        android:text="Button" />

</FrameLayout>
```

3. As you can see, the layout file contains a single FrameLayout container, within which we have a big button widget. If you run the application, you will see a screen similar to figure 3.8 -

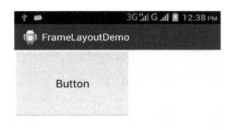

Figure 3.8: Running FrameLayoutDemo application

4. You can see that the button widget is anchored to the top left of the FrameLayout. Next, we will add a new TextView widget to our FrameLayout container -

```
<FrameLayout xmlns:android="http://schemas.android.com/apk/res/android"
    android:layout_width="fill_parent"
    android:layout_height="fill_parent" >

    <Button
        android:id="@+id/button1"
        android:layout_width="204dp"
        android:layout_height="128dp"
        android:text="Button" />

    <TextView
        android:id="@+id/textView1"
        android:layout_width="wrap_content"
        android:layout_height="wrap_content"
        android:text="This is a textview!" />

</FrameLayout>
```

5. Re-run the application and you will get a result similar to figure 3.9 -

Figure 3.9: FrameLayout with two views

You can see that the new TextView widget appears on top of the existing button widget,. This is because each new view is placed on top of existing views.

Typically you will want to add a FrameLayout within another container. With FrameLayout, you can animate a series of images - where you want to display a single image at a time. Other usages of FrameLayout might be to create visual effect - by creating a FrameLayout to display views on top of another layout.

ScrollView

You can use the ScrollView container to contain a single view or a viewGroup that might be too big to fit on your device's display screen. Using ScrollView is very simple -

```xml
<?xml version="1.0" encoding="utf-8"?>
<LinearLayout xmlns:android="http://schemas.android.com/apk/res/android"
    android:layout_width="match_parent"
    android:layout_height="match_parent"
    android:orientation="vertical" >
```

145

```
<ScrollView
    android:layout_width="match_parent"
    android:layout_height="wrap_content" >

    <TextView
        android:layout_width="match_parent"
        android:layout_height="wrap_content"
        android:text="@string/my_long_text" />
</ScrollView>

</LinearLayout>
```

The above example shows how we can use a ScrollView to contain a TextView widget.

Adapting to Display Orientation

While running your application, the display orientation of the device might change. As an Android application developer, you need to be aware on how to manage the orientation change. When a device's orientation is changed, the current activity is destroyed and recreated. This can have several consequences. When the activity is recreated, it's view components might not fit well to adopt the new display screen. Also, users may lose their current running application state.

The portrait mode of device has more height and less width while the landscape mode has more width than height. While designing a layout, you might be in the habit of considering the portrait mode of the device - which means a more narrow width and longer height. When that layout is switched to landscape mode, you might find few problems, like extra spaces across the width and few views located at the bottom might be hidden.

Particularly if you use specific dimensions, (like fixed width for your widgets), when the layout is running in landscape mode, you will find lots of whitespace at the right side of the screen. The Android system will not scale the width to match the new orientation. Rather, it will use your specified dimensions. This problem can be solved by using relative dimensions. Instead of using absolute values for dimensions, you can take advantage of relative dimension values, like wrap_content, match_parent etc. In these cases, the Android system will figure out the available dimensions of the screen and scale the views to fit properly. Similarly, you should use weight property to split the available spaces among multiple components in proportions rather than setting absolute dimensions.

For example, the TableLayoutDemo application which was created a few sections earlier uses relative dimensions and as a result adopts well in both portrait and landscape mode (3.10) -

Figure 3.10: Running TableLayoutDemo application in both portrait and landscape mode

Besides, the RelativeLayout container enables you to anchor the views to the four edges of the screen and also arranges the views with respect to one another. Using these techniques will make your layout more adoptable to orientation changes. Our RelativeLayoutDemo application layout was created by anchoring the EditText widget to the top-left corner. The two buttons were positioned with respect to EditText. Thus running in landscape mode, we get the layout adopted to new screen dimensions (figure 3.11).

Figure 3.11: Running RelativeLayoutDemo application in landscape mode

Providing Alternative Layout Resources

For simple UI designs, using the practices mentioned in the previous section might work and make your layout adoptable for orientation changes. But as the UI design gets complicated, you will need to provide a separate layout design for portrait and landscape mode. This is how it is done.

- First you will create the layout design for portrait mode and put that under the res/layout directory.
- To put the alternative layout resource, create a new directory res/layout-land, which will hold layouts for landscape orientation.
- Then, create the layout for landscape orientation with the same file name and put that layout file under the res/layout-land directory.

Now when you install the application on a device, it will contain both versions of the layout design. Depending upon the orientation of the device, the right file will be chosen by the Android run time. So when the device is running in portrait mode, the layout file from res/layout directory will be used and if the device orientation is changed to landscape mode, the layout file from res/layout-land directory will be used.

Figure 3.12: Providing alternative layout

Managing Changes to Screen Orientation

In chapter 2, we have learned about activity life cycle methods. Whenever the display orientation is changed, the current activity is first destroyed and then recreated, which means a series of life cycle methods are called.

While the current activity is destroyed, the following life cycle methods are called -

* onPause()
* onStop()
* onDestroy()

Then when the activity is re-created, these set of life cycle methods are called -

* onCreate()
* onStart()
* onResume()

Understanding this behavior is important because it helps you to take necessary

149

measures to preserve the state of your activity when the orientation changes. Though the activity is destroyed and recreated when orientation of the device changes, users will expect to have uniform behavior from your application. The Android system takes care of some things for you for example. The text entered in EditText element will be preserved in the orientation change (though the EditText should have android:id attribute set). However, you will still need to take care of other things. You will need to save and restore the user interface, as well as the values of the variables.

Persisting State Information During Orientation Change

You can implement the onSaveInstanceState() method of your activity to save the state information in case of an orientation change. A Bundle object is passed as argument to this method. You will save state information within this Bundle object which can be retrieved later.

```
@Override
protected void onSaveInstanceState(Bundle outState) {
        super.onSaveInstanceState(outState);
        outState.putInt("currentIndex", currentIndex);
}
```

As you can see, we have saved an integer value to our Bundle object. You can retrieve state information saved to the Bundle from the onRestoreInstanceState() method. This method is called immediately after the onCreate() method is called -

```
@Override
protected void onRestoreInstanceState(Bundle savedInstanceState) {
        super.onRestoreInstanceState(savedInstanceState);
        currentIndex = savedInstanceState.getInt("currentIndex");
}
```

This is how you can retain state information in an orientation change.

Avoiding Activity Restart on Orientation Change

If you don't want to recreate your activity every time an orientation change occurs, you can disable this. All you have to do is in your AndroidManifest.xml file, in the <activity> node which you want to disable the orientation change, add the following attribute -

```
android:configChanges="orientation|keyboardHidden|screenSize"
```

You also have the option to handle the orientation change (or other configuration changes) by yourself. To do that, in addition to adding the above line to your AndroidManifest.xml file, you will need to implement the following method to your activity -

```
@Override
public void onConfigurationChanged(Configuration newConfig) {
        super.onConfigurationChanged(newConfig);

        if (getResources().getConfiguration().orientation ==
                        Configuration.ORIENTATION_LANDSCAPE) {
        //do something for landscape orientation

    } else {
        //do something else for portrait orientation
    }
}
```

You have seen how we have detected screen orientation from our activity. Now based on your own requirements, you can do whatever you want for a particular orientation mode (like inflating a different layout).

It is also possible to force the application to run on a particular orientation. You will need to add android:screenOrientation attribute to AndroidManifest.xml file to your <activity> node -

```
android:screenOrientation="portrait"
```

This will run the activity in portrait mode.

Utilizing The Action Bar

Android 3.0 (API level 11) introduced a new UI component, called Action Bar. It's a navigation panel which replaces the traditional title bar and facilitates you to provide a consistent pattern for your application icon, application name and other common actions of your activity. Figure 3.13 shows you the built-in Gmail application with action bar -

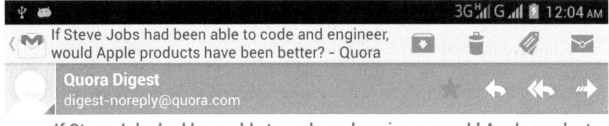

Figure 3.13: Built-in Gmail application with action bar

Showing or Hiding the Action Bar

The action bar is enabled by default in any activity that uses the Theme.Holo
theme (or few other themes that inherit from that theme). It requires minimum
SDK of 11 or higher.

In your AndroidManifest.xml file, you can set the minimum required SDK using
the <uses-sdk> tag. Here is how you can do that -

```
<uses-sdk
android:minSdkVersion="11"
android:targetSdkVersion="19" />
```

Set your application theme to your manifest file as follows -

```
<application
android:allowBackup="true"
android:icon="@drawable/ic_launcher"
android:label="@string/app_name"
android:theme="@android:style/Theme.Holo" >
```

If you don't want to show the action bar, you can use a theme with no action bar -

```
<application
    android:allowBackup="true"
    android:icon="@drawable/ic_launcher"
    android:label="@string/app_name"
    android:theme="@android:style/Theme.Holo.NoActionBar" >
```

Alternatively, you can choose to show or hide an action bar from your activity class at run time -

```
ActionBar actionBar = getActionBar();

//show action bar
actionBar.show();

//hide action bar
actionBar.hide();
```

In case you want to show/hide action bar at run time from an activity class, make sure you are using a compatible theme and also minSdkVersion is 11 or higher.

Adding Action Items

Now we will see how we can add action items to our action bar. We will create a new project to demonstrate this.

1. Create a new project ActionBarDemo with minimum SDK level 14.

2. We will define our action bar items within the XML file. Under the res/menu directory, you will find an XML file named "main.xml". Update the content of that file with the following code -

```
<menu xmlns:android="http://schemas.android.com/apk/res/android" >

  <item
    android:id="@+id/item_help"
    android:icon="@android:drawable/ic_menu_help"
    android:showAsAction="ifRoom"
```

```
        android:title="Help"/>

    <item
        android:id="@+id/item_about"
        android:icon="@android:drawable/ic_menu_info_details"
        android:showAsAction="ifRoom"
        android:title="About"/>

    <item
        android:id="@+id/item_refresh"
        android:showAsAction="ifRoom"
        android:title="Refresh"/>

    <item
        android:id="@+id/item_delete"
        android:showAsAction="ifRoom"
        android:title="Delete"/>

</menu>
```

We have added four items which will be displayed as action bar items.

3. Update the MainActivity.java file with the following code -

```
package com.iducate.actionbardemo;

import android.os.Bundle;
import android.app.Activity;
import android.view.Menu;
import android.view.MenuItem;
import android.widget.Toast;

public class MainActivity extends Activity {

    @Override
    protected void onCreate(Bundle savedInstanceState) {
        super.onCreate(savedInstanceState);
        setContentView(R.layout.activity_main);
    }

    @Override
    public boolean onCreateOptionsMenu(Menu menu) {
```

```java
        getMenuInflater().inflate(R.menu.main, menu);
        return true;
    }

    @Override
    public boolean onOptionsItemSelected(MenuItem item) {
        switch (item.getItemId()) {
        case R.id.item_about:
            Toast.makeText(this, "About item clicked!",
                            Toast.LENGTH_SHORT).show();
            return true;
        case R.id.item_delete:
            Toast.makeText(this, "Delete item clicked!",
                        Toast.LENGTH_SHORT).show();
            return true;
        case R.id.item_help:
            Toast.makeText(this, "Help item clicked!",
                            Toast.LENGTH_SHORT).show();
            return true;
        case R.id.item_refresh:
            Toast.makeText(this, "Refresh item clicked!",
                        Toast.LENGTH_SHORT).show();
            return true;
        }

        return false;
    }

}
```

4. If you run the application, you will see that our action bar contains some items (figure 3.14). Depending on your phone's screen size, the number of action items might vary. If your action bar has more items than it can actually fit, pressing the MENU button (either hardware menu button or soft menu button) will reveal the rest of the items. For devices without a dedicated MENU button, you will see an option with three dots. Clicking that will reveal the other options.

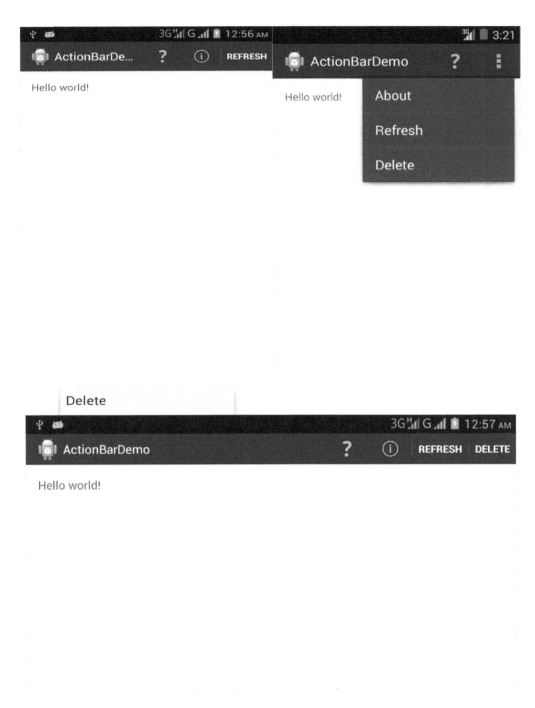

Figure 3.14: Running ActionBarDemo application

How it Works?

The action items of our action bar are defined within a XML menu resource under the res/menu directory -

```
<menu xmlns:android="http://schemas.android.com/apk/res/android" >
```

Under the root <menu> node, we have added <item> nodes for each action items -

```
<item
android:id="@+id/item_help"
android:icon="@android:drawable/ic_menu_help"
android:showAsAction="ifRoom"
android:title="Help"/>
```

We have set the id, title, icon etc attributes of each item. Notice the attribute android:showAsAction. We have set value for that attribute as "ifRoom", which specifies to show that item on action bar if there is enough room to fit that item. We could set that property value to "never", "always" or "withText" etc.

The onCreateOptionsMenu() method of Activity class inflates the menu items -

```
@Override
public boolean onCreateOptionsMenu(Menu menu) {
        getMenuInflater().inflate(R.menu.main, menu);
        return true;
}
```

The getMenuInflater() is used to return a MenuInflater object and we then call the inflate() method of the object with our main.xml menu identifier as argument. This is how the items are added to the action bar.

Now, if any of the action items are selected, the onOptionsItemSelected() method is called.

```
@Override
public boolean onOptionsItemSelected(MenuItem item) {
        switch (item.getItemId()) {
        case R.id.item_about:
                Toast.makeText(this, "About item clicked!",
                                Toast.LENGTH_SHORT).show();
                return true;
        case R.id.item_delete:
                Toast.makeText(this, "Delete item clicked!",
                                Toast.LENGTH_SHORT).show();
                return true;
        case R.id.item_help:
```

```
            Toast.makeText(this, "Help item clicked!",
                        Toast.LENGTH_SHORT).show();
                return true;
        case R.id.item_refresh:
            Toast.makeText(this, "Refresh item clicked!",
                    Toast.LENGTH_SHORT).show();
                return true;
        }

        return false;
    }
```

Within this method, we use a switch statement to identify which action item is clicked and then show a Toast message for the corresponding item.

Making an Application Icon Clickable

When your application consists of multiple activities, you will often want to make the application icon clickable to act as a home button. This is fairly simple -

```
getActionBar().setHomeButtonEnabled(true);
```

You simply need to call the setHomeButtonEnabled() of the action bar instance and set it equal to true.

Now you can handle the click event of that icon by adding a new case to the switch statement within the onOptionsItemSelected() method -

```
case android.R.id.home:
        //do some stuff here
        return true;
```

Notice the ID which is always android.R.id.home. Typically, you will want the application icon to act as a shortcut for the home button which will take the users to the main activity. A good practice is to create a new Intent object and set the flag Intent.FLAG_ACTIVITY_CLEAR_TOP which clears the back stack of activities. So after returning to the main activity, clicking the back button won't take the user back to previous activities. This is how it is done -

```
case android.R.id.home:
        Intent intent = new Intent(this, MainActivity.class);
```

```
intent.setFlags(Intent.FLAG_ACTIVITY_CLEAR_TOP);
startActivity(intent);
return true;
```

Creating a User Interface Programmatically

So far, we have created user interfaces using XML layout files. Defining a user interface using a XML layout file is the standard way and you will most likely to follow that practice. But it is entirely possible to create a user interface of an Android application programmatically without using XML file. This will be useful in situations where you need to create part of your UI dynamically at run time. The following example demonstrates how to do that.

1. Create a new project UIExample.

2. Update the MainActivity.java file with the following code -

```
package com.iducate.uiexample;

import android.app.Activity;
import android.os.Bundle;
import android.widget.Button;
import android.widget.LinearLayout;
import android.widget.TextView;

public class MainActivity extends Activity {

    @Override
    protected void onCreate(Bundle savedInstanceState) {
        super.onCreate(savedInstanceState);

        //layout params for LinearLayout
        LinearLayout.LayoutParams layoutParams = new
                    LinearLayout.LayoutParams(
                LinearLayout.LayoutParams.MATCH_PARENT,
                LinearLayout.LayoutParams.MATCH_PARENT);

        //create a new LinearLayout
        LinearLayout layout = new LinearLayout(this);
        layout.setOrientation(LinearLayout.VERTICAL);
        layout.setLayoutParams(layoutParams);
```

```
//layout params for widgets
LinearLayout.LayoutParams params = new
                        LinearLayout.LayoutParams(
            LinearLayout.LayoutParams.WRAP_CONTENT,
            LinearLayout.LayoutParams.WRAP_CONTENT);

//create a new TextView widget
TextView textView = new TextView(this);
textView.setText("This is a dynamically generated
                                TextView!");
textView.setLayoutParams(params);

//create a new Button widget
Button button = new Button(this);
button.setText("Click Me");
button.setLayoutParams(params);

//add the views to layout
layout.addView(textView);
layout.addView(button);

setContentView(layout);
    }

}
```

3. Now run the application, the application UI will look like figure 3.15 -

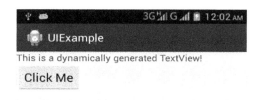

Figure 3.15: Running UIExample application

How it Works?

The whole user interface of our previous example is created programmatically. First we have created a LayoutParams object -

```
LinearLayout.LayoutParams layoutParams = new
            LinearLayout.LayoutParams(
        LinearLayout.LayoutParams.MATCH_PARENT,
        LinearLayout.LayoutParams.MATCH_PARENT);
```

This LinearParams object will be used by our LinearLayout container. Here, we set the width and height property of our LinearLayout. Both width and height are set to MATCH_PARENT so that our LinearLayout occupies the full screen area.

Next, we create a new LinearLayout object with the activity Context -

```
LinearLayout layout = new LinearLayout(this);
layout.setOrientation(LinearLayout.VERTICAL);
layout.setLayoutParams(layoutParams);
```

We also set the orientation of our LinearLayout to vertical and set the layout parameters.

Next, we create another LayoutParams object which will be used by our views -

```
LinearLayout.LayoutParams params = new
                                LinearLayout.LayoutParams(
                LinearLayout.LayoutParams.WRAP_CONTENT,
                LinearLayout.LayoutParams.WRAP_CONTENT);
```

We want our view widgets to occupy only the space required to accommodate their content. So we set both width and height as WRAP_CONTENT.

Next, we create a TextView widget and a Button widget with the LayoutParams defined earlier -

```
//create a new TextView widget
TextView textView = new TextView(this);        textView.setText("This is
a dynamically generated TextView!");
textView.setLayoutParams(params);

//create a new Button widget
Button button = new Button(this);
button.setText("Click Me");
button.setLayoutParams(params);
```

Next, we add the view widgets to our LinearLayout object -

```
//add the views to layout
layout.addView(textView);
layout.addView(button);
```

Finally, we add the LinearLayout object to our activity -

```
setContentView(layout);
```

This is how we generate the whole UI dynamically. As I mentioned earlier, start defining your UI within the XML layout and then generate dynamic UI components as you need.

Listening For UI Notifications

Users can interact with your application's UI in various ways like touch, button press, long press, swipe etc. Android offers you more than one way to intercept events resulting from user's interaction. Usually you will capture events from the specific View object that the user interacts with. Various View classes provide you with public callback methods that listen for relevant events. When a specific event occurs, the relevant callback method is called by the Android framework. To handle such events, the View class provides a collection of interfaces with callbacks. These interfaces are known as event listeners.

Registering Events For Views

User interaction with Views fire events. If you register an event listener for any View, once the event is fired, you handle that by implementing the corresponding callback method. We will see an example that shows us how to handle the button click event.

1. Create a new project called "UINotifications".

2. Update the activity_main.xml file (under the res/layout directory) with the following code which includes only a single button -

```xml
<LinearLayout xmlns:android="http://schemas.android.com/apk/res/android"
    android:layout_width="fill_parent"
    android:layout_height="fill_parent"
    android:orientation="vertical" >

    <Button
        android:id="@+id/btnClick"
        android:layout_width="wrap_content"
        android:layout_height="wrap_content"
        android:layout_gravity="center"
        android:text="Click Me" />

</LinearLayout>
```

3. Now update the MainActivity.java file with the following code -

```java
package com.iducate.uinotifications;

import android.app.Activity;
import android.os.Bundle;
```

```java
import android.view.View;
import android.view.View.OnClickListener;
import android.widget.Button;
import android.widget.Toast;

public class MainActivity extends Activity {

        @Override
        protected void onCreate(Bundle savedInstanceState) {
                super.onCreate(savedInstanceState);
                setContentView(R.layout.activity_main);

                Button button = (Button) findViewById(R.id.btnClick);
                button.setOnClickListener(new OnClickListener() {

                        @Override
                        public void onClick(View v) {
                                Toast.makeText(MainActivity.this,"Handling Button
                                        Click Event!", Toast.LENGTH_SHORT).show();
                        }
                });
        }

}
```

4. Now if you run the application, you will see a UI with a single button. Click the button and a Toast message will appear (figure 3.16) .

Figure 3.16: Running UINotifications application

How it Works?

Our layout file contains a single button. We want to listen to the click event of that button. From our MainActivity.java file, after we inflate the layout file, we find the reference of our Button view using the id by calling the findViewById() method -

```
Button button = (Button) findViewById(R.id.btnClick);
```

Next, we register a callback to our button element using setOnClickListener() –

```
button.setOnClickListener(new OnClickListener() {

        @Override
        public void onClick(View v) {
                Toast.makeText(MainActivity.this,"Handling Button
                        Click Event!", Toast.LENGTH_SHORT).show();
        }
    });
```

The setOnClickListener() expects a listener for the click event. We simply pass an anonymous inner class as a button click listener. The anonymous class needs to implement the onClick() method which will be fired every time a click event occur.

Instead of using an inner anonymous class, we could have declared a new anonymous class within our activity class and use that as our button click listener -

```
private OnClickListener btnClickListener = new OnClickListener()   {

        @Override
        public void onClick(View v) {
                Toast.makeText(MainActivity.this,"Handling Button
                        Click Event!", Toast.LENGTH_SHORT).show();
        }
};
```

We then pass that to onClickListener() -

```
button.setOnClickListener(btnClickListener);
```

There is yet another commonly used method for creating event handler by implement ing the OnClickListener interface to our activity class -

```
public class MainActivity extends Activity implements OnClickListener {
.
.
.


        @Override
        public void onClick(View v) {
                Toast.makeText(MainActivity.this, "Handling Button Click
                        Event!",Toast.LENGTH_SHORT).show();
        }
}
```

Once we implement the OnClickListener to our activity class, we need to provide an implementation of onClick() method of that interface. Next, we pass our activity as the button click listener -

```
button.setOnClickListener(this);
```

If you want to listen to events for multiple views, it would be better to create a anonymous class or implement an interface to your activity. For listening single views, its fine to use anonymous inner class.

Events Not Handled By Views

Its more common to handle events by corresponding Views and provide corresponding actions. But if that's not the case, you can use some methods provided by the Activity class to handle those events -

- onKeyDown() - Called when a key is pressed down and not handled by any of the views
- onKeyUp () - Called when a key is released and not handled by any of the views
- onTouchEvent() - Called when a screen touch event is not handled by any of the views under it
- onMenuItemSelected() - Called when a menu item is selected by user

You can overwrite these methods in your activity class and implement the action you want to perform. For example, the following skeleton code shows the onTouchEvent() method implementation -

```
@Override
public boolean onTouchEvent(MotionEvent event) {
    //do something
    return super.onTouchEvent(event);
}
```

Summary

In this chapter, we have learned about different ViewGroups which are the containers used in a UI design to hold different view widgets. We have also learned how we can handle orientation changes which are critical to ensure smooth user experience. Then, we learned about action bars, an important UI component to provide branding and navigation throughout the application. Finally we have learned how we can listen to different events and respond to them by invoking callbacks.

Chapter 4: Creating Your User Interface With Views

In this chapter, we will look at different views and learn how we can use them to design the user interface of our applications. We will learn about basic views like TextView, EditText, Button, Checkbox etc. We will also learn about picker views which lets users pick date or time. We will have a look at views that are used to create list of items and finally we will discuss about specialized fragments.

Using Basic Views

To design your application's UI, the Android platform provides a number of basic view widgets -

- TextView
- EditText
- Button
- ImageButton
- CheckBox
- ToggleButton
- RadioButton
- RadioGroup

Using the above view widgets, you can display text labels, get text input from users and also get user's input through check boxes or radio buttons. We will look at the above view widgets and how they respond to user interactions.

1. Create a new project named BasicViewsDemo.

2. Update the layout file activity_main.xml (under the res/layout directory) with the following code -

```
<LinearLayout xmlns:android="http://schemas.android.com/apk/res/android"
    android:layout_width="fill_parent"
```

```xml
    android:layout_height="fill_parent"
    android:orientation="vertical" >

    <TextView
        android:id="@+id/textView1"
        android:layout_width="wrap_content"
        android:layout_height="wrap_content"
        android:text="This is a TextView!" />

    <EditText
        android:id="@+id/editText1"
        android:layout_width="match_parent"
        android:layout_height="wrap_content"
        android:hint="Enter something here..." >
    </EditText>

    <Button
        android:id="@+id/button1"
        android:layout_width="wrap_content"
        android:layout_height="wrap_content"
        android:text="Button" />

    <ImageButton
        android:id="@+id/imageButton1"
        android:layout_width="wrap_content"
        android:layout_height="wrap_content"
        android:src="@drawable/ic_launcher" />

    <CheckBox
        android:id="@+id/checkBox1"
        android:layout_width="wrap_content"
        android:layout_height="wrap_content"
        android:text="CheckBox" />

    <ToggleButton
        android:id="@+id/toggleButton1"
        android:layout_width="wrap_content"
        android:layout_height="wrap_content"
        android:text="ToggleButton" />

    <RadioGroup
        android:id="@+id/radioGroup1"
        android:layout_width="wrap_content"
```

```
android:layout_height="wrap_content" >

    <RadioButton
        android:id="@+id/radio0"
        android:layout_width="wrap_content"
        android:layout_height="wrap_content"
        android:checked="true"
        android:text="Option 1" />

    <RadioButton
        android:id="@+id/radio1"
        android:layout_width="wrap_content"
        android:layout_height="wrap_content"
        android:text="Option 2" />

    <RadioButton
        android:id="@+id/radio2"
        android:layout_width="wrap_content"
        android:layout_height="wrap_content"
        android:text="Option 3" />
    </RadioGroup>

</LinearLayout>
```

3. Run the application and you will see a layout similar to figure 4.1 -

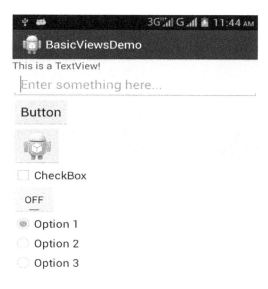

Figure 4.1: Running BasicViewsDemo application

How It Works?

In our layout file activity_main.xml, we have added all the basic views mentioned earlier. We haven't done anything to handle various user interaction events yet. First, we will get ourselves familiar with these view widgets.

We have used a LinearLayout container to hold all the different view widgets in vertical orientation -

```
<LinearLayout xmlns:android="http://schemas.android.com/apk/res/android"
    android:layout_width="fill_parent"
    android:layout_height="fill_parent"
    android:orientation="vertical" >
```

The first view widget we have used is a TextView widget -

```
    <TextView
    android:id="@+id/textView1"
    android:layout_width="wrap_content"
```

```
android:layout_height="wrap_content"
android:text="This is a TextView!" />
```

A TextView widget simply shows text information. This text information can't be changed by the users. You can see that we have set both the android:layout_width and the android:layout_height attributes of TextView widget to wrap_content , which means that this widget will take only the width and height needed to fit its content. The android:text attribute of TextView widget is the text label shown. The android:id attribute defines an id for this widget, which can be used from our Java code to programmatically access this TextView widget. Other view widgets have these attributes as well.

The next view widget we have in our layout file is an EditText widget -

```
<EditText
    android:id="@+id/editText1"
    android:layout_width="match_parent"
    android:layout_height="wrap_content"
    android:hint="Enter something here..." >
</EditText>
```

An EditText widget can be used to get text input from users. Our EditText widget has android:layout_width of match_parent which gives the EditText widget the same width as its parent container. Using the android:hint attribute, we can give a hint text which will disappear once the user starts typing.

The Button widget gives us a clickable button -

```
<Button
android:id="@+id/button1"
android:layout_width="wrap_content"
android:layout_height="wrap_content"
android:text="Button" />
```

The button label is set using the attribute android:text. If you want to use an image as a button label, Android provides you another widget, the ImageButton widget -

```
<ImageButton
android:id="@+id/imageButton1"
android:layout_width="wrap_content"
android:layout_height="wrap_content"
```

```
android:src="@drawable/ic_launcher" />
```

The ImageButton widget's android:src attribute is used to set a drawable resource which is used as a button label. This image is stored under the res/drawable directory.

Next, we use the CheckBox widget -

```
<CheckBox
android:id="@+id/checkBox1"
android:layout_width="wrap_content"
android:layout_height="wrap_content"
android:text="CheckBox" />
```

With a CheckBox widget, you can provide a check box control. As always, the android:text attribute is used to set the label for the check box.

The ToggleButton widget provides a button like control that can be toggled to ON or OFF states by user clicks -

```
<ToggleButton
android:id="@+id/toggleButton1"
android:layout_width="wrap_content"
android:layout_height="wrap_content"
android:text="ToggleButton" />
```

Finally, our layout contains three RadioButton widgets which are contained within a RadioGroup widget -

```
<RadioGroup
android:id="@+id/radioGroup1"
android:layout_width="wrap_content"
android:layout_height="wrap_content" >

<RadioButton
    android:id="@+id/radio0"
    android:layout_width="wrap_content"
    android:layout_height="wrap_content"
    android:checked="true"
    android:text="Option 1" />
```

```
    <RadioButton
        android:id="@+id/radio1"
        android:layout_width="wrap_content"
        android:layout_height="wrap_content"
        android:text="Option 2" />

    <RadioButton
        android:id="@+id/radio2"
        android:layout_width="wrap_content"
        android:layout_height="wrap_content"
        android:text="Option 3" />
</RadioGroup>
```

Using a RadioGroup widget, you can provide multiple options through RadioButtons for users to choose one option.

Handling View Events

In this section, we will attach various event handlers to different view widgets and then see how to handle those events. We will use the same project created in the previous section.

Adding a TextWatcher to EditText

First, we will see how we can add a TextWatcher to our EditText and update the TextView with the text entered in EditText while the user is typing.

1. Update the ActivityMain.java file with the following code -

```
package com.iducate.basicviewsdemo;

import android.app.Activity;
import android.os.Bundle;
import android.text.Editable;
import android.text.TextWatcher;
import android.widget.EditText;
import android.widget.TextView;

public class MainActivity extends Activity {

    @Override
```

```java
protected void onCreate(Bundle savedInstanceState) {
    super.onCreate(savedInstanceState);
    setContentView(R.layout.activity_main);

    final TextView mTextView = (TextView)

    findViewById(R.id.textView1);
    EditText mEditText = (EditText) findViewById(R.id.editText1);
    mEditText.addTextChangedListener(new TextWatcher() {

                @Override
                public void onTextChanged(CharSequence s, int start,
                            int before, int count) {
                    mTextView.setText(s);
                }

                @Override
                public void beforeTextChanged(CharSequence arg0, int
                            arg1, int arg2, int arg3) {
                    // TODO Auto-generated method stub

                }

                @Override
                public void afterTextChanged(Editable arg0) {
                    // TODO Auto-generated method stub

                }
        });
    }

}
```

2. Now run the application and start typing in EditText field. You will see the TextView widget above the EditText is updated every time you enter some text in EditText field (figure 4.2) -

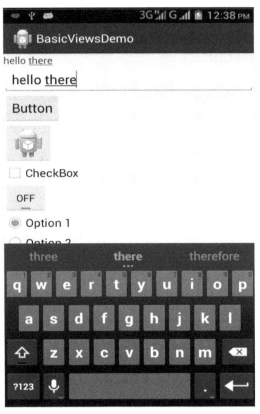

Figure 4.2: TextWatcher attached to EditText

How It Works?

After the layout file is inflated, we get reference to the TextView and EditText widgets, so that we can access them programmatically -

```
final TextView mTextView = (TextView)findViewById(R.id.textView1);
EditText mEditText = (EditText) findViewById(R.id.editText1);
```

Next, we add a TextWatcher to the EditText instance, so whenever the text of this widget is changed, the TextWatcher's callback methods is called. We have passed a TextWatcher object as an anonymous inner class. Within the onTextChanged() callback method, we set the text of TextView with the updated text -

```
@Override
public void onTextChanged(CharSequence s, int start,
                    int before, int count
{                           mTextView.setText(s);
}
```

Setting OnClickListener to Button

Now we will see how we can set an OnClickListener to our Button widget -

1. Update the MainActivity.java with the following code -

```java
package com.iducate.basicviewsdemo;

import android.app.Activity;
import android.os.Bundle;
import android.view.View;
import android.view.View.OnClickListener;
import android.widget.Button;
import android.widget.Toast;

public class MainActivity extends Activity {

    @Override
    protected void onCreate(Bundle savedInstanceState) {
        super.onCreate(savedInstanceState);
        setContentView(R.layout.activity_main);

        Button mButton = (Button) findViewById(R.id.button1);
        mButton.setOnClickListener(new OnClickListener() {

            @Override
            public void onClick(View view) {
                Toast.makeText(MainActivity.this, "The Button is
                    clicked!",Toast.LENGTH_SHORT).show();
            }
        });
    }

}
```

2. Run the application and click the Button widget. You will see a Toast message appear (figure 4.3) -

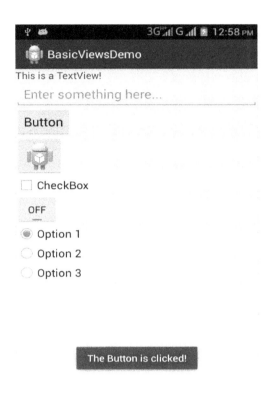

Figure 4.3: Toast message appears on Button click

How It Works?

We first get a reference to our Button widget -

```
Button mButton = (Button) findViewById(R.id.button1);
```

Next, we add a OnClickListener to our Button instance and pass an OnClickLinstner object as an anonymous inner class -

```
mButton.setOnClickListener(new OnClickListener() {

    @Override
    public void onClick(View view) {
        Toast.makeText(MainActivity.this, "The Button is
                clicked!",Toast.LENGTH_SHORT).show();
    }
});
```

The onClick() callback method is called when a button press event occurs. Within that onClick() method, we show a Toast message which indicates the button click.

178

Setting OnClickListener to ImageButton

The OnClickListener for ImageButton widget acts similarly as the Button widget -

1. Update the MainActivity.java file with the following code -

```java
package com.iducate.basicviewsdemo;

import android.app.Activity;
import android.os.Bundle;
import android.view.View;
import android.view.View.OnClickListener;
import android.widget.ImageButton;
import android.widget.Toast;

public class MainActivity extends Activity {

    @Override
    protected void onCreate(Bundle savedInstanceState) {
        super.onCreate(savedInstanceState);
        setContentView(R.layout.activity_main);

        ImageButton mImageButton = (ImageButton)
                        findViewById(R.id.imageButton1);
        mImageButton.setOnClickListener(new OnClickListener() {

            @Override
            public void onClick(View view) {
                Toast.makeText(MainActivity.this,
                    "The ImageButton is clicked!",
                                Toast.LENGTH_SHORT).show();
            }
        });
    }

}
```

2. Run the application and click the ImageButton widget. You will get a Toast message similar to figure 4.4 -

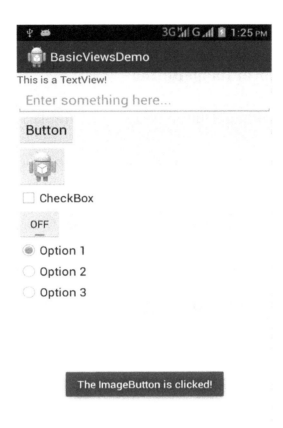

Figure 4.4: Toast message shown on ImageButton click

How It Works?

The OnClickListener for ImageButton works similarly as it works for the Button widget. Here instead of getting the reference to Button widget, we get a reference to ImageButton widget -

ImageButton mImageButton = (ImageButton)

findViewById(R.id.imageButton1);

Then we set OnClickListener to this instance of ImageButton widget in exactly the same way we did for Button widget.

Setting OnCheckedChangeListener to CheckBox

A CheckBox can be in either checked or unchecked state. The OnCheckedChangeListener can handle the state change of a CheckBox widget. Let's add an OnCheckedChangeListener to our CheckBox widget -

1. Update MainActivity.java file with the following code -

```java
package com.iducate.basicviewsdemo;

import android.app.Activity;
import android.os.Bundle;
import android.widget.CheckBox;
import android.widget.CompoundButton;
import android.widget.CompoundButton.OnCheckedChangeListener;
import android.widget.Toast;

public class MainActivity extends Activity {

    @Override
    protected void onCreate(Bundle savedInstanceState) {
        super.onCreate(savedInstanceState);
        setContentView(R.layout.activity_main);

        CheckBox mCheckBox = (CheckBox)
                            findViewById(R.id.checkBox1);
        mCheckBox.setOnCheckedChangeListener(new
                        OnCheckedChangeListener() {

            @Override
            public void onCheckedChanged(CompoundButton
                            buttonView,boolean isChecked) {
                Toast.makeText(MainActivity.this,
                    "CheckBox state: " + isChecked,
                            Toast.LENGTH_SHORT).show();
            }
        });

    }

}
```

2. Run the application and click the CheckBox widget to make it checked. You will notice a Toast message is shown (figure 4.5).

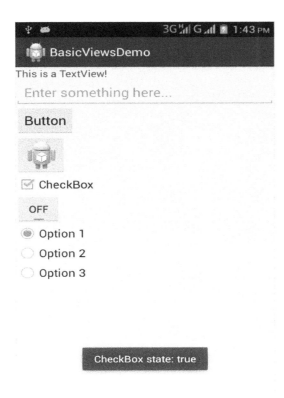

Figure 4.5: Toast message shown on CheckBox state change

How It Works?

First we get a reference to our CheckBox widget instance -

CheckBox mCheckBox = (CheckBox) findViewById(R.id.checkBox1);

Then we set an OnCheckedChangeListener to our CheckBox widget and pass in an anonymous inner OnCheckedChangeListener object instance -

```
mCheckBox.setOnCheckedChangeListener(new OnCheckedChangeListener() {

    @Override
    public void onCheckedChanged(CompoundButton buttonView,boolean
            isChecked) {
        Toast.makeText(MainActivity.this, "CheckBox state: " +
                        isChecked, Toast.LENGTH_SHORT).show();
    }
});
```

Whenever the state of the check box is changed, the callback method

182

onCheckedChanged() will be called with the buttonView and state of the check box (true for checked and false for unchecked) as arguments.

Listening to a ToggleButton State Change

ToggleButton can be in one of two states – ON or OFF. As the name suggests, clicking on ToggleButton will toggle the state. Let's see how we can add a listener to ToggleButton.

1. Update the MainActivity.java with the following code -

```java
package com.iducate.basicviewsdemo;

import android.app.Activity;
import android.os.Bundle;
import android.widget.CompoundButton;
import android.widget.CompoundButton.OnCheckedChangeListener;
import android.widget.Toast;
import android.widget.ToggleButton;

public class MainActivity extends Activity {

    @Override
    protected void onCreate(Bundle savedInstanceState) {
        super.onCreate(savedInstanceState);
        setContentView(R.layout.activity_main);

        ToggleButton tButton = (ToggleButton)

findViewById(R.id.toggleButton1);
        tButton.setOnCheckedChangeListener(new
                                OnCheckedChangeListener() {

            @Override
            public void onCheckedChanged(CompoundButton
                                buttonView, boolean isChecked) {
                Toast.makeText(MainActivity.this,
                    "ToggleButton State: " + isChecked,
                        Toast.LENGTH_SHORT).show();
            }
        });

    }
```

}

2. Run the application. You will initially see the ToggleButton in OFF state. Click the ToggleButton. You will see the button label changed from OFF to ON and a Toast message appearing to indicate that the ToggleButton state is changed (figure 4.6).

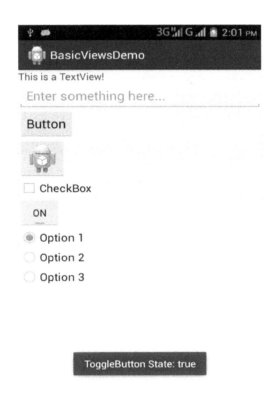

Figure 4.6: ToggleButton state change

How It Works?

After we inflate the layout file, we get a reference to our ToggleButton instance -

ToggleButton tButton = (ToggleButton)

findViewById(R.id.toggleButton1);

To listen to the state change of our ToggleButton, we attach an OnCheckedChangeListener to our ToggleButton instance and pass a OnCheckedChangeListener object as an anonymous inner class -

```java
tButton.setOnCheckedChangeListener(new
                                   OnCheckedChangeListener() {

    @Override
    public void onCheckedChanged(CompoundButton buttonView,
            boolean isChecked) {
        Toast.makeText(MainActivity.this, "ToggleButton State:
            " + isChecked, Toast.LENGTH_SHORT).show();
    }
});
```

Once the state of our ToggleButton is changed, the OnCheckedChanged() callback method is called. This callback method of our listener will have two arguments – the buttonView and the state of the toggle button as boolean.

For both CheckBox and ToggleButton widgets, the OnCheckedChangeListener is imported from android.widget.CompoundButton.OnCheckedChangeListener class.

You will see in the next section that we will use OnCheckedChangeListener for RadioGroup, imported from android.widget.RadioGroup.OnCheckedChangeListener class.

Adding OnCheckedChangeListener to RadioGroup

The RadioGroup widget let's the user choose an option from multiple alternatives. In this section, we will see how we can add OnCheckedChangeListener to our RadioGroup, which will listen to the change of a RadioGroup option.

1. Update the MainActivity.java file with the following code -

```java
package com.iducate.basicviewsdemo;

import android.app.Activity;
import android.os.Bundle;
import android.widget.RadioGroup;
import android.widget.RadioGroup.OnCheckedChangeListener;
import android.widget.Toast;

public class MainActivity extends Activity {
```

```java
@Override
protected void onCreate(Bundle savedInstanceState) {
        super.onCreate(savedInstanceState);
        setContentView(R.layout.activity_main);

        RadioGroup radioGroup = (RadioGroup)

findViewById(R.id.radioGroup1);
        radioGroup.setOnCheckedChangeListener(new
                                OnCheckedChangeListener() {

            @Override
            public void onCheckedChanged(RadioGroup group, int
            checkedId) {
                switch (checkedId) {
                case R.id.radio0:
                    Toast.makeText(MainActivity.this, "Option 1
                        selected",Toast.LENGTH_SHORT).show();
                    break;
                case R.id.radio1:
                    Toast.makeText(MainActivity.this, "Option 2
                        selected", Toast.LENGTH_SHORT).show();
                    break;
                case R.id.radio2:
                    Toast.makeText(MainActivity.this, "Option 3
                        selected", Toast.LENGTH_SHORT).show();
                    break;
                }
            }
        });

    }
}
```

2. Run the application and select an option from RadioGroup. Figure 4.7 shows a Toast message appearing once the 2nd option is selected -

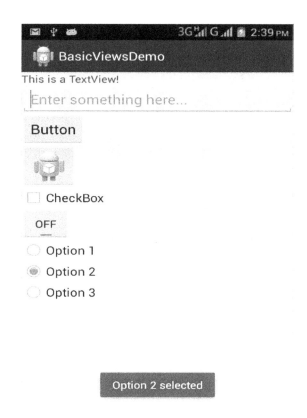

Figure 4.7: Second option of RadioGroup selected

How It Works?

First we get the reference of our RadioGroup instance by its id -

RadioGroup radioGroup = (RadioGroup) findViewById(R.id.radioGroup1);

Then, we add OnCheckedChangeListener to this RadioGroup instance and pass an OnCheckedChangeLister object as an anonymous inner class -

```
radioGroup.setOnCheckedChangeListener(new
                         OnCheckedChangeListener() {

    @Override
    public void onCheckedChanged(RadioGroup group, int
        checkedId) {
        switch (checkedId) {
        case R.id.radio0:
            Toast.makeText(MainActivity.this, "Option 1
                selected",Toast.LENGTH_SHORT).show();
```

```
                    break;
          case R.id.radio1:
                    Toast.makeText(MainActivity.this, "Option 2
                             selected", Toast.LENGTH_SHORT).show();
                    break;
          case
R.id.radio2:
     Toast.makeText(MainActivity.this, "Option
3                                  selected", Toast.LENGTH_SHORT).show();
                    break;
               }
          }
     });
```

When the checked RadioButton of our RadioGroup is changed, the callback
method onCheckedChanged() will be fired. This method will have two arguments.
The first one is the RadioGroup view and the second one is the id of the checked
RadioButton. We use the switch statement to compare the RadioButton widget's id
and thus detect which RadioButton is checked.

ProgressBar View

The ProgressBar widget facilitates us to provide visual feedback to the users
regarding ongoing tasks. This way, you can update users about the progress of long
running background tasks (like a file download from Internet). We will create a
new project to demonstrate this view widget.

1. Create a new project named ProgressBarDemo.

2. Add a new ProgressBar widget to the layout file activity_main.xml, so that the
layout file looks like this -

```
<RelativeLayout          xmlns:android="http://schemas.android.com/apk/res/
android"
    xmlns:tools="http://schemas.android.com/tools"
    android:layout_width="match_parent"
    android:layout_height="match_parent" >

    <ProgressBar
       android:id="@+id/progressBar1"
       style="@android:style/Widget.ProgressBar.Horizontal"
```

```
        android:layout_width="match_parent"
        android:layout_height="wrap_content"
        android:layout_alignParentLeft="true"
        android:layout_alignParentTop="true"
        android:padding="6dp" />

</RelativeLayout>
```

3. Update the MainActivity.java activity file with the following code -

```
package com.iducate.progressbardemo;

import android.app.Activity;
import android.os.AsyncTask;
import android.os.Bundle;
import android.os.SystemClock;
import android.widget.ProgressBar;

public class MainActivity extends Activity {

    private ProgressBar mProgressBar;

    @Override
    protected void onCreate(Bundle savedInstanceState) {
        super.onCreate(savedInstanceState);
        setContentView(R.layout.activity_main);

        mProgressBar = (ProgressBar)

findViewById(R.id.progressBar1);

        new MyTask().execute();
    }

    public class MyTask extends AsyncTask<Void, Integer, Void> {
        @Override
        protected Void doInBackground(Void... params) {

            for(int i=1; i <= 10; i++) {
                publishProgress(i*10);
                SystemClock.sleep(500);
            }
```

```
            return null;
        }


        @Override
        protected void onProgressUpdate(Integer... values) {
            mProgressBar.setProgress(values[0]);
        }
    }

}
```

4. Run the application, and you will see a progress bar similar to figure 4.8 -

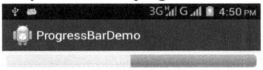

Figure 4.8: ProgressBarDemo application

How It Works?

The layout file contains a ProgressBar widget -

```
<ProgressBar
android:id="@+id/progressBar1"
style="@android:style/Widget.ProgressBar.Horizontal"
```

```
android:layout_width="match_parent"
android:layout_height="wrap_content"
android:layout_alignParentLeft="true"
android:layout_alignParentTop="true"
android:padding="6dp" />
```

Along with some other attributes, we have set a style attribute and id for this ProgressBar widget.

In Android, long running tasks should run on a separate thread. Within our MainActivity.java class, you will notice an inner class named MyTask. The MyTask class is a subclass of AsyncTask class. AsyncTask class provides us the facility to run long running background tasks in a separate thread and also the facility to update the main UI thread with ease.

The doInBackground() method of AsyncTask will run the long running background tasks. For our demo application, to simulate a long running task, we loop through the numbers from 1 to 10 and made a delay of 500 milliseconds between each step.

```
@Override
protected Void doInBackground(Void... params) {

        for(int i=1; i <= 10; i++) {
                publishProgress(i*10);
                SystemClock.sleep(500);
        }

        return null;
}
```

The code inside doInBackgroud() will run on a separate thread. Within each loop iteration of doInBackground() method, we do two things. Call publishProgress() method and make a delay of 500 milliseconds.

A call to the publishProgress() method will invoke the onProgressUpdate() method of AsyncTask class -

```
@Override
protected void onProgressUpdate(Integer... values) {
        mProgressBar.setProgress(values[0]);
}
```

191

Within this onProgressUpdate() method, we update the progress bar. This method runs on the Main UI thread.

After having the MyTask class set up, we create a new instance of this class and call the execute() method -

```
new MyTask().execute();
```

From the onCreate() method of our activity class, we instantiate a new instance of our MyTask class and call it's execute() method. This will start executing MyTask class.

AsyncTask class has two other methods you can use –

```
@Override
protected void onPreExecute() {
    // TODO Auto-generated method stub
    super.onPreExecute();
}

@Override
protected void onPostExecute(Void result) {
    // TODO Auto-generated method stub
    super.onPostExecute(result);
}
```

Both these methods also run on the main UI thread. The onPreExecute() method is called before the doInBackgroud() method. Within the onPreExecute() method, you will likely do some background setup before starting the tasks.

On the other hand, the onPostExecute() method is called once the background task of doInBackground() method finishes. This method will get the result as parameter. Within this method call, you will likely update the UI with the result.

AutoCompleteTextView Widget

The AutoCompleteTextView widget is a text input control quite similar to

EditText. But unlike EditText widget, the AutoCompleteTextView widget shows a list of completion suggestions automatically while the user is typing. The next example will demonstrate how to do that.

1. Create a new project called AutoCompleteTextViewDemo.

2. Update the layout file activity_main.xml with the following code -

```xml
<LinearLayout xmlns:android="http://schemas.android.com/apk/res/android"
    android:layout_width="fill_parent"
    android:layout_height="fill_parent"
    android:orientation="vertical" >

    <TextView
        android:id="@+id/textView1"
        android:layout_width="wrap_content"
        android:layout_height="wrap_content"
        android:text="Enter name of your country" />

    <AutoCompleteTextView
        android:id="@+id/autoCompleteTextView1"
        android:layout_width="match_parent"
        android:layout_height="wrap_content" >

        <requestFocus />
    </AutoCompleteTextView>

</LinearLayout>
```

3. Update the MainActivity.java file with the following code -

```java
package com.iducate.autocompletetextviewdemo;

import android.app.Activity;
import android.os.Bundle;
import android.widget.ArrayAdapter;
import android.widget.AutoCompleteTextView;

public class MainActivity extends Activity {

    private String[] countries = { "Albania", "Algeria", "Armenia",
            "Andora","Angola", "Argentina", "Australia", "Bahrain",
```

```
            "Bangladesh", "Barbados", "Brazil", "China", "Denmark",
            "Egypt", "France", "Ghana", "Hong Kong", "India", "Italy",
            "United Kingdom", "United States", "United Arab  Emirates"    };

    @Override
    protected void onCreate(Bundle savedInstanceState) {
            super.onCreate(savedInstanceState);
            setContentView(R.layout.activity_main);

            AutoCompleteTextView acCountry = (AutoCompleteTextView)
                    findViewById(R.id.autoCompleteTextView1);

            ArrayAdapter<String> adapter = new
                                    ArrayAdapter<String>(this,

    android.R.layout.simple_list_item_1, countries);

            acCountry.setAdapter(adapter);
    }

}
```

4. Run the application and you will see a layout with a text label and a text input
   area (similar to EditText). Start typing and after you a couple of characters, you
   will see a list of suggestions appear (figure 4.9) -

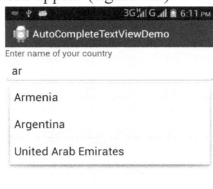

How It Works?

The AutoCompleteTextView is a subclass of EditText. In addition to letting the user type some text, it can give suggestions for completion. These suggestions needs to be attached with the AutoCompleteTextView via an Adapter object.

First, we create an array of strings which we want to show as suggestion texts -

```
private String[] countries = { "Albania", "Algeria", "Armenia",
        "Andora","Angola", "Argentina", "Australia", "Bahrain",
        "Bangladesh", "Barbados", "Brazil", "China", "Denmark",
        "Egypt", "France", "Ghana", "Hong Kong", "India", "Italy",
        "United Kingdom", "United States", "United Arab  Emirates"    };
```

Then we get a reference to the AutoCompleteTextView instance -

```
AutoCompleteTextView acCountry = (AutoCompleteTextView)
                findViewById(R.id.autoCompleteTextView1);
```

We have both the data source (completion suggestions) and the AutoCompleteTextView instance. Now we need to glue them together using an Adapter object. For that, we create an ArrayAdapter (since our data source is an array of strings) -

```
ArrayAdapter<String> adapter = new ArrayAdapter<String>(this,
        android.R.layout.simple_list_item_1, countries);
```

The ArrayAdapter constructor takes three parameters. The first one is the Context object. We pass our activity class as Context. The second parameter is the resource id of the suggestion list individual item's layout. We pass a built-in layout provided by Android, which only has a TextView. The third parameter is the data source, our array of countries.

Finally we set the adapter to our AutoCompleteTextView -
```
acCountry.setAdapter(adapter);
```

Using Picker Views

Sometimes you will need to let users select date and time from your application. Android provides two picker views, DatePicker and TimePicker for that purpose. The following sections will demonstrate the usage of both view widgets.

TimePicker View

The TimePicker view widget let's your users select the time of the day. Follow the steps below to see how it works -

1. Create a new project named TimePickerDemo.

2. Update the layout file activity_main.xml with the following code -

```
<LinearLayout xmlns:android="http://schemas.android.com/apk/res/android"
   android:layout_width="fill_parent"
   android:layout_height="fill_parent"
   android:orientation="vertical" >

   <TimePicker
      android:id="@+id/timePicker1"
      android:layout_width="wrap_content"
      android:layout_height="wrap_content" />

   <Button
      android:id="@+id/button1"
      android:layout_width="wrap_content"
      android:layout_height="wrap_content"
      android:onClick="showTime"
      android:text="Show Time" />

</LinearLayout>
```

3. Update the MainActivity.java file with the following code -

```
package com.iducate.timepickerdemo;

import android.app.Activity;
import android.os.Bundle;
import android.view.View;
```

```
import android.widget.TimePicker;
import android.widget.Toast;

public class MainActivity extends Activity {

    private TimePicker timePicker;

    @Override
    protected void onCreate(Bundle savedInstanceState) {
        super.onCreate(savedInstanceState);
        setContentView(R.layout.activity_main);

        timePicker = (TimePicker) findViewById(R.id.timePicker1);
    }

    public void showTime(View v) {
        int hour = timePicker.getCurrentHour();
        int minute = timePicker.getCurrentMinute();

        Toast.makeText(this, "Time Selected: " + hour + ":" +
                minute, Toast.LENGTH_LONG).show();
    }

}
```

4. Run the application. You will see a screen with a TimePicker widget and a Button widget below the TimePicker. Select any arbitrary time and click the button. you will see a Toast message with the selected time -

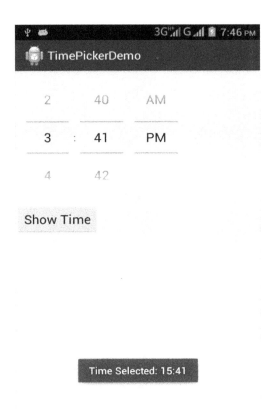

Figure 4.10: Selected time shown as Toast message

How It Works?

Our layout file contains a TimePicker widget -

```
<TimePicker
android:id="@+id/timePicker1"
android:layout_width="wrap_content"
android:layout_height="wrap_content" />
```

We need to set the android:id attribute to access it programmatically and get the selected time.

We also have a Button widget. We want to show the selected time when someone clicks the button -

```
<Button
android:id="@+id/button1"
android:layout_width="wrap_content"
android:layout_height="wrap_content"
```

```
android:onClick="showTime"
android:text="Show Time" />
```

The Button widget's android:onClick attribute is set to showTime, which means we can handle the button click from our activity class's showTime() method.

Within our MainActivity.java file, we need to access the TimePicker from more than one place. That's why we create a member variable for the TimePicker instance -

```
private TimePicker timePicker;
```

Within the onCreate() method of our activity, we get a reference of that TimerPicker instance -

```
timePicker = (TimePicker) findViewById(R.id.timePicker1);
```

Finally, we implement the showTime() method to handle the button click event -

```
public void showTime(View v) {
        int hour = timePicker.getCurrentHour();
        int minute = timePicker.getCurrentMinute();

        Toast.makeText(this, "Time Selected: " + hour + ":" +
                minute, Toast.LENGTH_LONG).show();
}
```

Within the showTime() method, we get the selected hour and minute by calling getCurrentHour() and getCurrentMinute() methods of the TimePicker instance. We then show the selected time as a Toast message.

DatePicker View

Using the DatePicker view widget, users can select any date conveniently from your application's UI. Let's see how the DatePicker widget is used.

1. Create a new project named DatePickerDemo.

2. Update the layout file activity_main.xml, to include a DatePicker and a Button widget -

```xml
<LinearLayout xmlns:android="http://schemas.android.com/apk/res/android"
    android:layout_width="fill_parent"
    android:layout_height="fill_parent"
    android:orientation="vertical" >

    <DatePicker
        android:id="@+id/datePicker1"
        android:layout_width="wrap_content"
        android:layout_height="wrap_content" />

    <Button
        android:id="@+id/button1"
        android:layout_width="wrap_content"
        android:layout_height="wrap_content"
        android:onClick="showDate"
        android:text="Show Date" />

</LinearLayout>
```

3. Update the MainActivity.java file with the following code -

```java
package com.iducate.datepickerdemo;

import android.app.Activity;
import android.os.Bundle;
import android.view.View;
import android.widget.DatePicker;
import android.widget.Toast;

public class MainActivity extends Activity {

    private DatePicker datePicker;

    @Override
    protected void onCreate(Bundle savedInstanceState) {
        super.onCreate(savedInstanceState);
        setContentView(R.layout.activity_main);

        datePicker = (DatePicker) findViewById(R.id.datePicker1);
    }

    public void showDate(View v) {
        int month = datePicker.getMonth() + 1;
```

```
        int day = datePicker.getDayOfMonth();
        int year = datePicker.getYear();

        Toast.makeText(this, "Date Selected: " + month + "/" + day
                            + "/" + year, Toast.LENGTH_LONG).show();
    }

}
```

4. Run the application. You will get a screen with a calender-like interface. Select
   any date and click the button. You will get a Toast message with selected date -

Figure 4.11: Toast message with selected date

How It Works?

The layout file contains a DatePicker widget -

```
    <DatePicker
    android:id="@+id/datePicker1"
    android:layout_width="wrap_content"
    android:layout_height="wrap_content" />
```

Below the DatePicker widget, there is a Button widget. When someone clicks this button, a Toast message with the selected date is shown -

```
<Button
android:id="@+id/button1"
android:layout_width="wrap_content"
android:layout_height="wrap_content"
android:onClick="showDate"
android:text="Show Date" />
```

The button click is handled by showDate() method of MainActivity class because we have android:onClick attribute of Button widget set to "showDate".

Now, within our MainActivity.java class, we create a member variable of type DatePicker -

```
private DatePicker datePicker;
```

and then get a reference of our DatePicker widget -

```
datePicker = (DatePicker) findViewById(R.id.datePicker1);
```

Finally, we implement the showDate() method -

```
public void showDate(View v) {
        int month = datePicker.getMonth() + 1;
        int day = datePicker.getDayOfMonth();
        int year = datePicker.getYear();

        Toast.makeText(this, "Date Selected: " + month + "/" + day
                        + "/" + year, Toast.LENGTH_LONG).show();
}
```

This method get the selected day, month and year from our DatePicker instance. We then show a Toast message with these date information.

Showing TimePicker and DatePicker as Dialog

While the TimePicker and DatePicker views enable users to select time and date, those widgets take up much space of the UI. Wouldn't it be more convenient if users could select time and date after which the widgets disappear? Let's create a new project to demonstrate how to do it.

1. Create a new project DateTimeDialogDemo.

2. Update the layout file activity_main.xml with the following code -

```xml
<LinearLayout xmlns:android="http://schemas.android.com/apk/res/android"
    android:layout_width="fill_parent"
    android:layout_height="fill_parent"
    android:orientation="vertical" >

    <Button
        android:id="@+id/btnTime"
        android:layout_width="match_parent"
        android:layout_height="wrap_content"
        android:onClick="setTime"
        android:text="Set Time" />

    <Button
        android:id="@+id/btnDate"
        android:layout_width="match_parent"
        android:layout_height="wrap_content"
        android:onClick="setDate"
        android:text="Set Date" />

</LinearLayout>
```

3. Update the MainActivity.java file with the following code -

```java
package com.iducate.datetimedialogdemo;

import java.util.Calendar;

import android.app.Activity;
import android.app.DatePickerDialog;
import android.app.DatePickerDialog.OnDateSetListener;
import android.app.TimePickerDialog;
import android.app.TimePickerDialog.OnTimeSetListener;
import android.os.Bundle;
import android.view.View;
import android.widget.DatePicker;
import android.widget.TimePicker;
```

```java
import android.widget.Toast;

public class MainActivity extends Activity {

        private Calendar calendar = Calendar.getInstance();

        @Override
        protected void onCreate(Bundle savedInstanceState) {
                super.onCreate(savedInstanceState);
                setContentView(R.layout.activity_main);
        }

        public void setTime(View v) {
                new TimePickerDialog(MainActivity.this, tListener,
                                calendar.get(Calendar.HOUR_OF_DAY),
                                calendar.get(Calendar.MINUTE), false).show();
        }

        public void setDate(View v) {
                new DatePickerDialog(MainActivity.this, dListener,
                                calendar.get(Calendar.YEAR),

calendar.get(Calendar.MONTH),
                                calendar.get(Calendar.DAY_OF_MONTH)).show();
        }

        TimePickerDialog.OnTimeSetListener tListener = new
                        OnTimeSetListener() {

                @Override
                public void onTimeSet(TimePicker view, int hourOfDay, int
                        minute) {
                        Toast.makeText(MainActivity.this, "Time Selected: " +
                                hourOfDay + ":" + minute,
                                        Toast.LENGTH_SHORT).show();
                }
        };

        DatePickerDialog.OnDateSetListener dListener = new
                        OnDateSetListener() {

                @Override
                public void onDateSet(DatePicker view, int year, int
```

```
                    monthOfYear, int dayOfMonth) {
                Toast.makeText(
                    MainActivity.this, "Date Selected: " +
                            monthOfYear + "/" + dayOfMonth + "/" +
year,                   Toast.LENGTH_SHORT).show();
            }
        };

}
```

4. Now run the application, you will see a screen with two buttons -

Figure 4.12: Running DateTimeDialogDemo application

5. If you click the "Set Time" button, a TimePickerDialog will open. Set the time and close the dialog by clicking "Done". You will get a Toast message with the time you just set -

Figure 4.13: TimePickerDialog

6. Similarly, if you click the "Set Date" button, a DatePickerDialog will appear -

Figure 4.14: DatePickerDialog

How It Works?

Our layout is simple consists of just two buttons. When someone clicks those buttons, the TimePickerDialog and DatePickerDialog will appear. The first button's android:onClick attribute is set to "setTime", so the click event will be handled by the method setTime() -

```
<Button
    android:id="@+id/btnTime"
    android:layout_width="match_parent"
    android:layout_height="wrap_content"
    android:onClick="setTime"
    android:text="Set Time" />
```

The other button's android:onClick is set to "setDate" and the setDate() method of MainActivity class will handle the corresponding click event -

```
<Button
    android:id="@+id/btnDate"
    android:layout_width="match_parent"
    android:layout_height="wrap_content"
    android:onClick="setDate"
    android:text="Set Date" />
```

Within the setTime() method, we create a new instance of TimePickerDialog -

```
public void setTime(View v) {
        new TimePickerDialog(MainActivity.this, tListener,
                calendar.get(Calendar.HOUR_OF_DAY),
                calendar.get(Calendar.MINUTE), false).show();
}
```

The TimePickerDialog constructor takes a number of parameters. The first parameter is the Context object where we pass our Activity in. The second parameter is an instance of OnTimeSetListener. We will look at that a while later. The third and fourth parameters provide initial values of hour and minute to the TimePickerDialog. The final parameter is a boolean which indicates whether the time is shown in 24 hours convention or not. False indicates that we don't want the 24 hours format. We next call the show() method of TimePickerDialog to show the dialog window.

Now let's go back to OnTimeSetListener. It has a method onTimeSet() that is fired as soon as the time is set -

```
TimePickerDialog.OnTimeSetListener tListener = new
```

```
        OnTimeSetListener() {

    @Override
    public void onTimeSet(TimePicker view, int hourOfDay, int
            minute) {
        Toast.makeText(MainActivity.this, "Time Selected: " +
            hourOfDay + ":" + minute,
                                    Toast.LENGTH_SHORT).show();
    }
};
```

The onTimeSet() method has selected hour and minute as parameter. Within the implementation of that onTimeSet() method, we show a Toast message using these time values.

Now let's see how the DatePickerDialog is working. The setDate() method creates a new instance of DatePickerDialog -

```
public void setDate(View v) {
    new DatePickerDialog(MainActivity.this, dListener,
            calendar.get(Calendar.YEAR),

calendar.get(Calendar.MONTH),
            calendar.get(Calendar.DAY_OF_MONTH)).show();
}
```

The DatePickerDialog takes in a few parameters. The first is the Context object. The rest of the parameters except the second parameter provide initial values of day, month and year to DatePickerDialog. The second parameter is the OnDateSetListener object, which has a callback method onDateSet(). It is fired when the user sets the date from the DatePickerDialog window -

```
DatePickerDialog.OnDateSetListener dListener = new
            OnDateSetListener() {

    @Override
    public void onDateSet(DatePicker view, int year, int
            monthOfYear, int dayOfMonth) {
        Toast.makeText(
            MainActivity.this, "Date Selected: " +
                    monthOfYear + "/" + dayOfMonth + "/" +
year,                Toast.LENGTH_SHORT).show();
```

```
        }
    };
```

The onDateSet() method will have the selected day, month and year as parameter. Using these values, we show a Toast message.

Using List Views to Display Long Lists

Often you need to display a list of items in your application. Android provides you two views for this purpose – ListView and Spinner. The following sections show how you can use both of them.

ListView Widget

With the ListView widget, you can display a list of items in a vertically scrolling list. Many applications that are shipped with Android, use the ListView widget. For example – the Contacts application, Messaging application, Gmail application etc use the ListView widget.

Let's create a new project to demonstrate the usage of the ListView widget.

1. Create a new project called ListViewDemo.

2. Update the MainActivity.java file with the following code -

```
package com.iducate.listviewdemo;

import android.app.ListActivity;
import android.os.Bundle;
import android.view.View;
import android.widget.ArrayAdapter;
import android.widget.ListView;
import android.widget.Toast;

public class MainActivity extends ListActivity {

    private String[] countries = { "Albania", "Algeria", "Armenia",
            "Andora", "Angola", "Argentina", "Australia", "Bahrain",
            "Bangladesh", "Barbados", "Brazil", "China", "Denmark",
            "Egypt", "France","Ghana", "Hong Kong", "India", "Italy",
            "United Kingdom", "United States", "United Arab Emirates"
```

```
};

@Override
protected void onCreate(Bundle savedInstanceState) {
        super.onCreate(savedInstanceState);

        ArrayAdapter<String> adapter = new
                                ArrayAdapter<String> (this,

android.R.layout.simple_list_item_1, countries);

        setListAdapter(adapter);
}

@Override
protected void onListItemClick(ListView l, View v, int position,
        long id) {
        Toast.makeText(this, "Item clicked: " +

countries[position],Toast.LENGTH_SHORT).show();
}

}
```

3. Now run the application and you will get a list of items (country names). If you click any item from the list, a Toast message with that item will appear (figure 4.15) -

211

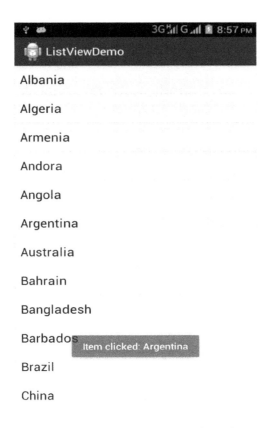

Figure 4.15: Running ListViewDemo

How It Works?

The MainActivity class doesn't extent the subclass Activity. Instead, it extends ListActivity class -

```
public class MainActivity extends ListActivity
```

ListActivity itself is a child class of Activity class. It is specially useful for displaying a list of items. If you haven't noticed yet, our MainActivity class doesn't inflate any layout file. The ListActivity class provides a layout to display a full screen list.

We have started by defining a string array which is an array of country names. To hook our data source (countries array) with the layout, we need an Adapter object -

```
ArrayAdapter<String> adapter = new ArrayAdapter<String> (this,
        android.R.layout.simple_list_item_1, countries);
```

We have created an instance of ArrayAdapter object. This ArrayAdapter instance takes Context object as first parameter which in this case is simply the activity class. The second parameter takes a layout resource id. This is the layout for each item of the list. We want to display a piece of text (a country name) per list item. So we have chosen a layout with a TextView. This layout comes with the Android system. The third parameter is the countries array.

Next, we call the setListAdapter() method of ListActivity class to set adapter for our list -

```
setListAdapter(adapter);
```

We have implemented another ListActivity method, onListItemClick() -

```
@Override
protected void onListItemClick(ListView l, View v, int position, long id) {
    Toast.makeText(this, "Item clicked: " +

countries[position],Toast.LENGTH_SHORT).show();
}
```

This method is called every time a list item is clicked. Within that method, we show a Toast notification with the item clicked.

Storing List Items in strings.xml

Instead of storing list items in our activity class as array, we can store them in strings.xml file as a string-array. We can easily rewrite the previous example to use strings.xml file as our source for list items. Here is how you can add a string-array of countries (with first few items of our array) -

```
<string-array name="countries">
<item>Albanai</item>
<item>Algeria</item>
<item>Armenia</item>
<item>Andora</item>
<item>Angola</item>
<item>Argentina</item>
</string-array>
```

In our MainActivity.java file, instead of creating an array of countries, we can programmatically retrieve the countries from our strings.xml file. The highlighted lines show the changes made from the previous version -

```
package com.iducate.listviewdemo;

import android.app.ListActivity;
import android.os.Bundle;
import android.view.View;
import android.widget.ArrayAdapter;
import android.widget.ListView;
import android.widget.Toast;

public class MainActivity extends ListActivity {

    private String[] countries;

    @Override
    protected void onCreate(Bundle savedInstanceState) {
        super.onCreate(savedInstanceState);

        countries =

getResources().getStringArray(R.array.countries);

        ArrayAdapter<String> adapter = new
                                    ArrayAdapter<String>(this,

android.R.layout.simple_list_item_1, countries);

        setListAdapter(adapter);
    }

    @Override
    protected void onListItemClick(ListView l, View v, int position,
        long id) {
        Toast.makeText(this, "Item clicked: " +

countries[position],Toast.LENGTH_SHORT).show();
    }

}
```

Enabling Multi-item Support

To enable multi-item support for our ListView, we first need to get a reference to our ListView object. We then call setChoiceMode() method of ListView to enable multi-item support -

```
@Override
protected void onCreate(Bundle savedInstanceState) {
    super.onCreate(savedInstanceState);

    ArrayAdapter<String> adapter = new ArrayAdapter<String>(this,
        android.R.layout.simple_list_item_checked, countries);

    ListView listView = getListView();
    listView.setChoiceMode(ListView.CHOICE_MODE_MULTIPLE);

    setListAdapter(adapter);
}
```

We can get the reference to our ListView widget programmatically by calling the getListView() method. We then call the setChoiceMode() method of ListView instance and set the multi-item select mode by passing the parameter ListView.CHOICE_MODE_MULTIPLE . Now we will be able to select multiple items -

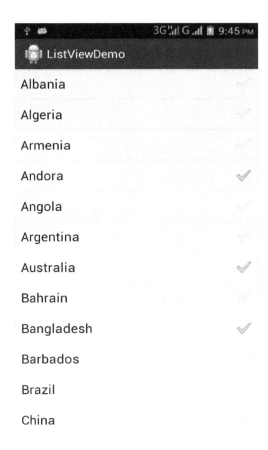

Figure 4.16: ListView with multi-item selected

Get Selected List Items

Since we have enabled multi-item selection in our ListView, let's see how we can see all the selected items. We will add a new button to show all the selected items.

1. Since we will need to add a button to our layout, we need to use a layout file. We will use the default generated activity_main.xml layout. Update the activity_main.xml with the following code -

```
<LinearLayout xmlns:android="http://schemas.android.com/apk/res/android"
    android:layout_width="fill_parent"
    android:layout_height="fill_parent"
    android:orientation="vertical" >

    <Button
        android:id="@+id/button1"
        android:layout_width="wrap_content"
```

```xml
        android:layout_height="wrap_content"
        android:layout_gravity="center"
        android:onClick="showSelectedItems"
        android:text="Get Selected Items"/>

    <ListView
        android:id="@+id/android:list"
        android:layout_width="match_parent"
        android:layout_height="wrap_content" >
    </ListView>

</LinearLayout>
```

2. Now update the MainActivity.java with the following code -

```java
package com.iducate.listviewdemo;

import android.app.ListActivity;
import android.os.Bundle;
import android.view.View;
import android.widget.ArrayAdapter;
import android.widget.ListView;
import android.widget.Toast;

public class MainActivity extends ListActivity {

    private String[] countries = { "Albania", "Algeria", "Armenia",
            "Andora", "Angola", "Argentina", "Australia", "Bahrain",
            "Bangladesh", "Barbados", "Brazil", "China", "Denmark",
            "Egypt", "France","Ghana", "Hong Kong", "India", "Italy",
            "United Kingdom", "United States", "United Arab Emirates"
    };

    @Override
    protected void onCreate(Bundle savedInstanceState) {
        super.onCreate(savedInstanceState);
        setContentView(R.layout.activity_main);

        ArrayAdapter<String> adapter = new
                                ArrayAdapter<String>(this,

    android.R.layout.simple_list_item_checked, countries);
```

```
                ListView listView = getListView();
                listView.setChoiceMode(ListView.CHOICE_MODE_MULTIPLE);

                setListAdapter(adapter);
        }

        public void showSelectedItems(View v) {
                ListView listView = getListView();
                String itemsSelected = "Selected items: \n";
                for (int i = 0; i < listView.getCount(); i++) {
                        if (listView.isItemChecked(i)) {
                                itemsSelected += listView.getItemAtPosition(i) +
                                                                "\n";
                        }
                }
                Toast.makeText(this, itemsSelected,
                                        Toast.LENGTH_LONG).show();
        }

        @Override
        protected void onListItemClick(ListView l, View v, int position,
                long id) {
                Toast.makeText(this, "Item clicked: " +
                                        countries[position],
Toast.LENGTH_SHORT).show();
        }

}
```

3. Now run the application. Select a few items and click the button to get the selected items -

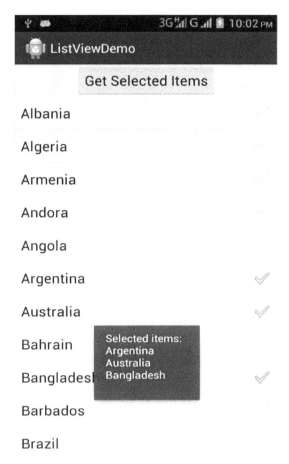

Figure 4.17: Getting selected items from ListView

How It Works?

Unlike the previous list examples where we had only a screen list, this example has a Button widget. That's why we need to provide our layout file. Within our layout file, we have a Button widget for we want to get the selected list items when users click this button.

```
<Button
android:id="@+id/button1"
android:layout_width="wrap_content"
android:layout_height="wrap_content"
android:layout_gravity="center"
android:onClick="showSelectedItems"
android:text="Get Selected Items"/>
```

The click event of this button will be handled by showSelectedItems() method of activity class.

To display the list of items, we have a ListView widget -

```
<ListView
android:id="@+id/android:list"
android:layout_width="match_parent"
android:layout_height="wrap_content" >
</ListView>
```

We set the android:id attribute to the id of android:list. This way, we access this ListView widget from our ListActivity by calling the getListView() method -

```
ListView listView = getListView();
```

Now, let's have a look at the showSelectedItems() method which handles the button click event and shows the selected multiple list items -

```
public void showSelectedItems(View v) {
    ListView listView = getListView();
    String itemsSelected = "Selected items: \n";
    for (int i = 0; i < listView.getCount(); i++) {
        if (listView.isItemChecked(i)) {
            itemsSelected += listView.getItemAtPosition(i) +
                                                        "\n";
        }
    }
    Toast.makeText(this, itemsSelected,
                            Toast.LENGTH_LONG).show();
}
```

We loop through all the selected items and append them together to show them as a Toast message.

Spinner View

Using the Spinner widget, we show a list of items as a drop down list. This might be more convenient because unlike the ListView, it takes a smaller space to display a Spinner widget. Let's create a new project to demonstrate the usage of the Spinner widget.

1. Create a new project SpinnerViewDemo.

2. Update the layout file activity_main.xml to include a Spinner widget -

```xml
<LinearLayout xmlns:android="http://schemas.android.com/apk/res/android"
    android:layout_width="fill_parent"
    android:layout_height="fill_parent"
    android:orientation="vertical" >

    <Spinner
        android:id="@+id/spinner1"
        android:layout_width="match_parent"
        android:layout_height="wrap_content" />

</LinearLayout>
```

3. Update the MainActivity.java file with the following code -

```java
package com.iducate.spinnerviewdemo;

import android.app.Activity;
import android.os.Bundle;
import android.view.View;
import android.widget.AdapterView;
import android.widget.AdapterView.OnItemSelectedListener;
import android.widget.ArrayAdapter;
import android.widget.Spinner;
import android.widget.Toast;

public class MainActivity extends Activity {

    private String[] items = { "Item 1", "Item 2", "Item 3", "Item                4",
"Item 5", "Item 6", "Item 7" };

    @Override
    protected void onCreate(Bundle savedInstanceState) {
        super.onCreate(savedInstanceState);
        setContentView(R.layout.activity_main);

        Spinner spinner = (Spinner) findViewById(R.id.spinner1);

        ArrayAdapter<String> adapter = new
                                        ArrayAdapter<String>(this,
```

```
        android.R.layout.simple_spinner_dropdown_item, items);

        spinner.setAdapter(adapter);

        spinner.setOnItemSelectedListener(new
                                OnItemSelectedListener() {

            @Override
            public void onItemSelected(AdapterView<?> arg0, View
                    arg1, int position, long arg3) {
                Toast.makeText(MainActivity.this,
                    "Item selected: " + items[position],
                        Toast.LENGTH_SHORT).show();
            }

            @Override
            public void onNothingSelected(AdapterView<?> arg0) {
                // TODO Auto-generated method stub
            }
        });
    }
}
```

4. Run the application and you will see a screen with a Spinner widget. You will only see the first item of the spinner widget listed. Click the spinner widget to reveal all the other options. You will see a drop down list of items appear. If you select any item, a Toast message will be shown.

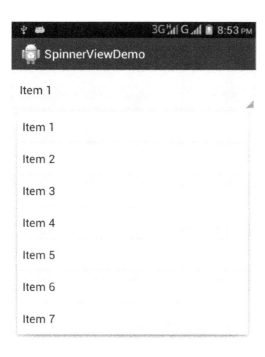

Figure 4.18: Spinner widget with drop down items

How It Works?

Our layout file contains a Spinner widget -

```
<Spinner
android:id="@+id/spinner1"
android:layout_width="match_parent"
android:layout_height="wrap_content" />
```

From our MainActivity.java file, we get reference to this Spinner widget by it's id -

```
Spinner spinner = (Spinner) findViewById(R.id.spinner1);
```

Like we did previously for ListView, we create an ArrayAdapter -

```
ArrayAdapter<String>          adapter          =          new
                    ArrayAdapter<String>(this,
```

```
android.R.layout.simple_spinner_dropdown_item,                    items);
```

Then, we need to glue the Spinner instance with data source via the adapter -

```
spinner.setAdapter(adapter);
```

Finally, we want to get notified every time a item of Spinner is selected. We do this by setting an OnItemSelectedListener to our Spinner instance -

```
spinner.setOnItemSelectedListener(new
                                OnItemSelectedListener() {

        @Override
        public void onItemSelected(AdapterView<?> arg0, View
                arg1, int position, long arg3) {
            Toast.makeText(MainActivity.this,
                "Item selected: " + items[position],

Toast.LENGTH_SHORT).show();
        }

        @Override
        public void onNothingSelected(AdapterView<?> arg0) {
            // TODO Auto-generated method stub
        }
    });
```

We pass an OnItemSelectedListener instance as an anonymous inner class. The onItemSelected() method of this listener is fired when an item of Spinner widget is selected. We show a Toast message in this method with the selected item.

Understanding Specialized Fragments

In the previous chapter, we have learned about fragments. All the fragments we have used are subclasses of the base Fragment class. In the same way that we have specialized the activity classes (like ListActivity for displaying list of items), we have specialized fragment classes as well – DialogFragment, ListFragment, PreferenceFragment etc. All of them are child classes of the Fragment class. The following sections will discuss more about these specialized fragment classes.

Just a reminder about the minimum required SDK for fragments.

Unless you don't use support library version of fragment classes, you should set minimum required SDK to 11 or above for the next few example projects.

Using DialogFragment

With the DialogFragment, you can create a floating dialog window. This can be helpful to get user confirmation on particular tasks. You create a dialog fragment by extending the DialogFragment base class. Follow the steps bellow to create a new project, which demonstrates the usage of DialogFragment.

1. Create a new project named DialogFragmentDemo.

2. Create a new fragment class MyDialogFragment.java, under the src directory (under default project package) with the following code -

```java
package com.iducate.dialogfragmentdemo;

import android.app.AlertDialog;
import android.app.Dialog;
import android.app.DialogFragment;
import android.content.DialogInterface;
import android.os.Bundle;

public class MyDialogFragment extends DialogFragment {

    @Override
    public Dialog onCreateDialog(Bundle savedInstanceState) {

        AlertDialog.Builder alerDialogBuilder = new
                        AlertDialog.Builder(
                getActivity()).setTitle("Confirmation")
                .setMessage("Are you sure?")
                .setPositiveButton("Yes", pListener)
                .setNegativeButton("No", nListener);

        return alerDialogBuilder.create();
    }

    DialogInterface.OnClickListener pListener = new
                        DialogInterface.OnClickListener() {
```

```java
        @Override
        public void onClick(DialogInterface arg0, int arg1) {
            // these will be executed when user click Yes button
        }
    };

    DialogInterface.OnClickListener nListener = new
                        DialogInterface.OnClickListener() {

        @Override
        public void onClick(DialogInterface arg0, int arg1) {
            // these will be executed when user click No button
        }
    };
}
```

3. Now update the layout file (activity_main.xml) of our activity class with the following code -

```xml
<LinearLayout xmlns:android="http://schemas.android.com/apk/res/android"
    android:layout_width="fill_parent"
    android:layout_height="fill_parent"
    android:orientation="vertical" >

    <Button
        android:layout_width="wrap_content"
        android:layout_height="wrap_content"
        android:onClick="showDialog"
        android:text="Show Dialog" />

</LinearLayout>
```

4. Finally, update the MainActivity.java file with the following code -

```java
package com.iducate.dialogfragmentdemo;

import android.app.Activity;
import android.os.Bundle;
import android.view.View;

public class MainActivity extends Activity {
```

```
@Override
protected void onCreate(Bundle savedInstanceState) {
       super.onCreate(savedInstanceState);
       setContentView(R.layout.activity_main);
}

public void showDialog(View v) {
       new MyDialogFragment().show(getFragmentManager(),
```

"MyFragment");
       }

}

5. Now, run the application. You will see a screen with a button. Click that button and a dialog will appear -

Figure 4.19: Running DialogFragmentDemo application

How It Works?

The layout file of our activity contains a single button -

```
<Button
    android:layout_width="wrap_content"
    android:layout_height="wrap_content"
    android:onClick="showDialog"
    android:text="Show Dialog" />
```

We want to show the dialog fragment when user clicks this button. The button click event is handled by showDialog() method of MainActivity.java class.

The MyDialogFragment class extends the DialogFragment base class -

```
public class MyDialogFragment extends DialogFragment {
```

We overwrite the onCreateDialog() method of DialogFragment class, which is called after onCreate() but before onCreateView() -

```
@Override
public Dialog onCreateDialog(Bundle savedInstanceState) {

    AlertDialog.Builder alerDialogBuilder = new
                        AlertDialog.Builder(
            getActivity()).setTitle("Confirmation")
            .setMessage("Are you sure?")
            .setPositiveButton("Yes", pListener)
            .setNegativeButton("No", nListener);

    return alerDialogBuilder.create();
}
```

Within this onCreateDialog() method, we have created an alert dialog with two buttons and set the different attributes of dialog window (like - title, message etc). To handle the "Yes" and "No" button clicks of dialog window, we have created two listener objects -

```
DialogInterface.OnClickListener pListener = new
                        DialogInterface.OnClickListener() {

    @Override
```

```
        public void onClick(DialogInterface arg0, int arg1) {
                // these will be executed when user click Yes button
        }
    };
```

The above listener's onClick() method will be fired when user clicks the "Yes" button. We have left the implementation of this method empty. You can choose to do whatever you want within this method. Similarly, we have another listener to handle the "No" button click -

```
    DialogInterface.OnClickListener nListener = new
                        DialogInterface.OnClickListener() {

        @Override
        public void onClick(DialogInterface arg0, int arg1) {
                // these will be executed when user click No button
        }
    };
```

Finally, let's see the showDialog() method implementation of MainActivity.java class -

```
    public void showDialog(View v) {
        new MyDialogFragment().show(getFragmentManager(),

"MyFragment");
    }
```

Within this method, we create a new instance of our MyDialogFragment class and call the show() method to display the alert dialog.

Using PreferenceFragment

Most Android applications offers preference screens to allow users to personalize app settings. The PreferenceActivity, which is a special type of Activity class, is capable of handling a preference screen. Android 3.0 or later also provides support for PreferenceFragment, which can be used for the same purpose.

1. Create a new project named PreferenceFragmentDemo.

2. We will create our preference screen as an XML resource file which will be

placed under res/xml directory. Create the res/xml directory if that isn't already there under your project structure. Within that res/xml directory, create an XML file named prefs.xml with the following code -

```xml
<?xml version="1.0" encoding="utf-8"?>
<PreferenceScreen xmlns:android="http://schemas.android.com/apk/res/android" >

    <CheckBoxPreference
        android:key="checkBoxPref"
        android:summary="CheckBox Preference"
        android:title="CheckBox" />

    <EditTextPreference
        android:key="editTextPref"
        android:summary="EditText Preference"
        android:title="EditText" />

</PreferenceScreen>
```

3. Create a new PreferenceFragment class under the src directory (under default project package) with the following content -

```java
package com.iducate.preferencefragmentdemo;

import android.os.Bundle;
import android.preference.PreferenceFragment;

public class MyPreferenceFragment extends PreferenceFragment {

    @Override
    public void onCreate(Bundle savedInstanceState) {
        super.onCreate(savedInstanceState);
        addPreferencesFromResource(R.xml.prefs);
    }
}
```

4. Finally, update the MainActivity.java file with the following code -

```java
package com.iducate.preferencefragmentdemo;
```

```
import android.app.Activity;
import android.app.FragmentManager;
import android.os.Bundle;

public class MainActivity extends Activity {

    @Override
    protected void onCreate(Bundle savedInstanceState) {
        super.onCreate(savedInstanceState);

        FragmentManager fragmentManager = getFragmentManager();
        fragmentManager.beginTransaction()
            .replace(android.R.id.content, new

MyPreferenceFragment()).commit();
    }
}
```

5. Now, run the application. You will get a preference screen with a CheckBox and an EditText preference. Save your preference and exit the application with the back button. When you return again, notice that your previous preference settings were saved.

Figure 4.20: Running PreferenceFragmentDemo application

How It Works?

The preference screen of your application's prefs.xml root element is a
PreferenceScreen -

```
<PreferenceScreen xmlns:android="http://schemas.android.com/apk/res/
android" >

  <CheckBoxPreference
    android:key="checkBoxPref"
    android:summary="CheckBox Preference"
    android:title="CheckBox" />

  <EditTextPreference
    android:key="editTextPref"
    android:summary="EditText Preference"
    android:title="EditText" />
```

`</PreferenceScreen>`

This preference screen has two elements. A `CheckBoxPreference` and an `EditTextPreference` preference. This preference screen is used by our fragment class.

Our fragment class extends PreferenceFragment class instead of extending the base Fragment class -

```
public class MyPreferenceFragment extends PreferenceFragment {
```

Within our MyPreferenceFragment class, we overwrite a single method, the onCreate() method -

```
@Override
public void onCreate(Bundle savedInstanceState) {
        super.onCreate(savedInstanceState);
        addPreferencesFromResource(R.xml.prefs);
}
```

This onCreate() method simply calls the addPreferencesFromResource() method, which adds our preference xml file.

Now, within our MainActivity.java class, we add the fragment dynamically -

```
@Override
protected void onCreate(Bundle savedInstanceState) {
        super.onCreate(savedInstanceState);

        FragmentManager fragmentManager = getFragmentManager();
        fragmentManager.beginTransaction()
                .replace(android.R.id.content, new

MyPreferenceFragment()).commit();
}
```

This is how it works. The preferences saved persist after you leave the application or even after you restart the device.

The preference settings are saved in an XML file which is private to this particular application. Specifically, it is stored under the directory

233

/data/data/com.iducate.preferencefragmentdemo/shared_prefs

From a hardware device, users can't directly access this file (unless the device is rooted). But for emulators, you can easily check the file from the DDMS perspective. Switch to the File Explorer tab and browse through the directory structure to locate the above mentioned path.

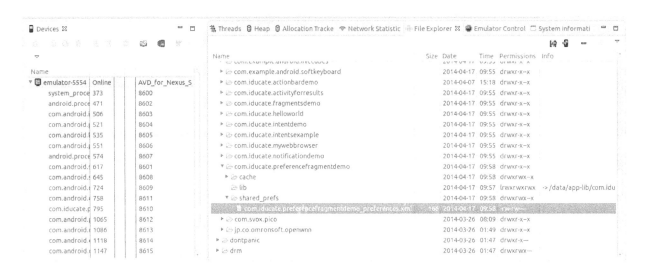

Figure 4.21: Locating preference file

Using ListFragment

ListFragment can be used to display a long list of items. This fragment contains a ListView widget. Let's see how we can use it.

1. Create a new project named ListFragmentDemo.

2. Create a new fragment class named MyListFragment.java under the src directory (under default project pacakge) with the following content -

```
package com.iducate.listfragmentdemo;

import android.app.ListFragment;
import android.os.Bundle;
import android.view.View;
import android.widget.ArrayAdapter;
import android.widget.ListView;
import android.widget.Toast;
```

```java
public class MyListFragment extends ListFragment {

    private String[] items = { "Item 1", "Item 2", "Item 3", "Item
                                4", "Item 5", "Item 6", "Item 7" };

    @Override
    public void onCreate(Bundle savedInstanceState) {
        super.onCreate(savedInstanceState);

        ArrayAdapter<String> adapter = new
                                ArrayAdapter<String>(getActivity(),
                    android.R.layout.simple_list_item_1, items);

        setListAdapter(adapter);
    }

    @Override
    public void onListItemClick(ListView l, View v, int position,        long
id) {
        Toast.makeText(getActivity(), "Item clicked: " +
                                items[position],
Toast.LENGTH_SHORT).show();
    }
}
```

3. Update the MainActivity.java file with the following code -

```java
package com.iducate.listfragmentdemo;

import android.app.Activity;
import android.app.FragmentManager;
import android.os.Bundle;

public class MainActivity extends Activity {

    @Override
    protected void onCreate(Bundle savedInstanceState) {
        super.onCreate(savedInstanceState);

        FragmentManager fragmentManager = getFragmentManager();
            fragmentManager.beginTransaction()
                .replace(android.R.id.content, new
```

```
        MyListFragment()).commit();
        }

}
```

4. Run the application and you will see a screen with a list of items. Clicking any item will show a Toast message with that item text -

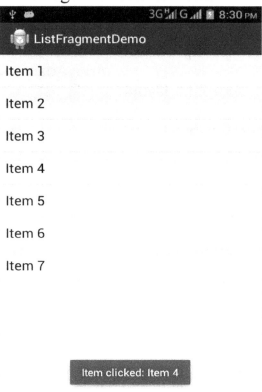

Figure 4.22: Running ListFragmentDemo application

How It Works?

Our fragment class extends ListFragment -

```
public class MyListFragment extends ListFragment {
```

Within this fragment class, we define an array of strings to be used as list items.

We overwrite the onCreate() method of our MyListFragment class -

```
@Override
public void onCreate(Bundle savedInstanceState) {
        super.onCreate(savedInstanceState);

        ArrayAdapter<String> adapter = new
                                ArrayAdapter<String>(getActivity(),
                android.R.layout.simple_list_item_1, items);

        setListAdapter(adapter);
}
```

Within this method, we create an ArrayAdapter and call the setListAdapter() method to set the adapter for our list. This process is very similar to what we have seen with the ListActivity example.

To handle the click of any item of our list, we overwrite the onListItemClick() method -

```
@Override
public void onListItemClick(ListView l, View v, int position,          long
id) {
        Toast.makeText(getActivity(), "Item clicked: " +
                                items[position],
Toast.LENGTH_SHORT).show();
    }
```

Finally, we dynamically add the fragment from our MainActivity class -

```
@Override
protected void onCreate(Bundle savedInstanceState) {
        super.onCreate(savedInstanceState);

        FragmentManager fragmentManager = getFragmentManager();
            fragmentManager.beginTransaction()
                    .replace(android.R.id.content, new

MyListFragment()).commit();
    }
```

Summary

In this chapter, we have looked at some commonly used views and also learned how to handle various user interaction events associated with those views. Android provides you a lot of flexibility for designing the application's UI. With the basics of different views covered in this chapter, you will hopefully keep on practicing and experimenting with your UI design.

Chapter 5: Displaying Pictures and Menus with Views

In this chapter, we will discuss about view widgets that enable us to display images. Using several example projects, we will demonstrate what Android offers us for working with images. We will then learn about another useful and commonly used user interface component – the menu. Finally, we will discuss a few more views to do things like displaying web content within our application, adding clock etc.

Using Image Views to Display Pictures

We have so far used a number of view widgets which mostly deal with text information. Android provides a rich collection of view widgets to display images like ImageView, Gallery, ImageSwitcher, GridView etc.

The following sections will discuss these view widgets in detail.

ImageView Widget

The ImageView widget let's us display images. It is quite easy to use the ImageView widget! Let's see how to do this.

```xml
<LinearLayout xmlns:android="http://schemas.android.com/apk/res/android"
    android:layout_width="fill_parent"
    android:layout_height="fill_parent"
    android:orientation="vertical" >

    <ImageView
        android:id="@+id/imageView1"
        android:layout_width="wrap_content"
        android:layout_height="wrap_content"
        android:src="@drawable/image1" />

</LinearLayout>
```

The image you want to display needs to be placed within the res/drawable-xxxx directories (where drawable-xxxx indicates drawable directories for different screen densities like drawable-hdpi, drawable-xhdpi etc). The image we want to display within the ImageView widget should be referenced by android:src attribute. In our above example, we want to display an image "image1.jpg", so we reference that image by @drawable/image1 .

Figure 5.1 shows a sample screen with an ImageView widget -

Figure 5.1: ImageView widget

Gallery View

The Gallery widget can be used to show images in a horizontal scrolling list. We will create a new project which will demonstrate the usage of Gallery widget to display a set of images. We will also use an ImageView widget which will display the selected image from the Gallery widget.

1. Create a new project named GalleryExample.

2. Update the layout file activity_main.xml to include a Gallery widget and an

ImageView widget -

```xml
<LinearLayout xmlns:android="http://schemas.android.com/apk/res/android"
    android:layout_width="fill_parent"
    android:layout_height="fill_parent"
    android:orientation="vertical" >

    <Gallery
        android:id="@+id/gallery1"
        android:layout_width="match_parent"
        android:layout_height="wrap_content" />

    <ImageView
        android:id="@+id/imageView1"
        android:layout_width="wrap_content"
        android:layout_height="wrap_content"
        android:layout_gravity="center"/>

</LinearLayout>
```

3. Create a new file attr.xml under the res/values directory with following content -

```xml
<?xml version="1.0" encoding="utf-8"?>
<resources>

    <declare-styleable name="Gallery1">
        <attr name="android:galleryItemBackground" />
    </declare-styleable>

</resources>
```

4. Prepare a set of images that you want to display within the Gallery widget. Name the images as image1.jpg, image2.jpg, image3.jpg etc (you can use png images as well). For our example project, we will be using 5 JPEG images. The source code of the project provided with the book will have these images. Find these images under the res/drawable-hdpi directory (or you can use your own images if you like, just rename the image files to be consistent). Whatever the case, put the 5 images under the res/drawable-hdpi directory (If you want to put more images, you need to update the reference to those images in MainActivity.java file. The member variable imageIdArr is the array that contain the ids of these images).

5. Finally, update the MainActivity.java file with the following code -

241

```
package com.iducate.galleryexample;

import android.app.Activity;
import android.content.Context;
import android.content.res.TypedArray;
import android.os.Bundle;
import android.view.View;
import android.view.ViewGroup;
import android.widget.AdapterView;
import android.widget.AdapterView.OnItemClickListener;
import android.widget.BaseAdapter;
import android.widget.Gallery;
import android.widget.ImageView;

public class MainActivity extends Activity {

        private Integer[] imageIdArr = {
                R.drawable.image1, R.drawable.image2, R.drawable.image3,
                R.drawable.image4, R.drawable.image5,
        };

        @Override
        protected void onCreate(Bundle savedInstanceState) {
                super.onCreate(savedInstanceState);
                setContentView(R.layout.activity_main);

                Gallery gallery = (Gallery) findViewById(R.id.gallery1);

                gallery.setAdapter(new ImageAdapter(this));
                gallery.setOnItemClickListener(new OnItemClickListener() {

                        @Override
                        public void onItemClick(AdapterView<?> parent, View v,
                                        int position, long id) {
                                ImageView imageView = (ImageView)
findViewById(R.id.imageView1);
                                imageView.setImageResource(imageIdArr[position]);
                        }
                });
        }
```

```java
public class ImageAdapter extends BaseAdapter {

    Context context;
    int itemBackground;

    public ImageAdapter(Context context) {
        this.context = context;

        // set style
        TypedArray typedArray =

obtainStyledAttributes(R.styleable.Gallery1);
        itemBackground = typedArray.getResourceId(


R.styleable.Gallery1_android_galleryItemBac
                                 kground, 0);
        typedArray.recycle();
    }

    @Override
    public int getCount() {
        return imageIdArr.length;
    }

    @Override
    public Object getItem(int position) {
        return position;
    }

    @Override
    public long getItemId(int position) {
        return position;
    }

    @Override
    public View getView(int position, View convertView,
                    ViewGroup parent) {
        ImageView imageView;

        if (convertView == null) {
            imageView = new ImageView(context);
            imageView.setImageResource(imageIdArr[position]);
```

```
        imageView.setScaleType(ImageView.ScaleType.FIT_XY);

        imageView.setLayoutParams(new

Gallery.LayoutParams(180, 150));
            } else {
              imageView = (ImageView) convertView;
            }

            imageView.setBackgroundResource(itemBackground);
            return imageView;
        }

    }

}
```

6. Run the application and you will see a Gallery widget appearing with a set of images. Select any image and that image will appear at the ImageView widget under the Gallery widget (figure 5.2).

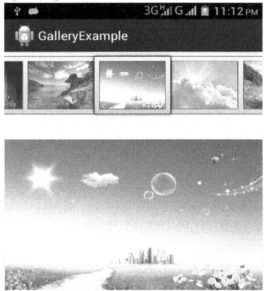

How It Works?

Our application layout file activity_main.xml contains two widgets. A Gallery widget and an ImageView widget -

```
<Gallery
android:id="@+id/gallery1"
android:layout_width="match_parent"
android:layout_height="wrap_content" />

<ImageView
android:id="@+id/imageView1"
android:layout_width="wrap_content"
android:layout_height="wrap_content"
android:layout_gravity="center"/>
```

We have used the Gallery widget to display a set of images in a horizontal scrolling list. We want to be able to select an image from the Gallery and then display that image within the ImageView widget.

Within the MainActivity.java file, we create a member variable named **imageIdArr** which is an Integer array. We store the ids of the image to be displayed within this array.

```
private Integer[] imageIdArr = {
        R.drawable.image1, R.drawable.image2, R.drawable.image3,
        R.drawable.image4, R.drawable.image5,
};
```

We need an Adapter to connect the Gallery view with the list of images. We extend the BaseAdapter class and create a new ImageAdapter class. Since we create an ImageAdapter by extending the BaseAdapter class, our ImageAdapter class need to implement the following methods -

- getCount() - which need to return the image counts
- getItem() - this method will return the item
- getItemId() - will return the ID of an item
- getView() - this method will return an ImageView view

245

Most of the above method implementations are quite straightforward. We will take a look at the getView() method implementation –

```java
@Override
public View getView(int position, View convertView,
                        ViewGroup parent) {
    ImageView imageView;

    if (convertView == null) {
        imageView = new ImageView(context);
        imageView.setImageResource(imageIdArr[position]);
        imageView.setScaleType(ImageView.ScaleType.FIT_XY);

        imageView.setLayoutParams(new
                                Gallery.LayoutParams(180,
150));
    } else {
        imageView = (ImageView) convertView;
    }

    imageView.setBackgroundResource(itemBackground);
    return imageView;
}
```

The getView() method is responsible for returning a View at a particular position. We should return the ImageView object instance in this case.

After we define ImageAdapter, we need to set this adapter for our Gallery instance -

```java
gallery.setAdapter(new ImageAdapter(this));
```

We also attach an OnItemClickListener to the gallery instance -

```java
gallery.setOnItemClickListener(new OnItemClickListener() {

    @Override
    public void onItemClick(AdapterView<?> parent, View v,
            int position, long id) {
        ImageView imageView = (ImageView)

findViewById(R.id.imageView1);
```

```
                    imageView.setImageResource(imageIdArr[position]);
        }
    });
```

The onItemClick() method will be fired when any item of the Gallery is clicked. Within this method, we set the clicked image to the ImageView widget.

ImageSwitcher View

In our previous example, we have seen how we can use the Gallery widget together with the ImageView widget to display a series of thumbnail images as an image gallery and then select any image to display that within ImageView widget. Although it works well, we sometimes feel it annoying because the images appear abruptly within the ImageView widget. Wouldn't it be better if we could add an animation while the image transition happens? In that case, we could use a ImageSwitcher widget with a Gallery widget.

Let's see How It Works. We will update our previous example project.

1. Update the activity_main.xml layout file. We want to add an ImageSwitcher widget instead of an ImageView widget -

```xml
<LinearLayout xmlns:android="http://schemas.android.com/apk/res/android"
    android:layout_width="fill_parent"
    android:layout_height="fill_parent"
    android:orientation="vertical" >

    <Gallery
        android:id="@+id/gallery1"
        android:layout_width="match_parent"
        android:layout_height="wrap_content" />
    <ImageSwitcher
        android:id="@+id/imageSwicher1"
        android:layout_width="wrap_content"
        android:layout_height="wrap_content"
        android:layout_gravity="center" />

</LinearLayout>
```

2. Update the MainActivity.java file with the highlighted code. The highlighted code indicates the changed content from the previous version -

```java
package com.iducate.galleryexample;

import android.app.Activity;
import android.content.Context;
import android.content.res.TypedArray;
import android.os.Bundle;
import android.view.View;
import android.view.ViewGroup;
import android.view.ViewGroup.LayoutParams;
import android.view.animation.AnimationUtils;
import android.widget.AdapterView;
import android.widget.AdapterView.OnItemClickListener;
import android.widget.BaseAdapter;
import android.widget.Gallery;
import android.widget.ImageSwitcher;
import android.widget.ImageView;
import android.widget.ViewSwitcher.ViewFactory;

public class MainActivity extends Activity {

    private Integer[] imageIdArr = {
        R.drawable.image1, R.drawable.image2,R.drawable.image3,
        R.drawable.image4, R.drawable.image5,
    };

    private ImageSwitcher imageSwitcher;

    @Override
    protected void onCreate(Bundle savedInstanceState) {
        super.onCreate(savedInstanceState);
        setContentView(R.layout.activity_main);

        imageSwitcher = (ImageSwitcher)

findViewById(R.id.imageSwicher1);
        imageSwitcher.setFactory(new ViewFactory() {

            @Override
            public View makeView() {
                ImageView imageView = new

ImageView(MainActivity.this);
```

```java
            imageView.setScaleType(
                    ImageView.ScaleType.FIT_CENTER);
            imageView.setLayoutParams(new

ImageSwitcher.LayoutParams(
                    LayoutParams.MATCH_PARENT,

LayoutParams.MATCH_PARENT));
            return imageView;
        }
    });

    imageSwitcher.setInAnimation(
        AnimationUtils.loadAnimation(this,
                    android.R.anim.fade_in));
    imageSwitcher.setOutAnimation(
        AnimationUtils.loadAnimation(this,
                    android.R.anim.fade_out));

    Gallery gallery = (Gallery) findViewById(R.id.gallery1);

    gallery.setAdapter(new ImageAdapter(this));
    gallery.setOnItemClickListener(new OnItemClickListener() {

        @Override
        public void onItemClick(AdapterView<?> parent, View v,
                    int position, long id) {
                imageSwitcher.setImageResource(
                                imageIdArr[position]);
        }
    });
}

public class ImageAdapter extends BaseAdapter {

    Context context;
    int itemBackground;

    public ImageAdapter(Context context) {
        this.context = context;

        // set style
        TypedArray typedArray =
```

249

```java
        obtainStyledAttributes(R.styleable.Gallery1);
            itemBackground = typedArray.getResourceId(


R.styleable.Gallery1_android_galleryItemBac
                                kground, 0);
            typedArray.recycle();
        }

        @Override
        public int getCount() {
            return imageIdArr.length;
        }

        @Override
        public Object getItem(int position) {
            return position;
        }

        @Override
        public long getItemId(int position) {
            return position;
        }

        @Override
        public View getView(int position, View convertView,
                        ViewGroup parent) {
            ImageView imageView;

            if (convertView == null) {
                imageView = new ImageView(context);
                imageView.setImageResource(imageIdArr[position]);
                imageView.setScaleType(ImageView.ScaleType.FIT_XY);

                imageView.setLayoutParams(new

Gallery.LayoutParams(180, 150));
            } else {
                imageView = (ImageView) convertView;
            }

            imageView.setBackgroundResource(itemBackground);
```

```
            return imageView;
        }

    }

}
```

3. Now run the application. If you select the images from the Gallery, you will notice that the transition between images are more smooth and animated.

Figure 5.3: Running GalleryExample application

How It Works?

Instead of the ImageView widget, our layout file now contains ImageSwitcher widget -

```
<ImageSwitcher
android:id="@+id/imageSwicher1"
android:layout_width="wrap_content"
android:layout_height="wrap_content"
android:layout_gravity="center" />
```

Within our MainActivity.java file, after we take the reference of our ImageSwitcher widget, we call the setFactory() method of the ImageSwitcher instance -

```
imageSwitcher = (ImageSwitcher)findViewById(R.id.imageSwicher1);
imageSwitcher.setFactory(new ViewFactory() {

    @Override
    public View makeView() {
        ImageView imageView = new ImageView(MainActivity.this);
        imageView.setScaleType(ImageView.ScaleType.FIT_CENTER);
        imageView.setLayoutParams(new
ImageSwitcher.LayoutParams(LayoutParams.MATCH_PARENT,
                    LayoutParams.MATCH_PARENT));
        return imageView;
    }
});
```

The setFactory() method takes an instance of ViewFactory which need to create views to be used with the ImageSwitcher widget. The makeView() method of ViewFactory takes care of this task. This method creates a new ImageView to be added in the ImageSwitcher view.

Same as before, we implement the ImageAdapter class, a subclass of BaseAdapter and bind it with the Gallery widget.

We set animation for ImageSwitcher so that when an image transition takes place, we will get a nice animated effect -

```
imageSwitcher.setInAnimation(
    AnimationUtils.loadAnimation(this,android.R.anim.fade_in));
imageSwitcher.setOutAnimation(
    AnimationUtils.loadAnimation(this,android.R.anim.fade_out));
```

Finally, we want to display the selected image within the ImageSwitcher view -

```
gallery.setOnItemClickListener(new OnItemClickListener() {

    @Override
```

```
        public void onItemClick(AdapterView<?> parent, View v,
                int position, long id) {
            imageSwitcher.setImageResource(imageIdArr[position]);
        }
    });
```

We add the OnItemClickListener to the Gallery instance and within the onItemClick() method, we set the selected image to be displayed within the ImageSwitcher.

GridView

With GridView, you can display items (images) in a two dimensional scrolling grid. The next example will demonstrate the use of GridView.

1. Create a new project GridViewExample.
2. Update the layout file activity_main.xml to include a GridView -

```xml
<LinearLayout xmlns:android="http://schemas.android.com/apk/res/android"
    android:layout_width="fill_parent"
    android:layout_height="fill_parent"
    android:orientation="vertical" >

    <GridView
        android:id="@+id/gridView1"
        android:layout_width="match_parent"
        android:layout_height="wrap_content"
        android:columnWidth="90dp"
        android:gravity="center"
        android:horizontalSpacing="10dp"
        android:numColumns="auto_fit"
        android:stretchMode="columnWidth"
        android:verticalSpacing="10dp" />

</LinearLayout>
```

3. We will use the same images we have used in our previous example. Put the images in res/drawable-hdpi directory.

4. Now update the MainActivity.java file with the following code -

```java
package com.iducate.gridviewexample;

import android.app.Activity;
import android.content.Context;
import android.os.Bundle;
import android.view.View;
import android.view.ViewGroup;
import android.widget.AdapterView;
import android.widget.AdapterView.OnItemClickListener;
import android.widget.BaseAdapter;
import android.widget.GridView;
import android.widget.ImageView;
import android.widget.Toast;

public class MainActivity extends Activity {

    private Integer[] imageIdArr = {
            R.drawable.image1, R.drawable.image2,R.drawable.image3,
            R.drawable.image4, R.drawable.image5,
    };

    @Override
    protected void onCreate(Bundle savedInstanceState) {
        super.onCreate(savedInstanceState);
        setContentView(R.layout.activity_main);

        GridView gridView = (GridView)

findViewById(R.id.gridView1);
        gridView.setAdapter(new ImageAdapter(this));

        gridView.setOnItemClickListener(new OnItemClickListener() {

            @Override
            public void onItemClick(AdapterView<?> parent, View
                    view, int position, long id) {
                Toast.makeText(MainActivity.this,
                        "Image " + (position + 1) + " selected",
                        Toast.LENGTH_SHORT).show();
            }
        });
    }
```

```java
public class ImageAdapter extends BaseAdapter {

    Context context;

    public ImageAdapter(Context context) {
        this.context = context;
    }

    @Override
    public int getCount() {
        return imageIdArr.length;
    }

    @Override
    public Object getItem(int position) {
        return position;
    }

    @Override
    public long getItemId(int position) {
        return position;
    }

    @Override
    public View getView(int position, View convertView,
                    ViewGroup parent) {
        ImageView imageView;
        if (convertView == null) {
            imageView = new ImageView(context);
            imageView.setImageResource(imageIdArr[position]);
            imageView.setScaleType(
                ImageView.ScaleType.CENTER_CROP);

            imageView.setLayoutParams(
                new GridView.LayoutParams(85, 85));
            imageView.setPadding(5, 5, 5, 5);
        } else {
            imageView = (ImageView) convertView;
        }
        imageView.setImageResource(imageIdArr[position]);
        return imageView;
    }
```

```
    }

}
```

5. Run the application and you will see a GridView displaying all the images. When you click any image, you will see a Toast notification.

Figure 5.4: GridView example

How It Works?

The layout file activity_main.xml contains a GridView widget -

```
<GridView
    android:id="@+id/gridView1"
    android:layout_width="match_parent"
    android:layout_height="wrap_content"
    android:columnWidth="90dp"
    android:gravity="center"
    android:horizontalSpacing="10dp"
    android:numColumns="auto_fit"
    android:stretchMode="columnWidth"
```

```
android:verticalSpacing="10dp" />
```

We can control the different aspects of GridView like column width, number of columns in each row, spacing etc using different attributes.

To connect the GridView with images, we need an adapter class. Like the previous example, we implement a new ImageAdapter class which extends BaseAdapter class. The ImageAdapter implementation is mostly the same except for a few tweaks in getView() method -

```java
public View getView(int position, View convertView,
                ViewGroup parent) {

    ImageView imageView;

    if (convertView == null) {
        imageView = new ImageView(context);
        imageView.setImageResource(imageIdArr[position]);
        imageView.setScaleType(
                        ImageView.ScaleType.CENTER_CROP);

        imageView.setLayoutParams(
            new GridView.LayoutParams(85, 85));
            imageView.setPadding(5, 5, 5, 5);
    } else {
        imageView = (ImageView) convertView;
    }
    imageView.setImageResource(imageIdArr[position]);
    return imageView;
}
```

Within this getView() method, we specify size of images and a few other things. Then as usual, we return ImageView.

We also add an OnItemClickListener to our GridView instance to handle a click event -

```java
gridView.setOnItemClickListener(new OnItemClickListener() {

    @Override
    public void onItemClick(AdapterView<?> parent, View
            view, int position, long id) {
```

```
                    Toast.makeText(MainActivity.this,
                        "Image " + (position + 1) + " selected",
                        Toast.LENGTH_SHORT).show();
            }
        });
```

The onItemClick() method is fired when a user will clicks an image from the grid. Within this method, we show a Toast notification.

Using Menus With Views

Menus are a common user interface component of Android applications. They are useful for providing additional options a user can perform. Using menus, you provide a consistent user experience throughout your application.

Prior to Android 3.0 (API level 11), Android devices used to have dedicated Menu button. Beginning with Android 3.0 however, it's not the case anymore.

The two main types of menus in Android platform are -

- Options Menu – Options menu is the place where you would like to have actions that are global to your app. If the application runs on Android 2.3 or lower, users can reveal the options menu by pressing the Menu button. On the other hand, if the application is running on Android 3.0 or higher, options menus are presented by the action bar (which you have already learned in Chapter 3) as a combination of on-screen action items and overflow options. Figure 5.5 shows an options menu of default browser application.

- Context Menu – A Context menu is a floating menu which is revealed when user long-clicks on an element. A Context menu provides some actions that are related to the selected element. Figure 5.6 shows a context menu, which represents some action when user long-clicks on any image on the default browser application.

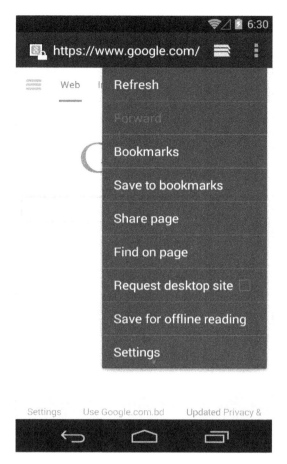

Figure 5.5: Options Menu

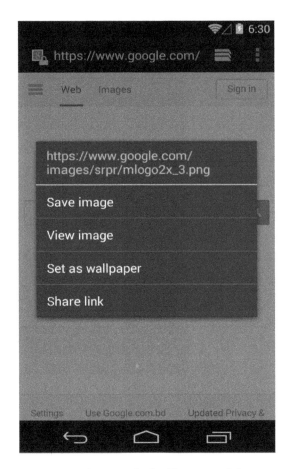

Figure 5.6: Context Menu

Defining Menus in XML

For all menu types, Android provides a standard XML format to define menu items. The common practice is to define your menu and menu items in a XML menu resource and then inflate that menu resource in your activity. Let's see a sample menu resource -

```xml
<?xml version="1.0" encoding="utf-8"?>
<menu xmlns:android="http://schemas.android.com/apk/res/android" >
  <item
    android:id="@+id/itemAdd"
    android:icon="@android:drawable/ic_menu_add"
    android:showAsAction="ifRoom"
    android:title="Add"/>
  <item
    android:id="@+id/itemDelete"
    android:icon="@android:drawable/ic_menu_delete"
    android:title="Delete"/>
```

```
</menu>
```

You will create the XML menu resource under the res/menu directory. The <menu> element should be the container for your menu items. Each individual menu item is defined using the <item> element. The <item> element can have several attributes to set different properties, like title of the item, icon, whether the item will be shown on action bar (when action bar is available) etc.

Creating a Options Menu

In this section, we will see how to create an options menu. Let's create a new project.

1. Create a new project OptionsMenuDemo.

2. Create a new menu resource named "main_menu.xml" and put it under the res/menu directory. The main_menu.xml file should have the following menu items -

```xml
<?xml version="1.0" encoding="utf-8"?>
<menu xmlns:android="http://schemas.android.com/apk/res/android" >

    <item
        android:id="@+id/itemAdd"
        android:icon="@android:drawable/ic_menu_add"
        android:showAsAction="ifRoom"
        android:title="Add"/>
    <item
        android:id="@+id/itemEdit"
        android:icon="@android:drawable/ic_menu_edit"
        android:title="Edit"/>
    <item
        android:id="@+id/itemDelete"
        android:icon="@android:drawable/ic_menu_delete"
        android:title="Delete"/>
    <item
        android:id="@+id/itemSearch"
        android:icon="@android:drawable/ic_menu_search"
        android:title="Search"/>
    <item
        android:id="@+id/itemHelp"
```

```
        android:icon="@android:drawable/ic_menu_help"
        android:title="Help"/>

</menu>
```

3. Now update the activity file MainActivity.java with the following code -

```java
package com.iducate.optionsmenudemo;

import android.os.Bundle;
import android.app.Activity;
import android.view.Menu;
import android.view.MenuInflater;
import android.view.MenuItem;
import android.widget.Toast;

public class MainActivity extends Activity {

    @Override
    protected void onCreate(Bundle savedInstanceState) {
        super.onCreate(savedInstanceState);
        setContentView(R.layout.activity_main);
    }

    @Override
    public boolean onCreateOptionsMenu(Menu menu) {
        MenuInflater inflater = getMenuInflater();
        inflater.inflate(R.menu.main_menu, menu);
        return true;
    }

    @Override
    public boolean onOptionsItemSelected(MenuItem item) {
        switch (item.getItemId()) {
        case R.id.itemAdd:
            Toast.makeText(this, "Menu Item Clicked: Add",
                    Toast.LENGTH_SHORT).show();
            return true;
        case R.id.itemEdit:
            Toast.makeText(this, "Menu Item Clicked: Edit",
                    Toast.LENGTH_SHORT).show();
```

```
            return true;
        case R.id.itemDelete:
            Toast.makeText(this, "Menu Item Clicked: Delete",
                    Toast.LENGTH_SHORT).show();
            return true;
        case R.id.itemSearch:
            Toast.makeText(this, "Menu Item Clicked: Search",
                    Toast.LENGTH_SHORT).show();
            return true;
        case R.id.itemHelp:
            Toast.makeText(this, "Menu Item Clicked: Help",
                     Toast.LENGTH_SHORT).show();
            return true;
        default:
            return false;
        }

    }

}
```

4. Run the application. Depending upon whether you are running the application on a pre-Android 3.0 device or post-Android 3.0 device, the options menu may appear differently.

If the application is running on Android 3.0 or later device, you will see some items appearing on the action bar and also a overflow option. Clicking on that overflow option will reveal other items (figure 5.7).

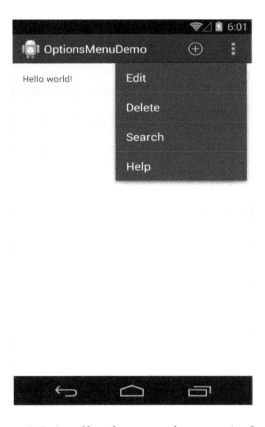

Figure 5.7 Application running on *Android 3.0 or later*

If the application is running on Android 2.3 or lower, press the menu button to reveal the option items (figure 5.8).

Hello world!

Figure 5.8: Application running on Android 2.3 or earlier

Click any option item and you will see a Toast notification with the item name.

How It Works?

First, we have created a XML menu resource for our options menu. The root element of XML menu resource file is the <menu> element -

```
<menu xmlns:android="http://schemas.android.com/apk/res/android" >
```

Under the <menu> element, we have defined all the menu items -

```
<item
android:id="@+id/itemAdd"
android:icon="@android:drawable/ic_menu_add"
android:showAsAction="ifRoom"
android:title="Add"/>
```

The <item> element is used to define an individual menu item. We have provided several attributes for the <item> element.

The android:id attribute is used to set an id for our menu item. This id can be used later when we want to detect which menu item is clicked.

The android:icon attribute sets the icon for the menu item. Put the icon files under the res/drawable directories and then reference them using @drawable notation. In our example, we have used icon resources provided by the Android platform.

The android:title attribute sets the title for the menu item.

The attribute android:showAsAction specifies whether this menu item should appear in the action bar (in case action bar is available).

This is how we define our menu items in the XML file.

After defining the menu items in the XML resource file, to display the options menu, we need to implement onCreateOptionsMenu() method in our activity class -

```
@Override
public boolean onCreateOptionsMenu(Menu menu) {
        MenuInflater inflater = getMenuInflater();
        inflater.inflate(R.menu.main_menu, menu);
        return true;
}
```

Within this method, we need to inflate the XML menu resource. To inflate a menu resource, we need the MenuInflater object. We call the getMenuInflater() method to get an instance of MenuInflater. We call the inflate() method of MenuInflater instance with the menu resource id as argument.

Finally, to handle the menu item clicks, we implement onOptionsItemSelected() method -

```
@Override
public boolean onOptionsItemSelected(MenuItem item) {
        switch (item.getItemId()) {
        case R.id.itemAdd:
            Toast.makeText(this, "Menu Item Clicked: Add",
                    Toast.LENGTH_SHORT).show();
            return true;
```

```
case R.id.itemEdit:
        Toast.makeText(this, "Menu Item Clicked: Edit",
                    Toast.LENGTH_SHORT).show();
        return true;
case R.id.itemDelete:
        Toast.makeText(this, "Menu Item Clicked: Delete",
                Toast.LENGTH_SHORT).show();
        return true;
case R.id.itemSearch:
        Toast.makeText(this, "Menu Item Clicked: Search",
                Toast.LENGTH_SHORT).show();
        return true;
case R.id.itemHelp:
        Toast.makeText(this, "Menu Item Clicked: Help",
                    Toast.LENGTH_SHORT).show();
        return true;
default:
        return false;
}

}
```

Within this method, we use menu item id to determine which menu item is clicked. Though we show a Toast notification in our implementation, you can replace the toast with your own code to suit your application requirements.

Creating a Context Menu

In this section, we will learn how to create a floating context menu. As we have discussed earlier, a context menu is associated with a particular view element and is revealed when user long-clicks on that element.

1. Create a new project called ContextMenuDemo.

2. Create a new XML menu resource named "menu.xml" under the res/menu directory. We will use this menu resource as our context menu. The menu.xml file should look like the following code listing -

```
<?xml version="1.0" encoding="utf-8"?>
<menu xmlns:android="http://schemas.android.com/apk/res/android" >
```

```xml
    <item
      android:id="@+id/itemOption1"
      android:title="Option 1"/>
    <item
      android:id="@+id/itemOption2"
      android:title="Option 2"/>
    <item
      android:id="@+id/itemOption3"
      android:title="Option 3"/>
</menu>
```

3. In our layout file, we add a button element. We want to reveal the context menu when user long-clicks on this button element. Update the activity_main.xml layout file (under the res/layout directory) with the following code -

```xml
<LinearLayout xmlns:android="http://schemas.android.com/apk/res/android"
    android:layout_width="fill_parent"
    android:layout_height="fill_parent"
    android:orientation="vertical" >

    <Button
      android:id="@+id/button1"
      android:layout_width="wrap_content"
      android:layout_height="wrap_content"
      android:text="Button" />
</LinearLayout>
```

4. Finally, update the MainActivity.java file with the following code -

```java
package com.iducate.contextmenudemo;

import android.app.Activity;
import android.os.Bundle;
import android.view.ContextMenu;
import android.view.MenuInflater;
import android.view.MenuItem;
import android.view.View;
import android.view.ContextMenu.ContextMenuInfo;
import android.widget.Button;
import android.widget.Toast;

public class MainActivity extends Activity {
```

```java
    @Override
    protected void onCreate(Bundle savedInstanceState) {
        super.onCreate(savedInstanceState);
        setContentView(R.layout.activity_main);

        Button button = (Button) findViewById(R.id.button1);
        button.setOnCreateContextMenuListener(this);
    }

    @Override
    public void onCreateContextMenu(ContextMenu menu, View v,
            ContextMenuInfo menuInfo) {
        super.onCreateContextMenu(menu, v, menuInfo);
        MenuInflater inflater = getMenuInflater();
        inflater.inflate(R.menu.menu, menu);
    }

    @Override
    public boolean onContextItemSelected(MenuItem item) {
        switch (item.getItemId()) {
        case R.id.itemOption1:
            Toast.makeText(this, "Item clicked: Option 1",
                        Toast.LENGTH_SHORT).show();
            return true;
        case R.id.itemOption2:
            Toast.makeText(this, "Item clicked: Option 2",
                        Toast.LENGTH_SHORT).show();
            return true;
        case R.id.itemOption3:
            Toast.makeText(this, "Item clicked: Option 3",
                        Toast.LENGTH_SHORT).show();
            return true;
        default:
            return false;
        }
    }

}
```

5. Run the application and you will see a screen with a single button element. Long-click on that button and a context menu associated with that button will be shown (figure 5.9). If you click any of the options, a Toast notification will

appear.

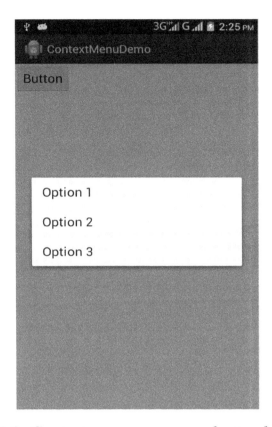

Figure 5.9: Context menu appear on button long-click

How It Works?

First we define an XML menu resource with the menu items for our context menu. The syntax for defining menu items for context menu is exactly the same as the options menu. In this case, we define our menu resource with three menu items.

Next, in our activity_main.xml file, we add a button element -

```
<Button
android:id="@+id/button1"
android:layout_width="wrap_content"
android:layout_height="wrap_content"
android:text="Button" />
```

We want to associate the context menu with this button element, so that when some user long-clicks the button element, a floating context menu will appear.

Next, in order to show the context menu, we implement onCreateContextMenu()

method in our activity class -

```
@Override
public void onCreateContextMenu(ContextMenu menu, View v,
        ContextMenuInfo menuInfo) {
    super.onCreateContextMenu(menu, v, menuInfo);
    MenuInflater inflater = getMenuInflater();
    inflater.inflate(R.menu.menu, menu);
}
```

Within this method, we inflate the XML menu resource. Inflating the XML menu resource for context menu is exactly the same as we did for options menu.

We then implement the onContextItemSelected() method to handle the click of a context menu item -

```
@Override
public boolean onContextItemSelected(MenuItem item) {
    switch (item.getItemId()) {
    case R.id.itemOption1:
        Toast.makeText(this, "Item clicked: Option 1",
                Toast.LENGTH_SHORT).show();
        return true;
    case R.id.itemOption2:
        Toast.makeText(this, "Item clicked: Option 2",
                Toast.LENGTH_SHORT).show();
        return true;
    case R.id.itemOption3:
        Toast.makeText(this, "Item clicked: Option 3",
                Toast.LENGTH_SHORT).show();
        return true;
    default:
        return false;
    }
}
```

Within this method implementation, we simply identify which menu item is clicked by the menu item id and then show a Toast notification.

Some Additional Views

Besides the standard views we have seen so far, Android provides some additional views for different tasks, like displaying web content, showing clock etc. In this section, we will learn about three more views – WebView, AnalogClock and DigitalClock.

WebView Widget

The WebView enables you to display HTML content in your application. It can be used for rendering HTML content from various sources, like content from RSS feeds, HTML email messages, ebooks and so on. The WebView widget can handle a wide range of HTML tags, as well as CSS and Javascript content. The following example demonstrates the usage of a WebView widget.

1. Create a new project named WebViewDemo.

2. Update the layout file activity_main.xml with the following code -

```
<LinearLayout xmlns:android="http://schemas.android.com/apk/res/android"
    android:layout_width="fill_parent"
    android:layout_height="fill_parent"
    android:orientation="vertical" >

    <WebView
        android:id="@+id/webView1"
        android:layout_width="wrap_content"
        android:layout_height="wrap_content" />

</LinearLayout>
```

3. Update the MainActivity.java file with the following code -

```
package com.iducate.webviewdemo;

import android.app.Activity;
import android.os.Bundle;
import android.webkit.WebView;

public class MainActivity extends Activity {

    private WebView webView;
```

272

```java
    @Override
    protected void onCreate(Bundle savedInstanceState) {
            super.onCreate(savedInstanceState);
            setContentView(R.layout.activity_main);

            webView = (WebView) findViewById(R.id.webView1);
            webView.loadUrl("http://www.android.com");
    }
}
```

4. In your AndroidManifest.xml file, you will need to add permission for INTERNET -

```xml
<?xml version="1.0" encoding="utf-8"?>
<manifest xmlns:android="http://schemas.android.com/apk/res/android"
    package="com.iducate.webviewdemo"
    android:versionCode="1"
    android:versionName="1.0" >

    <uses-sdk
        android:minSdkVersion="8"
        android:targetSdkVersion="19" />

    <uses-permission android:name="android.permission.INTERNET" />

    <application
        android:allowBackup="true"
        android:icon="@drawable/ic_launcher"
        android:label="@string/app_name"
        android:theme="@style/AppTheme" >
        <activity
            android:name="com.iducate.webviewdemo.MainActivity"
            android:label="@string/app_name" >
            <intent-filter>
                <action android:name="android.intent.action.MAIN" />

                <category

android:name="android.intent.category.LAUNCHER" />
            </intent-filter>
        </activity>
```

```
</application>

</manifest>
```

5. Run the application and you will get a screen similar to figure 5.10 -

Figure 5.10: Running WebViewDemo application

How It Works?

We want to use the WebView widget to load a web page. To do so, we need to add a WebView widget in our layout file -

```
<WebView
android:id="@+id/webView1"
        android:layout_width="wrap_content"
android:layout_height="wrap_content" />
```

Now, from our MainActivity class, we get a reference to WebView widget -

```
webView = (WebView) findViewById(R.id.webView1);
```

Then, we call the loadUrl() method of WebView instance with the URL to be loaded as argument -

```
webView.loadUrl("http://www.android.com");
```

Finally, since we need to use the INTERNET connection of the device, we will need to explicitly tell that in our AndroidManifest.xml file -

```
<uses-permission android:name="android.permission.INTERNET" />
```

Supporting Javascript

By default, Javascript is turned off in the WebView widget. But it can be easily enabled by calling the getSettings().setJavaScriptEnabled(true) method of WebView instance -

```
//enable javascript
webView.getSettings().setJavaScriptEnabled(true);
```

Alternatives for Loading Content

Instead of loading content from the web using the loadUrl() function, you can use the WebView widget for displaying local HTML content as well. This allows you to display a snippet of HTML (that is either received as part of parsing some RSS feed or generated by you dynamically) or display a local HTML file (such as HTML help manual which is installed with your application package).

First, let's display a snippet of HTML -

```
@Override
protected void onCreate(Bundle savedInstanceState) {
    super.onCreate(savedInstanceState);
    setContentView(R.layout.activity_main);

    webView = (WebView) findViewById(R.id.webView1);

    webView.loadData("<html><body><h2>Welcome</
```

275

```
h2><p>Hello                    there!</p></body></html>", "text/html",
"UTF-8");
    }
```

Here, we use the loadData() method of WebView widget instance to display a snippet of HTML code. The loadData() method takes three arguments. First is the snippet of HTML we want to display. The second one is the MIME type and the third argument is the character encoding. Figure 5.11 shows the content displayed by the WebView widget -

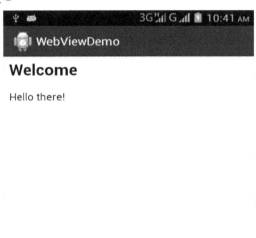

Figure 5.11: Displaying HTML snippet by WebView widget

If you want to display a local HTML file which you want to distribute with your application, you will need to put that HTML file under the **assets/** directory. Next, to display that file to your WebView widget, you call the loadUrl() method as follows -

```
@Override
protected void onCreate(Bundle savedInstanceState) {
        super.onCreate(savedInstanceState);
        setContentView(R.layout.activity_main);
```

276

```
            webView = (WebView) findViewById(R.id.webView1);
            webView.loadUrl("file:///android_asset/webpage.html");
        }
```

This will load the HTML file named webpage.html, which is stored under the assets directory.

AnalogClock and DigitalClock Views

With the AnalogClock and DigitalClock views, we can display the system time in our applications. The AnalogClick widget displays an analog clock with hours and minutes, while DigitalClock view displays time as a digital clock. Let's see how we can use these two views in our application.

1. Create a new project named ClockViewsDemo.

2. Update the layout file activity_main.xml, with following code -

```xml
<LinearLayout xmlns:android="http://schemas.android.com/apk/res/android"
    android:layout_width="fill_parent"
    android:layout_height="fill_parent"
    android:orientation="vertical" >

    <AnalogClock
        android:id="@+id/analogClock1"
        android:layout_width="wrap_content"
        android:layout_height="wrap_content" />

    <DigitalClock
        android:id="@+id/digitalClock1"
        android:layout_width="wrap_content"
        android:layout_height="wrap_content" />

</LinearLayout>
```

3. Run the application, you will see a screen similar to figure 5.12 -

277

Figure 5.12: Running ClockViewsDemo application

How It Works?

As you can see, displaying the AnalogClock and DigitalClock widgets are fairly straightforward and simple. We add the AnalogClock in our layout file as follows -

```
<AnalogClock
android:id="@+id/analogClock1"
android:layout_width="wrap_content"
android:layout_height="wrap_content" />
```

Next, we add the DigitalClock widget -

```
<DigitalClock
android:id="@+id/digitalClock1"
android:layout_width="wrap_content"
android:layout_height="wrap_content" />
```

Summary

In this chapter, we have learned about various view widgets which help us to display images within our application. The Android platform offers the ImageView,

ImageSwitcher, Gallery, GridView to facilitate image display within our application. Next, we learn about the options and context menu through practical examples. We have also used the WebView widget which is helpful for displaying web content within our application. Finally, we have used clock widgets to display system time.

Chapter 6: Keeping Data Persistent

In this chapter, we will learn how to store data persistently in Android applications. We will discuss about various persistent data storage mechanisms provided by the Android platform like SharedPreferences for storing key-value pairs, file based data storage mechanism and using SQLite for storing structured data.

Saving and Loading User Preferences

In many applications, you will need to store some user preference data. For example, if you have a game application, you might need to save some data persistently like high score, current game level, whether user prefers to keep sound on or off etc. These data needs to be persistent as users expect to have them in subsequent sessions of game play even if after their device is restarted.

Android provides several persistent data storage mechanisms to save data locally, like -

- Shared Preferences – which can be used to store primitive data in key-value pairs
- File based storage – using traditional file systems
- SQLite Databases – store structured data in a relational database management system

Shared preferences is a lightweight persistent data storage mechanism provided by the Android platform for storing application states, configuration options and other such informations. This functionality is provided by the SharedPreferences interface, which is part of the android.content package.

Preferences are stored in XML file as key-value pairs. The following data types are supported as preference settings values –

- Integer values

- Long values
- Float values
- Boolean values
- String values
- Set of multiple String values (added to API level 11)

Using Shared Preferences

In this section, we will see how to use SharedPreferences class to store some information and then retrieve that information.

1. Create a new project named PreferencesExample1.

2. Update the activity_main.xml layout file to include an EditText widget and two Button widgets -

```xml
<LinearLayout xmlns:android="http://schemas.android.com/apk/res/android"
    android:layout_width="fill_parent"
    android:layout_height="fill_parent"
    android:orientation="vertical" >

    <EditText
        android:id="@+id/editText1"
        android:layout_width="match_parent"
        android:layout_height="wrap_content"
        android:hint="Enter some text..." />

    <Button
        android:id="@+id/btnSave"
        android:layout_width="match_parent"
        android:layout_height="wrap_content"
        android:onClick="savePreferences"
        android:text="Save Preferences" />

    <Button
        android:id="@+id/btnLoad"
        android:layout_width="match_parent"
        android:layout_height="wrap_content"
        android:onClick="loadPreferences"
        android:text="Load Preferences" />

</LinearLayout>
```

3. Update the MainActivity.java file with the following code -

```java
package com.iducate.preferencesexample1;

import android.app.Activity;
import android.content.SharedPreferences;
import android.os.Bundle;
import android.preference.PreferenceManager;
import android.view.View;
import android.widget.EditText;
import android.widget.Toast;

public class MainActivity extends Activity {

    private EditText etPrefText;

    @Override
    protected void onCreate(Bundle savedInstanceState) {
        super.onCreate(savedInstanceState);
        setContentView(R.layout.activity_main);

        etPrefText = (EditText) findViewById(R.id.editText1);
    }

    public void savePreferences(View v) {
        String prefText = etPrefText.getText().toString();

        SharedPreferences prefs = PreferenceManager
                .getDefaultSharedPreferences(this);
        SharedPreferences.Editor editor = prefs.edit();
        editor.putString("prefText", prefText);
        editor.commit();
    }

    public void loadPreferences(View v) {
        SharedPreferences prefs = PreferenceManager
                .getDefaultSharedPreferences(this);

        String prefText = prefs.getString("prefText",
                "No preference text saved yet!");

        Toast.makeText(this, prefText, Toast.LENGTH_SHORT).show();
```

282

```
        }

}
```

4. Run the application. Enter some text to the EditText input area and click the "Save Preferences" button (figure 6.1) -

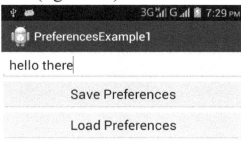

Figure 6.1: Running PreferencesExample1 application

5. Now press the back button to close the activity and then re-launch the application from the launcher menu. Click the "Load Preferences" button and you will see a Toast message with the text you previously saved as preference value (figure 6.2) -

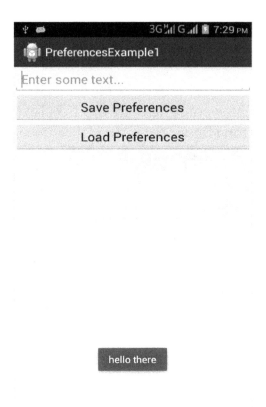

Figure 6.2: Loading preference value

How It Works?

When the user enters some text to the EditText and presses the "Save Preferences" button, the savePreferences() method of MainActivity class handles that button click. Within this savePreferences() method, we get an instance of SharedPreferences class by calling the getDefaultSharedPreferences() method of PreferenceManger class -

    SharedPreferences prefs = PreferenceManager
                    .getDefaultSharedPreferences(this);

We then call the edit() method of SharedPreferences instance -

    SharedPreferences.Editor editor = prefs.edit();

The edit() method call returns an instance of SharedPreferences.Editor which is used to add preference values to our preference XML file.

We then put our string value to the preference file by calling putString() method with a key called "prefText" and text value obtained from the EditText input box -

```
editor.putString("prefText", prefText);
```
Finally, to save changes, we need to call the commit() method -

```
editor.commit();
```

If you are targeting devices that run API level 9 or higher, instead of using commit(), you should use the apply() method. Unlike commit() which writes its preferences to persistent storage synchronously, apply() commits the changes to in-memory SharedPreferences immediately, but writes to disk asynchronously.

This is how we add preference values to the XML preference file. Now, if you are wondering where this preference file is saved, the default location for preference files is the directory

```
/data/data/<package-name>/shared_prefs
```

If you are using an AVD (or rooted device), switch to DDMS perspective, go to File Explorer tab and browse the location to see the preference file created (figure 6.3) -

Figure 6.3: Location of preference files

Now, let's see how we can retrieve the preference values. We again call the getDefaultSharedPreferences() method of PreferenceManager class to get an instance of SharedPreferences -

```
SharedPreferences prefs = PreferenceManager
                    .getDefaultSharedPreferences(this);
```

Then, depending upon the data type we are trying to retrieve (like – int, float, string etc), we call corresponding get<Type>() method (like – getInt(), getFloat(), getString() etc) to retrieve the value of a given key -

```
String prefText = prefs.getString("prefText",
                    "No preference text saved yet!");
```

Here, prefText is the key we use while saving the preference value. That's why we use the same key to retrieve that value. The second parameter of getString() is the default value, which will be used in case there is no entry found for any given key.

SharedPreferences files are private to the application package within which it is created.

Using Other Preference Files

The preceding example shows how we can use the default shared preference file for storing preference values. But we aren't limited to use that default shared preference file. We can use as many shared preference files as we want. In that case, instead of getting the default shared preference, we need to call the getSharedPrefences() method and provide the preference file name as argument -

SharedPreferences prefs =

getSharedPreferences("myPrefsFile",*MODE_PRIVATE*);

For both saving and retrieving preference values, we need to call getSharedPreferences() method with the appropriate preference file name.

Creating a User Preference Screen

We now understand how to store and retrieve shared preferences programmatically. This works well when you need to keep application state information. However if you want to create a settings screen for your users, it is recommended that you take advantage of the preference screen provided by the Android platform. Preference screens are XML resource files, which with the help of PreferenceActivity class provide users a settings screen consistent with the Android's standard settings screen. We will create a new project to demonstrate the usage of the preference screen.

1. Create a new project PreferencesExample2.

2. Create a new directory named xml under the res/ directory. Add a new preference resource file named prefs.xml under the res/xml directory with the following content -

```xml
<?xml version="1.0" encoding="utf-8"?>
<PreferenceScreen xmlns:android="http://schemas.android.com/apk/res/android" >
```

```xml
<EditTextPreference
    android:key="email"
    android:summary="Your email address"
    android:title="Email" />

<ListPreference
    android:entries="@array/gender_type"
    android:entryValues="@array/gender_values"
    android:key="gender"
    android:summary="Select a gender for your game character"
    android:title="Game Character Gender" />

<CheckBoxPreference
    android:key="sound"
    android:summary="Do you want to enable game sound?"
    android:title="Enable Sound?" />

</PreferenceScreen>
```

3. The preference resource file references to two string arrays. Add the highlighted lines to your strings.xml file (under the res/values directory) -

```xml
<?xml version="1.0" encoding="utf-8"?>
<resources>

    <string name="app_name">PreferencesExample2</string>
    <string name="action_settings">Settings</string>
    <string name="hello_world">Hello world!</string>

    <string-array name="gender_values">
        <item>male</item>
        <item>female</item>
    </string-array>

    <string-array name="gender_type">
        <item>Male</item>
        <item>Female</item>
    </string-array>

</resources>
```

4. Add a new activity named SettingsActivity.java, which extends the special Activity class PreferenceActivity -

package com.iducate.preferencesexample2;

import android.os.Bundle;
import android.preference.PreferenceActivity;
import android.preference.PreferenceManager;

public class SettingsActivity extends PreferenceActivity {

    @Override
    protected void onCreate(Bundle savedInstanceState) {
        super.onCreate(savedInstanceState);

        PreferenceManager manager = getPreferenceManager();
        manager.setSharedPreferencesName("my_prefs");

        addPreferencesFromResource(R.xml.prefs);
    }
}

5. We need to register this activity class in the AndroidManifest.xml file -

```
<?xml version="1.0" encoding="utf-8"?>
<manifest xmlns:android="http://schemas.android.com/apk/res/android"
  package="com.iducate.preferencesexample2"
  android:versionCode="1"
  android:versionName="1.0" >

  <uses-sdk
    android:minSdkVersion="8"
    android:targetSdkVersion="19" />

  <application
    android:allowBackup="true"
    android:icon="@drawable/ic_launcher"
    android:label="@string/app_name"
    android:theme="@style/AppTheme" >
    <activity
      android:name="com.iducate.preferencesexample2.MainActivity"
      android:label="@string/app_name" >
```

```
        <intent-filter>
            <action android:name="android.intent.action.MAIN" />

            <category android:name="android.intent.category.LAUNCHER" />
        </intent-filter>
    </activity>
    <activity android:name="com.iducate.preferencesexample2.SettingsActivity" >
    </activity>
</application>

</manifest>
```

6. In our activity_main.xml file, add two buttons -

```
<LinearLayout xmlns:android="http://schemas.android.com/apk/res/android"
    android:layout_width="fill_parent"
    android:layout_height="fill_parent"
    android:orientation="vertical" >

    <Button
        android:id="@+id/btnSetPrefs"
        android:layout_width="match_parent"
        android:layout_height="wrap_content"
        android:onClick="setPreferences"
        android:text="Set Preferences" />

    <Button
        android:id="@+id/btnGetPrefs"
        android:layout_width="match_parent"
        android:layout_height="wrap_content"
        android:onClick="getPreferences"
        android:text="Get Preferences" />

</LinearLayout>
```

7. Finally, update the MainActivity.java file with the following code -

```
package com.iducate.preferencesexample2;

import android.app.Activity;
import android.content.Intent;
import android.content.SharedPreferences;
```

```java
import android.os.Bundle;
import android.view.View;
import android.widget.Toast;

public class MainActivity extends Activity {

    @Override
    protected void onCreate(Bundle savedInstanceState) {
        super.onCreate(savedInstanceState);
        setContentView(R.layout.activity_main);
    }

    public void setPreferences(View v) {
        Intent intent = new Intent(this, SettingsActivity.class);
        startActivity(intent);
    }

    public void getPreferences(View v) {
        SharedPreferences prefs = getSharedPreferences(
                                        "my_prefs", MODE_PRIVATE);
        String email = prefs.getString("email", "");
        String gender = prefs.getString("gender", "");
        boolean soundEnabled = prefs.getBoolean("sound", false);

        Toast.makeText(this,"Email: " + email + "\nGender: " +                     gender
+ "\nSound Enabled: "+ soundEnabled,
        Toast.LENGTH_SHORT).show();
    }
}
```

8. Run the application and you will see a screen with two buttons (figure 6.4). If you click the first button ("Set Preferences" button), you will be taken to the preference screen (figure 6.5). The preference screen has three settings items. The first one is an EditTextPreference. If you click that option, a new dialog window will appear to let you enter an email address (figure 6.6). The second item of preference screen is a ListPreference. Click that item and a dialog will appear to let you choose an option (figure 6.7). Finally, the third preference let's you check or uncheck the option.

9. Once you are done with the preference settings, press the back button to return to the previous screen and then click the second button ("Get Preferences" button). You will see a Toast message with the preference values you have set on the

290

preference screen (figure 6.8).

Figure 6.4: Launcher activity   *Figure 6.5: Preference screen*

Figure 6.6: EditText Preference   *Figure 6.7: List Preference*

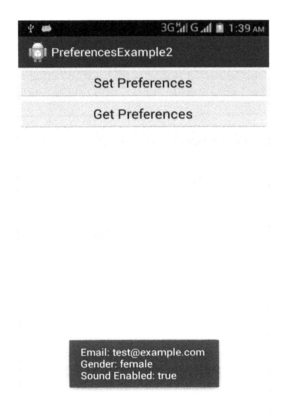

Figure 6.8: Getting preference values

How It Works?

We have created an XML preference resource file named prefs.xml, under the res/ xml directory. The root element of preference resource file is PreferenceScreen -

```
<PreferenceScreen
    xmlns:android="http://schemas.android.com/apk/res/android">
```

Under the root PreferenceScreen element, we add three preference settings items – an EditTextPreference item, a ListPreference item and a CheckBoxPreference item.

For example, this is how our EditTextPreference item looks like -

```
<EditTextPreference
android:key="email"
android:summary="Your email address"
android:title="Email" />
```

The preference items has a number of attributes. Some of them are item specific, but there are some common attributes for all types of preference items.

The android:key attribute specifies the key, which can be used to reference the preference item programmatically from our code.

The android:title attribute sets a title for that preference item.

The android:summary attribute can be used to set a brief summary about the preference item.

We want to display the preference screen from our SettingsActivity class. The SettingsActivity class extends the PreferenceActivity class. The PreferenceActivity class is a special activity that can handle a preference screen -

```
public class SettingsActivity extends PreferenceActivity {
```

Within the onCreate() method of the SettingsActivity class, we do two things. First, we get an instance of PreferenceManager class by calling the getPreferenceManager() method and then call the setSharedPreferencesName() method of manager object to set the name of the preference file. If we don't do that, the default shared preferences file will be used. The second thing we do is call the addPreferencesFromResource() method and pass the XML preference resource file as argument. This loads the XML preference resource file -

```
@Override
protected void onCreate(Bundle savedInstanceState) {
        super.onCreate(savedInstanceState);

        PreferenceManager manager = getPreferenceManager();
        manager.setSharedPreferencesName("my_prefs");
```

```
addPreferencesFromResource(R.xml.prefs);
    }
```

This is how we get the preference screen.

The code of MainActivity.java file should be straightforward to you at this point. To see the preference screen, user will click the "Set Preferences" button which is handled by setPreferences() method -

```
public void setPreferences(View v) {
        Intent intent = new Intent(this, SettingsActivity.class);
        startActivity(intent);
    }
```

This method simply calls the startActivity() method to start the SettingsActivity class.

The other method getPreferences(), loads the preference values from our preference file and shows a Toast notification -

```
public void getPreferences(View v) {
        SharedPreferences prefs = getSharedPreferences(
                                        "my_prefs", MODE_PRIVATE);
        String email = prefs.getString("email", "");
        String gender = prefs.getString("gender", "");
        boolean soundEnabled = prefs.getBoolean("sound", false);

        Toast.makeText(this,"Email: " + email + "\nGender: " +            gender
+ "\nSound Enabled: "+ soundEnabled,
    Toast.LENGTH_SHORT).show();
    }
```

This method should look familiar to you as this is how we retrieved preference values in our previous example project.

Persisting Data to Files

The SharedPreferences object works well for storing key-value pairs. They are typically well suited for saving preference information of applications, like – storing user ids, whether user prefers application sound to be on or off, font size, font color etc. However, you might want to use the traditional file system as persistent data storage. You can use both internal storage of the device and external storage (SD card) to store files.

Saving to Internal Storage

First, let's see how we can save files to the Android device's internal storage. We will create a new project to demonstrate this.

1. Create a new project FilesDemo.

2. Update the layout file activity_main.xml to include an EditText widget to take text input and two buttons -

```xml
<LinearLayout xmlns:android="http://schemas.android.com/apk/res/android"
    android:layout_width="fill_parent"
    android:layout_height="fill_parent"
    android:orientation="vertical" >
    <EditText
        android:id="@+id/etInput"
        android:layout_width="match_parent"
        android:layout_height="wrap_content"
        android:hint="Enter text here..." />

    <Button
        android:id="@+id/btnSave"
        android:layout_width="match_parent"
        android:layout_height="wrap_content"
        android:onClick="writeToFile"
        android:text="Save" />

    <Button
        android:id="@+id/btnLoad"
        android:layout_width="match_parent"
        android:layout_height="wrap_content"
        android:onClick="readFromFile"
        android:text="Load" />

</LinearLayout>
```

3. Update the MainActivity.java file with the following code -

```java
package com.iducate.filesdemo;

import java.io.BufferedReader;
import java.io.FileInputStream;
import java.io.FileNotFoundException;
import java.io.FileOutputStream;
import java.io.IOException;
import java.io.InputStreamReader;

import android.app.Activity;
import android.os.Bundle;
import android.view.View;
import android.widget.EditText;
import android.widget.Toast;

public class MainActivity extends Activity {

        private EditText etInput;

        @Override
        protected void onCreate(Bundle savedInstanceState) {
                super.onCreate(savedInstanceState);
                setContentView(R.layout.activity_main);

                etInput = (EditText) findViewById(R.id.etInput);
        }

        public void writeToFile(View v) {
                try {
                        String inputStr = etInput.getText().toString();
                        FileOutputStream fos = openFileOutput("myfile.txt",
                                                MODE_PRIVATE);
                        fos.write(inputStr.getBytes());
                        fos.flush();
                        fos.close();

                        Toast.makeText(this, "File saved successfuly!",
                                                Toast.LENGTH_SHORT).show();
                } catch (FileNotFoundException e) {
                        e.printStackTrace();
                } catch (IOException e) {
                        e.printStackTrace();
                }
```

```
        }

        public void readFromFile(View v) {
                try {
                        FileInputStream fis = openFileInput("myfile.txt");
                        StringBuffer stringBuffer = new StringBuffer();
                        BufferedReader bReader = new BufferedReader(
                                        new InputStreamReader(fis));
                        String strLine = null;

                        while ((strLine = bReader.readLine()) != null) {
                                stringBuffer.append(strLine + "\n");
                        }

                        bReader.close();
                        fis.close();

                        Toast.makeText(this, "File Content: \n" +
                                        stringBuffer.toString(),Toast.LENGTH_SHORT).show();

                } catch (FileNotFoundException e) {
                        e.printStackTrace();
                } catch (IOException e) {
                        e.printStackTrace();
                }
        }
}
```

4. Now run the application. Enter some text to the EditText field and press the "Save" button. The text content of EditText field will be saved to a file (figure 6.9) -

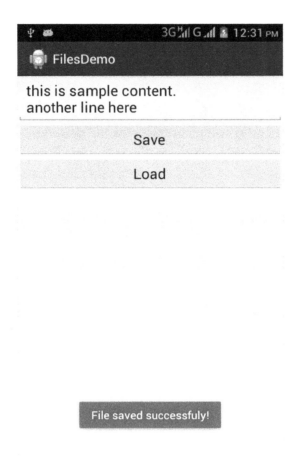

Figure 6.9: Writing to text file

5. Next, press the BACK button to exit the application and run again from the launcher menu. This time, click the "Load" button and you will see previously saved content in a Toast message (figure 6.10) -

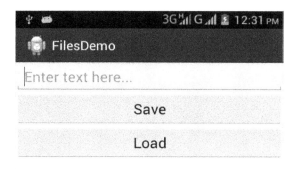

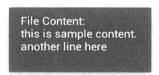

Figure 6.10: Reading from text file

How It Works?

The activity_main.xml layout file has an EditText widget -

```
<EditText
android:id="@+id/etInput"
android:layout_width="match_parent"
android:layout_height="wrap_content"
android:hint="Enter text here..." />
```

We will use this EditText widget to take text input from users and then write this content to a text file.

The layout file has two button widgets as well -

```
<Button
```

```
android:id="@+id/btnSave"
android:layout_width="match_parent"
android:layout_height="wrap_content"
android:onClick="writeToFile"
android:text="Save" />

   <Button
android:id="@+id/btnLoad"
android:layout_width="match_parent"
android:layout_height="wrap_content"
android:onClick="readFromFile"
android:text="Load" />
```

Upon clicking these two buttons, we want to perform two operations - write text to file and read text from file. The android:onClick attribute of these two buttons are set to "writeToFile" and "readFromFile". So you can guess, in our activity file, we will have two corresponding methods – writeToFile() and readFromFile().

First, let's have a look at the writeToFile() method implementation -

```
public void writeToFile(View v) {
     try {
             String inputStr = etInput.getText().toString();
             FileOutputStream fos = openFileOutput("myfile.txt",
                                        MODE_PRIVATE);
             fos.write(inputStr.getBytes());
             fos.flush();
             fos.close();

             Toast.makeText(this, "File saved successfuly!",
                                        Toast.LENGTH_SHORT).show();
     } catch (FileNotFoundException e) {
             e.printStackTrace();
     } catch (IOException e) {
             e.printStackTrace();
     }
}
```

This method will handle the click event of the "Save" button. Within this method, we take the text entered in EditText widget and save that into a text file. The openFileOutput() method opens a named file for writing with the specified mode. We have specified the mode as *MODE_PRIVATE* which indicates that this file can only be read from within the application -

```
FileOutputStream fos = openFileOutput("myfile.txt",MODE_PRIVATE);
```

The openFileOutput() method call returns a FileOutputStream object. We call the write() method of that FileOutputStream instance to write the text into a file -

```
fos.write(inputStr.getBytes());
```

To ensure write operation performs correctly, we call the flush() method and then finally call the close() method of the FileOutputStream object -

```
fos.flush();
fos.close();
```

The file created as a result of above process is stored under the directory -

/data/data/<package-name>/files

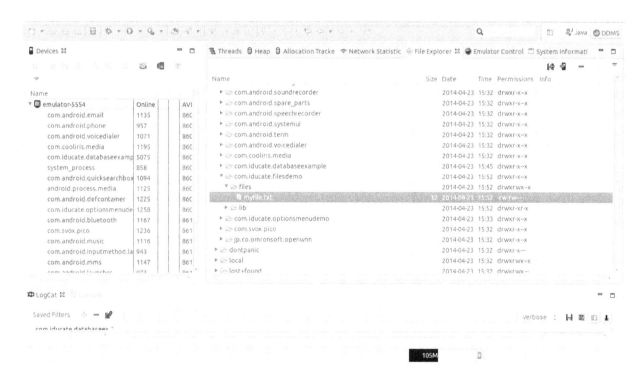

Figure 6.11: Path of myfile.tx file

Now, let's see how we read the file contents. We first call the openFileInput() method with the file name as argument. This method call returns a FileInputStream object -

```
    FileInputStream fis = openFileInput("myfile.txt");
```

We use the java.io.InputStreamReader and java.io.BufferedReader for reading our text file line by line and store it in a StringBuffer object -

```
    BufferedReader bReader = new BufferedReader(
                                        new InputStreamReader(fis));
    String strLine = null;

    while ((strLine = bReader.readLine()) != null) {
            stringBuffer.append(strLine + "\n");
    }
```

We finally we call the toString() method of StringBuffer object to get a string representation of file content and show that as a Toast message.

Saving to External Storage (SD Card)

The previous example showed how we can save files to the internal storage of our Android device. But we are not limited to writing files to internal storage only, Android let's us write files to external storage (SD card) as well. This is helpful because internal storage capacity is limited and sometimes depending upon the application requirements, you will need to utilize external storage.

In this section, we will see how we can write files to external storage. We will update the previous example project and make necessary changes so that it can write files to external storage instead of internal storage.

1. Update your MainActivity.java file with the following code. Highlighted lines reflect the changes made from the previous version –

```
package com.iducate.filesdemo;

import java.io.BufferedReader;
import java.io.File;
import java.io.FileInputStream;
import java.io.FileNotFoundException;
import java.io.FileOutputStream;
import java.io.IOException;
```

```java
import java.io.InputStreamReader;

import android.app.Activity;
import android.os.Bundle;
import android.os.Environment;
import android.view.View;
import android.widget.EditText;
import android.widget.Toast;

public class MainActivity extends Activity {

    private EditText etInput;

    @Override
    protected void onCreate(Bundle savedInstanceState) {
        super.onCreate(savedInstanceState);
        setContentView(R.layout.activity_main);

        etInput = (EditText) findViewById(R.id.etInput);
    }

    public void writeToFile(View v) {
        String inputStr = etInput.getText().toString();

        try {
            // find the root of external storage
            File root = Environment.getExternalStorageDirectory();

            File dir = new File(root.getAbsolutePath() +
                            "/MyFiles");
            dir.mkdirs();

            File file = new File(dir, "myfile.txt");

            FileOutputStream fos = new FileOutputStream(file);

            fos.write(inputStr.getBytes());
            fos.flush();
            fos.close();

            Toast.makeText(this, "File saved successfuly!",
                    Toast.LENGTH_SHORT).show();
        } catch (FileNotFoundException e) {
```

```
                e.printStackTrace();
        } catch (IOException e) {
                e.printStackTrace();
        }
    }


    public void readFromFile(View v) {
        try {
                // find the root of external storage
                File root = Environment.getExternalStorageDirectory();

                File dir = new File(root.getAbsolutePath() +
                                "/MyFiles");

                File file = new File(dir, "myfile.txt");

                FileInputStream fis = new FileInputStream(file);
                StringBuffer stringBuffer = new StringBuffer();
                BufferedReader bReader = new BufferedReader(
                        new InputStreamReader(fis));
                String strLine = null;

                while ((strLine = bReader.readLine()) != null) {
                        stringBuffer.append(strLine + "\n");
                }

                bReader.close();
                fis.close();

                Toast.makeText(this, "File Content: \n" +
                                stringBuffer.toString(),Toast.LENGTH_SHORT).show();

        } catch (FileNotFoundException e) {
                e.printStackTrace();
        } catch (IOException e) {
                e.printStackTrace();
        }
    }
}
```

2. We need to add a permission in order to write to the device's external storage. Open the AndroidManifest.xml file and add the WRITE_EXTERNAL_STORAGE permission -

```xml
<?xml version="1.0" encoding="utf-8"?>
<manifest xmlns:android="http://schemas.android.com/apk/res/android"
   package="com.iducate.filesdemo"
   android:versionCode="1"
   android:versionName="1.0" >

   <uses-sdk
      android:minSdkVersion="8"
      android:targetSdkVersion="19" />

   <uses-permission
android:name="android.permission.WRITE_EXTERNAL_STORAGE" />

   <application
      android:allowBackup="true"
      android:icon="@drawable/ic_launcher"
      android:label="@string/app_name"
      android:theme="@style/AppTheme" >
      <activity
         android:name="com.iducate.filesdemo.MainActivity"
         android:label="@string/app_name" >
         <intent-filter>
            <action android:name="android.intent.action.MAIN" />

            <category android:name="android.intent.category.LAUNCHER" />
         </intent-filter>
      </activity>
   </application>

</manifest>
```

3. Now run the application. The user interface of the application is exactly the same as in the previous version. The application will work the same way as it did previously (figure 6.12) but instead of using the internal storage, it will use the external storage of the device –

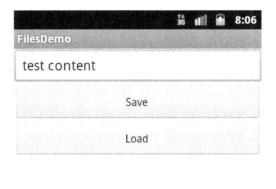

Figure 6.12: Writing to and reading from external storage

306

How It Works?

In order to use external storage (for both reading and writing files), we first need to get the path to the external storage. We call the getExternalStorageDirectory() method of the Environment class which returns the full path to the external storage of the device -

      File root = Environment.*getExternalStorageDirectory*();

For a real device typically, the path will be "/sdcard" and for AVD, it will be "/mnt/sdcard". But you should never use a hardcoded path because a manufacturer may choose to assign a different path name to the SD card.

We will write our file to a new directory. We create a directory named "MyFiles" in the SD card -

      File dir = new File(root.getAbsolutePath() + "/MyFiles");
      dir.mkdirs();

We then create a new file resource within the specified directory and create a new instance of the FileOutputStream class -

      File file = new File(dir, "myfile.txt");

      FileOutputStream fos = new FileOutputStream(file);

We finally write the content to file and save that -

      fos.write(inputStr.getBytes());
      fos.flush();
      fos.close();

Now, if you have already run the application and saved some content, you can switch to the DDMS perspective of Eclipse and go to File Explorer tab to browse the directory -

      /mnt/sdcard/MyFiles

and you will see the file myfile.txt created (figure 6.13).

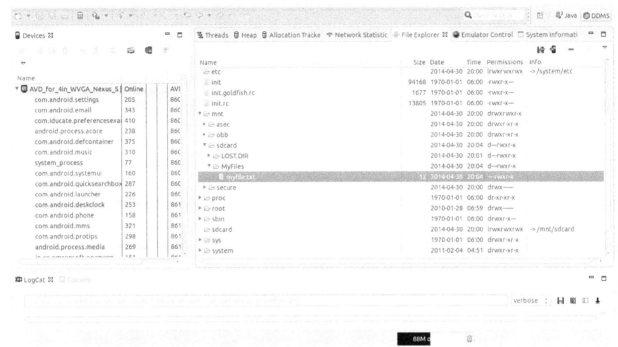

Figure 6.13: Browsing file in external storage

Now, to read the file from external storage, we will also need to get the path of the external storage. We create a new file resource and after that, we create a new instance of FileInputStream with that file resource. The rest of the steps are similar to reading from internal storage -

File root = Environment.*getExternalStorageDirectory*();

File dir = new File(root.getAbsolutePath() + "/MyFiles");
File file = new File(dir, "myfile.txt");

FileInputStream fis = new FileInputStream(file);

StringBuffer stringBuffer = **new** StringBuffer();
BufferedReader bReader = **new** BufferedReader(
                            new InputStreamReader(fis));
String strLine = **null**;

while ((strLine = bReader.readLine()) != **null**) {
        stringBuffer.append(strLine + "\n");
}

bReader.close();
fis.close();

Finally, we need to get permission from the Android system for writing to external storage. That's why we need to add the following uses-permission to our AndroidManifest.xml file -

```
<uses-permission
        android:name="android.permission.WRITE_EXTERNAL_STORAGE" />
```

Using Static Resources

In addition to creating and using files dynamically during runtime, we can also bundle some pre-created files to our application package. We can then use those files during run time from our application. Those files are stored under the res/raw directory (if that directory doesn't exist, you need to create it).

We can then access files stored in res/raw directory by calling the getResources() method which returns a Resource object. We then call the openRawResource() method -

```
getResources().openRawResource(R.raw.filename);
```

You can see that the openRawResource() method takes the resource id of resources stored in the res/raw directory. If you have a file named filename.txt under res/raw directory, the resource id for that file will be R.raw.filename.

Creating and Using Databases

We have already seen how we can use shared preferences and file system for storing persistent data. Now we will see yet another option to save persistent data on Android platform – the SQLite database. Using SQLite database, we can store structured data much more efficiently.

SQLite is a relational database which provides you many of the commonly used features of a full fledged database management system like MySQL, PostgreSQL, Oracle etc. SQLite is a self-contained, serverless, transactional database.

SQLite databases are private to the application which means, it can only be accessed by the application package within which it is created. The SQLite databases that you create programmatically from your Android application are stored under the directory -

/data/data/<package-name>/databases

In the next section, we will create a new project to demonstrate the usage of SQLite database in our Android application. In our example project, we will create a database table to hold information about employee records. To keep things simple, we will have only three fields -

- id – employee id, this will be an integer field. We will use this field as our primary key
- name – employee name which will be a text field
- email – employee email address. This will be a text field as well

This example project will be quite comprehensive. That's why we will break it down to several parts. We will start by creating the Employee class. After that, we will create a helper class to manage database operations. Later we will see how we can interact with our database and perform CRUD (create, read, update and delete) operations from our activity class.

Creating the Employee Class

First we will create a new class named Employee which will have three fields – id, name and email. We will define corresponding getter and setter methods for these fields. The three fields of Employee class corresponds to the three columns of our "employee" database table.

1. First, create a new project DatabaseExample.

2. Create a new java file Employee.java to the project package under the src directory. This file will represent the Employee class. Add the following code to this file -

```java
package com.iducate.databaseexample;

public class Employee {

    private int id;
    private String name;
    private String email;

    public Employee(int id, String name, String email) {
```

```java
        super();
        this.id = id;
        this.name = name;
        this.email = email;
    }

    public Employee(String name, String email) {
        this.name = name;
        this.email = email;
    }

    public int getId() {
        return id;
    }

    public String getName() {
        return name;
    }

    public void setName(String name) {
        this.name = name;
    }

    public String getEmail() {
        return email;
    }

    public void setEmail(String email) {
        this.email = email;
    }

    @Override
    public String toString() {
        return "Employee [id=" + id + ", name=" + name + ", email="
                + email + "]";
    }
}
}
```

How It Works?

We can see that in addition to getter and setter methods for our three fields, we have two constructor methods -

```java
public Employee(int id, String name, String email) {
    super();
    this.id = id;
    this.name = name;
    this.email = email;
}

public Employee(String name, String email) {
    this.name = name;
    this.email = email;
}
```

The first version of the constructor method takes all three fields as arguments, while the second version of constructor doesn't use id as an argument. The database helper class we are going to create in the next step will have a method to insert data. That method will take an Employee object and insert that into the database table. While inserting a new Employee record, we will not provide an employee id. Rather, we want our database to generate an auto-increment id for each employee. In that case, we will use the constructor without id argument to create a new Employee object.

On the other hand when we will retrieve records from database, we will have the values of employee id. In that case, we will use the other version of constructor to create Employee objects.

Finally, we define a toString() method for Employee class -

```java
@Override
public String toString() {
    return "Employee [id=" + id + ", name=" + name + ", email="
        + email + "]";
}
```

Creating the Database Helper Class

We will create a database helper class which will encapsulate all the complexities of handling database operations. We will create a helper class named DBAdapter, which will manage database creation, opening, closing and other operations like data insertion, deletion, access and update.

Let's add a new java file named DBAdapter.java to the package. Add the following code to DBAdapter.java -

```java
package com.iducate.databaseexample;

import android.content.ContentValues;
import android.content.Context;
import android.database.Cursor;
import android.database.SQLException;
import android.database.sqlite.SQLiteDatabase;
import android.database.sqlite.SQLiteOpenHelper;

public class DBAdapter {

    public static final String DB_NAME = "employee_db";
    public static final int DB_VERSION = 1;
    public static final String TABLE_NAME = "employee";
    public static final String C_ID = "_id";
    public static final String C_NAME = "name";
    public static final String C_EMAIL = "email";

    private static final String CREATE_TABLE_SQL = "create table " +
    TABLE_NAME + " ( " + C_ID + " integer primary key            autoincrement,
" + C_NAME + " text, " + C_EMAIL + " text)";

    private Context context;
    private DBHelper dbHelper;
    private SQLiteDatabase db;

    public DBAdapter(Context context) {
            this.context = context;
            dbHelper = new DBHelper();
    }

    //open database
    public void open() {
            db = dbHelper.getWritableDatabase();
    }

    //close database
    public void close() {
            db.close();
    }
```

```java
//insert an employee
public long insert(Employee employee) {
        ContentValues values = new ContentValues();
        values.put(C_NAME, employee.getName());
        values.put(C_EMAIL, employee.getEmail());
        return db.insert(TABLE_NAME, null, values);
}


//get all employee
public Cursor getAll() {
        return db.query(TABLE_NAME, null, null, null, null, null,
                                        null);
}


// update a record
public int update(long id, Employee employee) {
        ContentValues values = new ContentValues();
        values.put(C_NAME, employee.getName());
        values.put(C_EMAIL, employee.getEmail());
        return db.update(TABLE_NAME, values, C_ID + "= ?", new
                                String[] { id + "" });
}



// delete a record
public int delete(long id) {
        return db.delete(TABLE_NAME, C_ID + "= ?", new String[]
                                { id + "" });
}


//get a single record
public Cursor getEmployeeById(long id) {
        Cursor cursor = db.query(TABLE_NAME, null, C_ID + "= ?",
                        new String[] { id + "" }, null, null, null);

        if (cursor != null) {
                cursor.moveToFirst();
        }

        return cursor;
}
```

```java
private class DBHelper extends SQLiteOpenHelper {

    public DBHelper() {
        super(context, DB_NAME, null, DB_VERSION);
    }

    @Override
    public void onCreate(SQLiteDatabase db) {
        try {
            db.execSQL(CREATE_TABLE_SQL);
        } catch (SQLException e) {
            e.printStackTrace();
        }
    }

    @Override
    public void onUpgrade(SQLiteDatabase db, int oldVersion,
        int newVersion) {
        //your database upgrade logic goes here
        db.execSQL("DROP TABLE IF EXISTS "+TABLE_NAME);
        onCreate(db);
    }

}

}
```

How It Works?

You will notice that we have started by defining a bunch of constants -

```java
public static final String DB_NAME = "employee_db";
public static final int DB_VERSION = 1;
public static final String TABLE_NAME = "employee";
public static final String C_ID = "_id";
public static final String C_NAME = "name";
public static final String C_EMAIL = "email";
```

These constants represent different information like database name, database version, table name, different field names of our table etc. Instead of using hard coded values, we have chosen to define these as constants. You will notice that column names are declared as public static constants. This allows us to use

315

constant names for table column names instead of hard coded values and thus minimize the risk of mis-spelled column names.

We also declare a string constant for the SQL syntax of creating an employee table -

```
private static final String CREATE_TABLE_SQL = "create table " +
TABLE_NAME + " ( " + C_ID + " integer primary key                autoincrement,
" + C_NAME + " text, " + C_EMAIL + " text)";
```

Within the DBAdapter class, we have a private inner class named DBHelper which is a subclass of SQLiteOpenHelper class -

```
private class DBHelper extends SQLiteOpenHelper {

    public DBHelper() {
        super(context, DB_NAME, null, DB_VERSION);
    }

    @Override
    public void onCreate(SQLiteDatabase db) {
        try {
            db.execSQL(CREATE_TABLE_SQL);
        } catch (SQLException e) {
            e.printStackTrace();
        }
    }

    @Override
    public void onUpgrade(SQLiteDatabase db, int oldVersion,
        int newVersion) {
        //your database upgrade logic goes here
        db.execSQL("DROP TABLE IF EXISTS "+TABLE_NAME);
        onCreate(db);
    }

}
```

This DBHelper class helps us to manage the tasks of database creation and version management. Within our DBHelper class, we need to overwrite two methods – onCreate() and onUpgrade(). When we create a new instance of DBHelper class, it will check if the database already exists or not. If the database isn't created yet, the

316

onCreate() method - which will create a new database will be called. In the case where the database is already created, it will then check the current database version against the supplied version. If both version matches, nothing happens. If the supplied database version is greater than the currently installed version however, the onUpgrade() method will be called. Within this method, you will handle the upgrade logic for your database schema.

Though in our onUpgrade() method implementation we have simply dropped the current database table and then created it again, depending upon your application requirement, you might need to have some strategy of backing up previous data before dropping the existing table.

Now, the constructor of our DBAdapter class takes a Context object as argument -

```
public DBAdapter(Context context) {
        this.context = context;
        dbHelper = new DBHelper();
}
```

We also instantiate a new instance of DBHelper inner class within the constructor of DBAdapter class and we save that instance within a member variable. We will use this DBHelper instance for opening and closing of database.

We define two methods of DBAdapter class for opening and closing of database -

```
//open database
public void open() {
        db = dbHelper.getWritableDatabase();
}

//close database
public void close() {
        db.close();
}
```

We then add different methods to our DBAdapter class to perform read, insert, delete, and update operations. Let's have a look at them one by one.

The insert() method of our DBAdapter class is responsible for inserting a new record to our database table -

```
//insert an employee
```

```
public long insert(Employee employee) {
        ContentValues values = new ContentValues();
        values.put(C_NAME, employee.getName());
        values.put(C_EMAIL, employee.getEmail());
        return db.insert(TABLE_NAME, null, values);
}
```

You will notice that the insert() method takes an Employee object, retrieves the name and email fields from that object and insert those values into the database table.

We define a getAll() method which will be used for retrieving all records of employee table -

```
//get all employee
public Cursor getAll() {
        return db.query(TABLE_NAME, null, null, null, null, null,
                                        null);
}
```

The getAll() method returns a Cursor object which can be thought of as a pointer to the result set from database query. Returning a Cursor is more efficient.

To update an existing record, we define a method called update() -

```
// update a record
public int update(long id, Employee employee) {
        ContentValues values = new ContentValues();
        values.put(C_NAME, employee.getName());
        values.put(C_EMAIL, employee.getEmail());
        return db.update(TABLE_NAME, values, C_ID + "= ?", new
                                        String[] { id + "" });
}
```

This method takes employee id and the updated Employee object as arguments.

We define a delete() method which takes the employee id as argument to remove an existing record. -

```
// delete a record
public int delete(long id) {
```

```
                    return db.delete(TABLE_NAME, C_ID + "= ?", new String[]
                                        { id + "" });
        }
```

Finally, to get an individual employee with given id value, we define getEmployeeById() method, which takes employee id as argument and return a Cursor object -

```
        //get a single record
        public Cursor getEmployeeById(long id) {
                Cursor cursor = db.query(TABLE_NAME, null, C_ID + "= ?",
                                new String[] { id + "" }, null, null, null);

                if (cursor != null) {
                        cursor.moveToFirst();
                }

                return cursor;
        }
```

Using the Database Programmatically

Having created our DBAdapter helper class, we are ready to interact with our database from the activity class. In the following sections, we will see how we can perform CRUD (create, read, update and delete) operations to our database. In order to understand them better, we will do one operation at a time and then explain how it works. For all database operations, we will use the MainActivity.java activity class, which is generated while creating our project.

Inserting a New Record

Let's start with the insert operation. First, we will see how we can add a new record to our database.

1. Update the MainActivity.java file with the following code -

```
package com.iducate.databaseexample;

import android.app.Activity;
import android.os.Bundle;
```

319

```
public class MainActivity extends Activity {
        private DBAdapter dbAdapter;

        @Override
        protected void onCreate(Bundle savedInstanceState) {
                super.onCreate(savedInstanceState);
                setContentView(R.layout.activity_main);

                dbAdapter = new DBAdapter(this);

                //generate few employee objects
                Employee joe = new Employee("Joe Mile", "joe@example.com");
                Employee mike = new Employee("Mike Muster",

"mike@example.com");
                Employee john = new Employee("John Connor",

"connor@example.com");

                //insert new employee record to database
                dbAdapter.open();
                dbAdapter.insert(joe);
                dbAdapter.insert(mike);
                dbAdapter.insert(john);
                dbAdapter.close();

        }

}
```

2. Now run the application. At this point, our database should be created and three new records should be inserted to the employee table. We will verify that from the DDMS perspective.

How It Works?

We start by creating a new instance of DBAdapter class -

```
dbAdapter = new DBAdapter(this);
```

We then create a few Employee objects -

```
//generate few employee objects
Employee joe = new Employee("Joe Mile", "joe@example.com");
Employee mike = new Employee("Mike Muster", "mike@example.com");
Employee john = new Employee("John Connor", "connor@example.com");
```

We want to add these employee records to our database table.

We get a copy of a writable database by calling the open() method of the DBAdapter instance. We then call the insert() method of DBAdapter instance with Employee object as parameter. This insert() method will then retrieve Employee name and email address and insert that into the database table.

```
//insert new employee record to database
dbAdapter.open();
dbAdapter.insert(joe);
dbAdapter.insert(mike);
dbAdapter.insert(john);
dbAdapter.close();
```

At this point, you can go to the DDMS perspective of Eclipse and from the File Explorer tab, browse the directory /data/data/<package-name>/databases and you will see that the employee_db database is created (figure 6.14) -

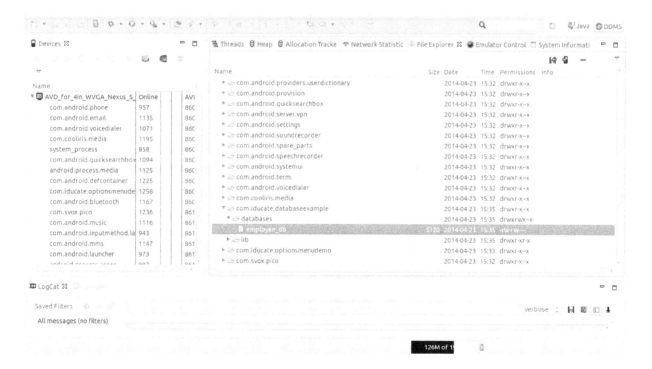

Figure 6.14: Viewing database from DDMS perspective

321

Retrieving all Records

Now let's update our MainActivity.java file to add code so that we can retrieve all the employee records from our database table.

1. Add the highlighted code to your MainActivity.java file -

```java
package com.iducate.databaseexample;

import android.app.Activity;
import android.database.Cursor;
import android.os.Bundle;
import android.widget.Toast;

public class MainActivity extends Activity {

    private DBAdapter dbAdapter;

    @Override
    protected void onCreate(Bundle savedInstanceState) {
        super.onCreate(savedInstanceState);
        setContentView(R.layout.activity_main);

        dbAdapter = new DBAdapter(this);
        dbAdapter.open();
        Cursor cursor = dbAdapter.getAll();
        if (cursor.getCount() > 0) {
            cursor.moveToFirst();
            int id;
            String name;
            String email;
            Employee employee;
            do {
                id = cursor.getInt(
                    cursor.getColumnIndex(DBAdapter.C_ID));
                name = cursor.getString(
                    cursor.getColumnIndex(DBAdapter.C_NAME));
                email = cursor.getString(
                    cursor.getColumnIndex(DBAdapter.C_EMAIL));
                employee = new Employee(id, name, email);
                Toast.makeText(this, employee.toString(),
```

```
Toast.LENGTH_SHORT).show();
            } while (cursor.moveToNext());
    }
    dbAdapter.close();
}

}
```

2. Now, if you run the application, you will see all employee records inserted so far being shown in a Toast message (figure 6.15) -

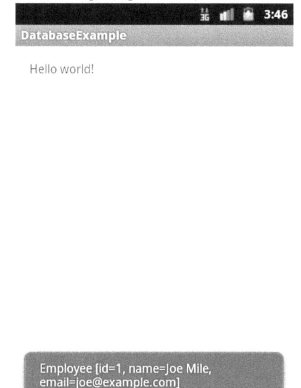

Figure 6.15: Retrieving database records

How It Works?

The getAll() method of DBAdapter helper class returns all the records of the database table in the form of a Cursor object -

```
Cursor cursor = dbAdapter.getAll();
```

We then check if there is any record returned by this Cursor object. If yes, we call the moveToFirst() method of Cursor object and loop through all the records and retrieve them -

```
if (cursor.getCount() > 0) {
        cursor.moveToFirst();
        int id;
        String name;
        String email;
        Employee employee;
        do {
                id = cursor.getInt(
                        cursor.getColumnIndex(DBAdapter.C_ID));
                name = cursor.getString(
                        cursor.getColumnIndex(DBAdapter.C_NAME));
                email = cursor.getString(
                        cursor.getColumnIndex(DBAdapter.C_EMAIL));
                employee = new Employee(id, name, email);
                Toast.makeText(this, employee.toString(),

Toast.LENGTH_SHORT).show();
        } while (cursor.moveToNext());
}
```

Retrieving a Single Record

To retrieve a single record by id, we call the getEmployeeById() method of the DBAdapter helper class.

1. Add the highlighted code to your MainActivity.java file -

```
package com.iducate.databaseexample;

import android.app.Activity;
import android.database.Cursor;
import android.os.Bundle;
import android.widget.Toast;

public class MainActivity extends Activity {

        private DBAdapter dbAdapter;
```

```java
@Override
protected void onCreate(Bundle savedInstanceState) {
        super.onCreate(savedInstanceState);
        setContentView(R.layout.activity_main);

        dbAdapter = new DBAdapter(this);

        dbAdapter.open();
        Cursor cursor = dbAdapter.getEmployeeById(1);

        if(cursor.getCount() > 0) {
                int id = cursor.getInt(
                        cursor.getColumnIndex(DBAdapter.C_ID));
                String name = cursor.getString(
                        cursor.getColumnIndex(DBAdapter.C_NAME));
                String email = cursor.getString(
                        cursor.getColumnIndex(DBAdapter.C_EMAIL));
                Employee employee = new Employee(id, name, email);
                Toast.makeText(this, employee.toString(),
                                        Toast.LENGTH_SHORT).show();
        }
        cursor.close();
        dbAdapter.close();
    }

}
```

2. Run the application and you will see that the employee record with specified id is retrieved from the database table -

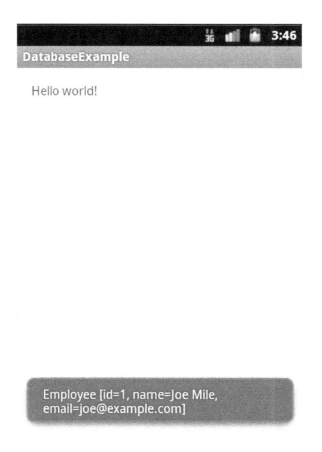

Figure 6.16: Retrieving single record from database table

How It Works?

We use the getEmployeeById() helper method of DBAdapter class to retrieve a single record from the database table -

```
Cursor cursor = dbAdapter.getEmployeeById(1);
```

This method returns a Cursor object. Similar to the previous getAll() method, we first check if there is any record returned by the Cursor. If there are any, we then retrieve that record -

```
if(cursor.getCount() > 0) {
        int id = cursor.getInt(
                cursor.getColumnIndex(DBAdapter.C_ID));
        String name = cursor.getString(
```

```
        cursor.getColumnIndex(DBAdapter.C_NAME));
    String email = cursor.getString(
        cursor.getColumnIndex(DBAdapter.C_EMAIL));
    Employee employee = new Employee(id, name, email);
    Toast.makeText(this, employee.toString(),
                                Toast.LENGTH_SHORT).show();
}
```

Updating a Record

So far, we have inserted and retrieved records. Now let's see how we can update an existing record.

1. Add the highlighted code to your MainActivity.java file -

```
package com.iducate.databaseexample;

import android.app.Activity;
import android.database.Cursor;
import android.os.Bundle;
import android.widget.Toast;

public class MainActivity extends Activity {

    private DBAdapter dbAdapter;

    @Override
    protected void onCreate(Bundle savedInstanceState) {
        super.onCreate(savedInstanceState);
        setContentView(R.layout.activity_main);

        dbAdapter = new DBAdapter(this);

        dbAdapter.open();
        Employee joe = new Employee("Joe Mile",
                                        "joe99@example.com");
        if(dbAdapter.update(1, joe) > 0) {
            Toast.makeText(this, "Record updated successfully",
                    Toast.LENGTH_SHORT).show();
        }
        dbAdapter.close();
    }
```

}

2. If you run the application, the database record with specified id will be updated.

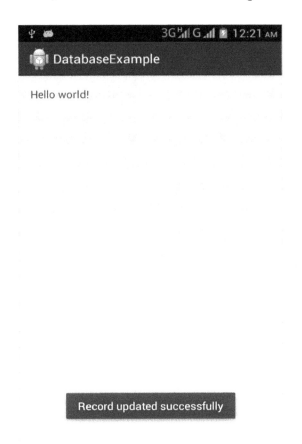

Figure 6.17: Updating an existing record

How It Works?

To update an existing record, we call the update() method of the DBAdapter helper class -

```
Employee joe = new Employee("Joe Mile", "joe99@example.com");
if(dbAdapter.update(1, joe) > 0) {
        Toast.makeText(this, "Record updated successfully",
                                        Toast.LENGTH_SHORT).show();
}
```

This update() method takes two arguments, the id of the record to be updated and the instance of Employee object which will have updated data. This method will return an integer value indicating how many rows are affected by the update operation. We simply check that return value is greater than zero to make sure that the record is successfully updated.

Deleting a Record

Finally, let's see how we can delete a record from our database table.

1. Add the highlighted lines to your MainActivity.java file -

```java
package com.iducate.databaseexample;

import android.app.Activity;
import android.database.Cursor;
import android.os.Bundle;
import android.widget.Toast;

public class MainActivity extends Activity {

        private DBAdapter dbAdapter;

        @Override
        protected void onCreate(Bundle savedInstanceState) {
                super.onCreate(savedInstanceState);
                setContentView(R.layout.activity_main);

                dbAdapter = new DBAdapter(this);

                //delete a record
                dbAdapter.open();
                if(dbAdapter.delete(2) > 0) {
                        Toast.makeText(this, "Record deleted successfully!",
                                Toast.LENGTH_SHORT).show();
                }
                dbAdapter.close();
        }

}
```

2. Now run the application. The record with the specified id should be removed from the database table.

Figure 6.18: Deleting record from database

How It Works?

In our DBAdapter helper class, we have defined a delete() method which we use in our MainActivity.java file to remove a record from database table -

```
if(dbAdapter.delete(2) > 0) {
        Toast.makeText(this, "Record deleted successfully!",
                Toast.LENGTH_SHORT).show();
}
```

This delete() method takes a single argument, which is the id of record to be removed. This method returns an integer value which indicates how many rows are removed. We check that the return value is greater than zero to make sure that the specified row is actually removed.

Upgrading a Database

We have learned how to work with SQLite database in Android. Sometimes, after you release your application, you might need to change your database schema to add some additional fields or even add a new table. In that case, you will need to increase the version number of your database. The DBAdapter helper class has a constant named *DB_VERSION* which indicates the database version number. You will need to increment that version number -

```
public class DBAdapter {

    public static final String DB_NAME = "employee_db";
    public static final int DB_VERSION = 2;
```

If the previous database version number was 1, we will change that to 2.

When there is an upgrade of the database version number, the onUpgrade() method of the DBHelper class (subclass of SQLiteOpenHelper class) will be called

```
@Override
public void onUpgrade(SQLiteDatabase db, int oldVersion, int newVersion) {
    //your database upgrade logic goes here
}
```

In the onUpgrade() method, you will handle your database upgrade logic. For example, backing up previous data and other things depending upon your application requirements.

Using a Pre-populated Database

So far, our discussion of SQLite database is about creating a database at runtime and then populating that database from application. This is the common scenario for many applications. However, there will be a time when you will need to ship a pre-populated SQLite database with your application.

In that case, you will have your SQLite database populated with existing data. You will need to bundle that database with the application package so that you can access that database from within your application. One way to accomplish this task is to put that pre-populated database in the assets/ directory. Then on the first start up, you will need to copy that database from assets directory to the /data/data/ <package-name>/databases/ directory.

The above mentioned method will work but you can use some external library to do your job more conveniently. There are many excellent libraries out there to help you accomplish your task. I would like to mention one particular library – the "Android SQLiteAssetHelper". This library is hosted in github -

https://github.com/jgilfelt/android-sqlite-asset-helper

Using this library is very easy. The github page mentioned above contains full documentation about how to use that library.

Choosing the Best Storage Option

Now we have discussed about different persistent data storage options. Let's see how we can choose the best storage option for our application.

- SharedPreferences are well suited for storing key-value pairs. If you find that the data you need to save can be represented as key-value pairs, you can use SharedPreferences.

- Internal storage of your device can be a good option when your application need to write some files (for example – download images from web, saving notes, saving audio record etc).

- If your application needs to store structured data, SQLite database then is the right option for you. It can handle large amount of structured data efficiently. You can use relational database design to store data in different tables. Using SQLite, operations like data retrieval, update, insertion, deletion can be done conveniently and efficiently.

Summary

Saving application data persistently is an important task for application development. The Android platform provides us different options for persistent storage. This chapter discusses them with example projects. Make sure you feel comfortable with these data storage options, because most of the applications you will develop in real life involves data storage and you will end up using one or more of the storage options mentioned in this chapter.

Chapter 7: Content Providers

In the previous chapter, we have learned about various persistent data storage mechanisms offered by the Android platform – shared preferences, file based data storage and SQLite databases. Those data storage mechanisms are private to the application package within which they are created. In this chapter, we will learn about Content Providers which enable us to share data among applications. We will have a look at different built-in content providers of Android. We will learn how to access data through content providers and we will also implement our own content provider that can be used for sharing data with other applications.

Sharing Data in Android

Content providers are the recommended way to share data across different Android application packages. Content providers offer a way to encapsulate data using URI instances as handles but the underlaying data source being hidden from users. The data might be stored in SQLite database, in flat files or even stored over the Internet. But the consumer applications of content providers need not to worry about data source, because content providers provide well defined interface for publishing and consuming data.

In Android, any URI that begins with the content:// scheme represents a resource served up by a content provider. The general format of the content URI is as follows -

> content://<authority>/<data_path>/<id>

Not all of the parts of the above format is always used, for example - <id> part is only used to get particular record. Let's see what are the different parts of content URI -

- The <authority> part of the content URI specifies the name of the content provider. For example – the authority of built-in Contacts provider is contacts. For third-party content providers, you will most likely provide a fully qualified name like, com.iducate.provider.
- The <data_path> part specifies the type of data requested. Again, if we go back to our Contacts content provider as an example, the data path would be

people. In that case, the URI will look like – content://contacts/people.
- The <id> part is optional, you will only use this part of content URI when you want to specify a specific record. For example, if you want to retrieve a contact from Contacts content provider with id 7, then the URI will look like – content://contacts/people/7.

Android expects these URI to be Uri objects, not strings. The Uri.parse() static method can be used to create a Uri object from the string representation discussed above. For example, for the Contacts content provider, we can get an Uri instance as follows -

Uri contactsUri = Uri.parse("content://contacts/people/");

The above example shows how we can get the base Uri for Contacts content provider. We provide the string representation of URI within the Uri.parse() method and that method returns an Uri instance.

Getting the Base Uri

We can use a hardcoded string as we did in our previous example and then pass that string to Uri.parse() method to get the base Uri of content providers. But this is not a good idea because the base Uri values for the content providers can change over time. There is a better way for getting the base Uri of the built-in content provider. Android provides a list of predefined constants to specify the base Uri for different built-in content providers. For example, to get the base Uri for Contacts represented as people, we can use *CONTENT_URI* constant of Contacts class -

Uri contactsUri = ContactsContract.Contacts.CONTENT_URI;

which maps to content://contacts/people/ and equivalent to writing -

Uri contactsUri = Uri.parse("content://contacts/people/");

Using constants to access base Uri is the recommended way for built-in content providers. For third-party content providers, it is also now a practice to provide a constant *CONTENT_URI* that maps to base Uri. But it may not be so always, in which case, you need to use the hardcoded method.

Built-in Content Providers

Android ships with a number of built-in content providers. You can make use of these content providers and integrate with your applications. You not only have ability to make use of the data from these content providers, you can also add, modify or remove data from them. Let's have a look at some useful content providers that are shipped with Android -

- AlarmClock – sets alarms with the alarm clock applications.
- Browser – gives access to browser history and bookmarks.
- CalenderContract – stores calender and event information.
- CallLog – stores sent and received calls information.
- ContactsContract – this is the phone contact database.
- MediaStore – Audio/visual data on the phone and external storage.
- SearchRecentSuggestions – stores search suggestions relevant to applications.
- Settings – stores system-wide devices settings and preferences.
- UserDictionary – a dictionary of user-defined words for use with predictive text input.
- VoicemailContract – a single unified place for the user to manage voicemail content from different sources.

Using a Content Provider

In this section, we will see how we can use a content provider. Though we will only see how to use the ContactsContract content provider, the usage pattern for all content providers are the same. Hopefully by learning how to use ContactsContract content provider, you will be able to gain sufficient knowledge to deal with other content providers as well. We will create a new project to demonstrate the usage of ContactsContract content provider which will output the contact name and phone number to the LogCat view.

Contacts in Android are saved in a complex way. You can save different types of contacts in your phone book. In addition to saving regular contact information like phone number, email etc, you can also import a whole variety of contact types, like – Gmail contacts, Skype contacts, Facebook contacts etc. Different types of contacts have different fields filled up. But you can't be assured that all contacts will have all fields filled up (like, you can't guarantee that all of your contact in your phone book will have a phone number). When you sync Skype contacts, you might not get a phone number for all Skype accounts. On the the other hand, a single contact can have multiple phone numbers or email addresses. You can see that data storage is not as straight forward, so you can expect the underlaying data storage to be slightly complex as well. We will not be discussing the underlaying data storage of ContactsContract. But just to give you some idea, it uses different tables for storing phone numbers, emails etc. So we will have to query more than once if we want to get email address or phone numbers. In our example project, we want to get display names and phone numbers. We will initially make a query to get display names and associated ids. Next, we will check if it has   phone number(s) and make another query to retrieve those phone numbers.

Let's now see how to do this.

1. First let's create a new project ContentProviderDemo.

2. Update the MainActivity.java file with the following code -

```
package com.iducate.contentproviderdemo;

import android.os.Bundle;
import android.provider.ContactsContract;
import android.util.Log;
import android.app.Activity;
import android.content.ContentResolver;
import android.database.Cursor;

public class MainActivity extends Activity {

        private static final String TAG = "ContentProviderDemo";

        @Override
        protected void onCreate(Bundle savedInstanceState) {
                super.onCreate(savedInstanceState);
                setContentView(R.layout.activity_main);

                ContentResolver cr = getContentResolver();
                Cursor cursor = cr.query(
                        ContactsContract.Contacts.CONTENT_URI, null,
                                                        null, null, null);

                if (cursor != null andand cursor.getCount() > 0) {
                        cursor.moveToFirst();
                        do {
                                int contactID = cursor.getInt(
                                cursor.getColumnIndex(
```

```
                    ContactsContract.Contacts._ID));
                int hasPhoneNumber = cursor.getInt(
                  cursor.getColumnIndex(
                    ContactsContract.Contacts.HAS_PHONE_NUMBER));
                String contactName = cursor.getString(
                  cursor.getColumnIndex(
                        ContactsContract.Contacts.DISPLAY_NAME));

                //if there is phone number for this contact
                if (hasPhoneNumber > 0) {
                        String[] projection = new String[]
{ ContactsContract.CommonDataKinds.Phone.NUMBER };
                        String selection =
ContactsContract.CommonDataKinds.Phone.CONTACT_ID
                                + "= ?";
                        String[] selectionArgs = { contactID + "" };
                        Cursor phoneCursor = cr.query(
          ContactsContract.CommonDataKinds.Phone.CONTENT_URI,
              projection, selection, selectionArgs, null);

                        if (phoneCursor != null andand
                                        phoneCursor.getCount() > 0)
{
                                phoneCursor.moveToFirst();
                                do {

                                        String phoneNumber = phoneCursor
                                                .getString(phoneCursor

.getColumnIndex(ContactsContract.CommonDataKinds.Phone.NUMBER));

                                        Log.d(TAG, "Name: " + contactName
                                + ", Phone Number: " + phoneNumber);
                                } while (phoneCursor.moveToNext());
                        }

                        phoneCursor.close();
                }

                } while (cursor.moveToNext());
        }

        cursor.close();
```

```
        }
}
```

3. To access ContactsContract content provider, we need *READ_CONTACTS* permission -

```xml
<?xml version="1.0" encoding="utf-8"?>
<manifest xmlns:android="http://schemas.android.com/apk/res/android"
    package="com.iducate.contentproviderdemo"
    android:versionCode="1"
    android:versionName="1.0" >

    <uses-sdk
        android:minSdkVersion="8"
        android:targetSdkVersion="19" />

    <uses-permission android:name="android.permission.READ_CONTACTS" />

    <application
        android:allowBackup="true"
        android:icon="@drawable/ic_launcher"
        android:label="@string/app_name"
        android:theme="@style/AppTheme" >
        <activity
         android:name="com.iducate.contentproviderdemo.MainActivity"
            android:label="@string/app_name" >
            <intent-filter>
                <action android:name="android.intent.action.MAIN" />

                <category android:name="android.intent.category.LAUNCHER" />
            </intent-filter>
        </activity>
    </application>

</manifest>
```

4. Now run the application and check your LogCat view. If you filter your LogCat view by the tag ContentProviderDemo , you will see all the contact name and associated phone numbers (figure 7.1) -

```
D 04-30 20:28:45.19 1552   1552  com.iducate.contentproviderdemo    ContentProviderDemo    Name: Andrew Perkin, Phone Number: 024-5631
D 04-30 20:28:45.22 1552   1552  com.iducate.contentproviderdemo    ContentProviderDemo    Name: Derek J., Phone Number: 025-632
D 04-30 20:28:45.22 1552   1552  com.iducate.contentproviderdemo    ContentProviderDemo    Name: Derek J., Phone Number: 033-452
D 04-30 20:28:45.25 1552   1552  com.iducate.contentproviderdemo    ContentProviderDemo    Name: Dan Wellman, Phone Number: 053-356
D 04-30 20:29:17.67 1586   1586  com.iducate.contentproviderdemo    ContentProviderDemo    Name: Andrew Perkin, Phone Number: 024-5631
```

Figure 7.1: LogCat view

How It Works?

First, we call getContentResolver() method, which returns a ContentResolver instance -

ContentResolver cr = getContentResolver();

Content resolver resolves an URI to a specific content provider.

Then, we call the query() method of content resolver instance, which returns a cursor object -

Cursor cursor = cr.query(ContactsContract.Contacts.*CONTENT_URI*,   **null**, **null, null, null**);

The query() method takes a number of arguments -

The first argument is the Uri of content provider. We use the CONTENT_URI constant to access the Uri object.

The second argument is the projection, which is a string array. This array should contain the name of the data columns we want to access. We could have defined a projection argument as follows -

```
String[] projection = new String[]     {
        ContactsContract.Contacts._ID,
        ContactsContract.Contacts.DISPLAY_NAME
};
```

If we passed this projection array as the second argument of the query() method, it would return only the _ID and *DISPLAY_NAME* columns. In our example project, we pass null as projection, so we will get all the columns.

The third argument is a string, which defines the selection condition. If we want to

339

filter some results, then we could do that by providing a selection string as follows -

> String selection = *ContactsContract.Contacts._ID* + " = ?";

Take a look at the selection string above. We have filtered by *_ID* column here but didn't provide a value for that column, instead we have used *?* . We will need to provide a corresponding value for that as fourth argument, in the form of selectionArgs array. However, if null is provided as selection string, it will return all results.

As mentioned in the above paragraph, the fourth argument of query() method is an array string which will provide the corresponding values for columns used in the selection argument -

> String[] selectionArgs = { contactID + "" };

Let's assume that the variable contactID holds the id of contact we want to retrieve. We will then construct an array of string with that contactID.

The final argument of query() method specifies the order of the results returned. If you want the result returned to be sorted in a particular order, provider the column name(s) as string in the form of fifth argument.

The next part is quite simple. As the query() method of content resolver object returns a cursor object, we can loop through the cursor in a similar way as we did in the previous chapter (for database query).

We loop through the cursor object and retrieve the column values of our interest, in this case *_ID* , *DISPLAY_NAME* and *HAS_PHONE_NUMBER* -

```
int contactID = cursor.getInt(cursor.getColumnIndex(
        ContactsContract.Contacts._ID));
int hasPhoneNumber = cursor.getInt(cursor.getColumnIndex(
        ContactsContract.Contacts.HAS_PHONE_NUMBER));
String contactName = cursor.getString(cursor.getColumnIndex(
        ContactsContract.Contacts.DISPLAY_NAME));
```

As mention in our previous discussion, the phone number isn't stored in the same table of the display name. Instead, it has a column *HAS_PHONE_NUMBER* which indicates if there is any phone number associated with this contact. If it has at least one phone number, we are interested in retrieving those numbers as well (there could be more than one number for each contact) -

```
if (hasPhoneNumber > 0) {
```

We need to make another query for retrieving phone numbers -

```
String[] projection = new String[]

{ ContactsContract.CommonDataKinds.Phone.NUMBER };
String selection =

ContactsContract.CommonDataKinds.Phone.CONTACT_ID + " = ?";
String[] selectionArgs = { contactID + "" };

Cursor phoneCursor = cr.query(
        ContactsContract.CommonDataKinds.Phone.CONTENT_URI,
                projection, selection, selectionArgs, null);
```

In this case, we are only interested in the phone number of the specified id. That's why we provide projection, selection and selectionArgs arguments to the second query() method.

We internally loop through the second cursor, retrieve phone number(s) and then output those numbers with the contact name as LogCat output -

```
do {

        String phoneNumber = phoneCursor.getString(
            phoneCursor.getColumnIndex(
                ContactsContract.CommonDataKinds.Phone.NUMBER));

        Log.d(TAG, "Name: " + contactName + ", Phone Number: " +
                                phoneNumber);
} while (phoneCursor.moveToNext());
```

If you are running this project in your emulator, make sure you add a few contacts in before you run the application.

Creating Your Own Content Providers

You can easily create your own content provider. To create your own content provider class, you need to extend the base ContentProvider class and override various methods.

In this section, we are going to create our own content provider which will store a list of student information. To store student data, our content provider needs a data source. We will use SQLite database as data source. The database will contain a single table with three fields -

- _id – student id
- name – student's name
- department – the department in which student is enrolled in

So, let's start to implement our content provider.

1. Create a new project MyContentProvider.

2. Add a new ContentProvider class named StudentsProvider.java, under the package name of src directory. Put the following code in that file -

```java
package com.iducate.mycontentprovider;

import android.content.ContentProvider;
import android.content.ContentUris;
import android.content.ContentValues;
import android.content.Context;
import android.content.UriMatcher;
import android.database.Cursor;
import android.database.SQLException;
import android.database.sqlite.SQLiteDatabase;
import android.database.sqlite.SQLiteOpenHelper;
import android.database.sqlite.SQLiteQueryBuilder;
import android.net.Uri;
import android.text.TextUtils;

public class StudentsProvider extends ContentProvider {

        private static final String PROVIDER_NAME =
```

```java
        "com.iducate.provider.Students";
        public static final Uri CONTENT_URI = Uri.parse("content://"
                                    + PROVIDER_NAME + "/students");

        public static final String _ID = "_id";
        public static final String NAME = "name";
        public static final String DEPARTMENT = "department";
        public static final int STUDENTS = 1;
        public static final int STUDENT_ID = 2;

        private static final UriMatcher uriMatcher;
        static {
                uriMatcher = new UriMatcher(UriMatcher.NO_MATCH);
                uriMatcher.addURI(PROVIDER_NAME, "students", STUDENTS);
                uriMatcher.addURI(PROVIDER_NAME, "students/#", STUDENT_ID);
        }

        @Override
        public boolean onCreate() {
                Context context = getContext();
                DBHelper dbHelper = new DBHelper(context);
                db = dbHelper.getWritableDatabase();
                return (db == null) ? false : true;
        }

        @Override
        public Cursor query(Uri uri, String[] projection, String selection, String[] selectionArgs,
String sortOrder) {
                SQLiteQueryBuilder queryBuilder = new SQLiteQueryBuilder();
                queryBuilder.setTables(TABLE_NAME);

                // if trying to retrieve a particular student, then add        // where clause
                if (uriMatcher.match(uri) == STUDENT_ID) {
                        queryBuilder.appendWhere(
                            _ID + " = " + uri.getPathSegments().get(1));
                }

                // when sortOrder isn't provider, set default sortOrder
                if (sortOrder == null || sortOrder == "") {
                        sortOrder = NAME;
                }

                Cursor cursor = queryBuilder.query(db, projection,
```

```
                    selection, selectionArgs, null, null, sortOrder);

        // register to notify a content URI for changes
        cursor.setNotificationUri(
                    getContext().getContentResolver(), uri);

        return cursor;
}




@Override
public Uri insert(Uri uri, ContentValues values) {
        long insertId = db.insert(TABLE_NAME, null, values);

        // when insert is successful
        if (insertId > 0) {
                Uri insertUri = ContentUris.withAppendedId(
                    CONTENT_URI, insertId);
                getContext().getContentResolver()
                        .notifyChange(insertUri, null);
                return insertUri;
        }

        throw new SQLException("Failed to insert new record");
}

@Override
public int update(Uri uri, ContentValues values, String                selection,
String[] selectionArgs) {

        int rowsUpdated = 0;

        switch (uriMatcher.match(uri)) {
        case STUDENTS:
                rowsUpdated = db.update(
                        TABLE_NAME, values, selection, selectionArgs);
                break;
        case STUDENT_ID:
                rowsUpdated = db.update(
                        TABLE_NAME, values, _ID + " = "
                        + uri.getPathSegments().get(1)
                        + (!TextUtils.isEmpty(selection) ? " AND ("
```

```java
                          + selection + ")" : ""), selectionArgs);
                break;
        default:
                throw new IllegalArgumentException(
                                "Unknow URI provide: " + uri);
        }

        getContext().getContentResolver().notifyChange(uri, null);
        return rowsUpdated;
    }

    @Override
    public int delete(Uri uri, String seletion, String[]                selectionArgs)
    {

        int rowsDeleted = 0;
        switch (uriMatcher.match(uri)) {
        case STUDENTS:
                rowsDeleted = db.delete(
                        TABLE_NAME, seletion, selectionArgs);
                break;
        case STUDENT_ID:
                rowsDeleted = db.delete(
                        TABLE_NAME, _ID + " = "
                        + uri.getPathSegments().get(1)
                        + (!TextUtils.isEmpty(seletion) ? " AND ("
                        + seletion + ")" : ""), selectionArgs);
                break;
        default:
                throw new IllegalArgumentException(
                                "Unknow URI provided: " + uri);
        }

        getContext().getContentResolver().notifyChange(uri, null);

        return rowsDeleted;
    }

    @Override
    public String getType(Uri uri) {
        switch (uriMatcher.match(uri)) {
        case STUDENTS:
                return "vnd.android.cursor.dir/vnd.iducate.students";
```

345

```java
        case STUDENT_ID:
                return "vnd.android.cursor.item/vnd.iducate/student";
        default:
                throw new IllegalArgumentException(
                        "Unsupprted URI provided: " + uri);
        }
}

// to help interact with database, we declare a helper class
private static final String DB_NAME = "students_db";
private static final String TABLE_NAME = "students";
private static final int DB_VERSION = 1;

private static final String CREATE_TABLE_SQL = "create table " +
TABLE_NAME + " ( " + _ID + " integer primary key
autoincrement, " + NAME + " text, " + DEPARTMENT + "                text);";

private SQLiteDatabase db;

private static class DBHelper extends SQLiteOpenHelper {
        public DBHelper(Context context) {
                super(context, DB_NAME, null, DB_VERSION);
        }

        @Override
        public void onCreate(SQLiteDatabase db) {
                db.execSQL(CREATE_TABLE_SQL);
        }

        @Override
        public void onUpgrade(SQLiteDatabase db, int oldVersion,
                int newVersion) {
                // database update logic goes here
                db.execSQL("DROP TABLE IF EXISTS " + TABLE_NAME);
                onCreate(db);
        }

        }

}
```

3. Like Activity classes, content providers are one of the main building blocks of Android. So we need to register them in the AndroidManifest.xml file -

```xml
<?xml version="1.0" encoding="utf-8"?>
<manifest xmlns:android="http://schemas.android.com/apk/res/android"
  package="com.iducate.mycontentprovider"
  android:versionCode="1"
  android:versionName="1.0" >

  <uses-sdk
    android:minSdkVersion="8"
    android:targetSdkVersion="19" />

  <application
    android:allowBackup="true"
    android:icon="@drawable/ic_launcher"
    android:label="@string/app_name"
    android:theme="@style/AppTheme" >
    <activity
      android:name="com.iducate.mycontentprovider.MainActivity"
      android:label="@string/app_name" >
      <intent-filter>
        <action android:name="android.intent.action.MAIN" />

        <category android:name="android.intent.category.LAUNCHER" />
      </intent-filter>
    </activity>

    <provider
      android:name="com.iducate.mycontentprovider.StudentsProvider"
      android:authorities="com.iducate.provider.Students" >
    </provider>
  </application>

</manifest>
```

How It Works?

We have created a new content provider class named StudentsProvider, which extends the base ContentProvider class. We have also overridden a number of methods -

- onCreate() - this method is called when the content provider is started
- getType() - this method returns the MIME type of the data at the given URI

347

- query() - when some client (user class) will request some data (either a single record or a set of records), this method will return a Cursor object as result
- insert() - adds a new record into the content provider
- update() - update an existing record of content provider
- delete() - this method will remove an existing record from content provider

As we have mentioned earlier in this chapter, we can use whatever data storage mechanism for example, SQLite database, file system or even network storage. We have used SQLite database for our StudentsProvider content provider.

We have started by defining some constant values in our StudentsProvider class -

```
private static final String PROVIDER_NAME = "com.iducate.provider.Students";
public static final Uri CONTENT_URI = Uri.parse("content://"
                                    + PROVIDER_NAME + "/students");


public static final String _ID = "_id";
public static final String NAME = "name";
public static final String DEPARTMENT = "department";
public static final int STUDENTS = 1;
public static final int STUDENT_ID = 2;
```

Notice the *CONTENT_URI* constant, which will return the base Uri of our content provider class. It is a good practice to provide a *CONTENT_URI* constant with the value of base Uri for the content provider.

We have also defined some other constant values, like database name, database version, table name and the field names of our database table. This will enable the client class (any class that uses our content provider class) to use constant names instead of hardcoded values.

Next, to help interact with our database, we have created a helper class, named DBHelper class which extends the SQLiteOpenHelper base class -

```
// to help interact with database, we declare a helper class
private static final String DB_NAME = "students_db";
private static final String TABLE_NAME = "students";
private static final int DB_VERSION = 1;

private static final String CREATE_TABLE_SQL = "create table " +
```

```
TABLE_NAME + " ( " + _ID + " integer primary key
autoincrement, " + NAME + " text, " + DEPARTMENT + "                     text);";

private SQLiteDatabase db;

private static class DBHelper extends SQLiteOpenHelper {
        public DBHelper(Context context) {
                super(context, DB_NAME, null, DB_VERSION);
        }

        @Override
        public void onCreate(SQLiteDatabase db) {
                db.execSQL(CREATE_TABLE_SQL);
        }

        @Override
        public void onUpgrade(SQLiteDatabase db, int oldVersion,
                int newVersion) {
                // database update logic goes here
                db.execSQL("DROP TABLE IF EXISTS " + TABLE_NAME);
                onCreate(db);
        }

}
```

In our previous chapter when we worked with SQLite database examples, we have used a similar DBHelper class. So the code should look familiar to you. We will create an instance of DBHelper class from within onCreate() method.

We have used an UriMatcher object to parse the content URI, which is passed to the content provider through ContentResolver. To initialize UriMatcher, we use static initializer -

```
private static final UriMatcher uriMatcher;
static {
        uriMatcher = new UriMatcher(UriMatcher.NO_MATCH);
        uriMatcher.addURI(PROVIDER_NAME, "students", STUDENTS);
        uriMatcher.addURI(PROVIDER_NAME, "students/#", STUDENT_ID);
}
```

By parsing the content URI, we will be able to identify whether a client has made request for a particular record or a set of records. For example -

content://com.iducate.provider.Students/students

requests all the student records, where -

content://com.iducate.provider.Students/students/2

requests a single student record with id 2.

Next, we override the getType() method, which returns the MIME type of the data of the given URI -

```
@Override
public String getType(Uri uri) {
        switch (uriMatcher.match(uri)) {
        case STUDENTS:
                return "vnd.android.cursor.dir/vnd.iducate.students";
        case STUDENT_ID:
                return "vnd.android.cursor.item/vnd.iducate/student";
        default:
                throw new IllegalArgumentException(
                        "Unsupprted URI provided: " + uri);
        }
}
```

We use UriMatcher object to detect whether a request is made for a set of records or a single record and then return the corresponding MIME type.

Next, we implement the onCreate() method of our StudentsProvider class -

```
@Override
public boolean onCreate() {
        Context context = getContext();
        DBHelper dbHelper = new DBHelper(context);
        db = dbHelper.getWritableDatabase();
        return (db == null) ? false : true;
}
```

Within the onCreate() method, we create a new instance of DBHelper class and open a connection to the database by calling the getWritableDatabase() method.

Next, we override the query() method which returns the result of our query as a Cursor object -

```java
@Override
public Cursor query(Uri uri, String[] projection, String selection, String[] selectionArgs,
String sortOrder) {
        SQLiteQueryBuilder queryBuilder = new SQLiteQueryBuilder();
        queryBuilder.setTables(TABLE_NAME);

        // if trying to retrieve a particular student, then add        // where clause
        if (uriMatcher.match(uri) == STUDENT_ID) {
            queryBuilder.appendWhere(
                _ID + " = " + uri.getPathSegments().get(1));
        }

        // when sortOrder isn't provider, set default sortOrder
        if (sortOrder == null || sortOrder == "") {
            sortOrder = NAME;
        }

        Cursor cursor = queryBuilder.query(db, projection,
                            selection, selectionArgs, null, null, sortOrder);

        // register to notify a content URI for changes
        cursor.setNotificationUri(
                    getContext().getContentResolver(), uri);

        return cursor;
    }
```

By matching the Uri passed to ContentResolver, we detect whether the request is made for a single record or a set of records. In case the request is made for retrieving a single student record, we add the where clause -

```java
        // if trying to retrieve a particular student, then add        // where clause
        if (uriMatcher.match(uri) == STUDENT_ID) {
            queryBuilder.appendWhere(
                _ID + " = " + uri.getPathSegments().get(1));
        }
```

We also check if any sorting criteria is set by the client. If not, we set a default value. We return the result as a Cursor object.

To add a new student record into our content provider, we have overridden the insert() method -

```
@Override
public Uri insert(Uri uri, ContentValues values) {
        long insertId = db.insert(TABLE_NAME, null, values);

        // when insert is successful
        if (insertId > 0) {
                Uri insertUri = ContentUris.withAppendedId(
                        CONTENT_URI, insertId);
                getContext().getContentResolver()
                        .notifyChange(insertUri, null);
                return insertUri;
        }

        throw new SQLException("Failed to insert new record");
}
```

The insert() method is fairly simple. We call the SQLiteDatabase object's insert() method to add a new record. Next, we call the notifyChange() method of ContentResolver class to notify registered observer classes about the newly entered student record.

To remove a student record, we override the delete() method -

```
@Override
public int delete(Uri uri, String seletion, String[]                    selectionArgs)
{

                int rowsDeleted = 0;
                switch (uriMatcher.match(uri)) {
                case STUDENTS:
                        rowsDeleted = db.delete(
                                TABLE_NAME, seletion, selectionArgs);
                        break;
                case STUDENT_ID:
                        rowsDeleted = db.delete(
                                TABLE_NAME, _ID + " = "
```

```
                        + uri.getPathSegments().get(1)
                        + (!TextUtils.isEmpty(seletion) ? " AND ("
                        + seletion + ")" : ""), selectionArgs);
                break;
        default:
                throw new IllegalArgumentException(
                                "Unknow URI provided: " + uri);
        }

        getContext().getContentResolver().notifyChange(uri, null);

        return rowsDeleted;
}
```

Similar to the insert operation, we need to notify the registered observer classes about the removal of the record. That's why we call the notifyChange() method of ContentResolver class. This delete() method returns the number of rows removed.

Finally, we override the update() method, which allows client classes to update a student record -

```
@Override
public int update(Uri uri, ContentValues values, String          selection,
String[] selectionArgs) {

        int rowsUpdated = 0;

        switch (uriMatcher.match(uri)) {
        case STUDENTS:
                rowsUpdated = db.update(
                        TABLE_NAME, values, selection, selectionArgs);
                break;
        case STUDENT_ID:
                rowsUpdated = db.update(
                        TABLE_NAME, values, _ID + " = "
                        + uri.getPathSegments().get(1)
                        + (!TextUtils.isEmpty(selection) ? " AND ("
                        + selection + ")" : ""), selectionArgs);
                break;
        default:
                throw new IllegalArgumentException(
                                "Unknow URI provide: " + uri);
```

```
        }

            getContext().getContentResolver().notifyChange(uri, null);
            return rowsUpdated;
    }
```

As with insert() and delete() methods, we also need to notify the observer classes about the update operation. So, we call the notifyChange() method of ContentResolver class after we complete the update operation.

To finish implementing our StudentsProvider class, we need to do one last task - register the content provider in AndroidManifest.xml file -

```
<provider

        android:name="com.iducate.mycontentprovider.StudentsProvider"
    android:authorities="com.iducate.provider.Students" >
</provider>
```

We need to provide at least two information – android:name and android:authorities. android:name is simply the content provider class name. We actually don't need to provide package name prefix (unless the content provider class is in another package). android:authorities is used to uniquely identify our content provider, thus we better use the reverse domain name convention as a prefix.

Using The Content Provider

Now that we have implemented our own content provider, let's use that content provider from within our application. We will use the same project from the previous section.

1. Update the layout file activity_main.xml with the following code -

```
<LinearLayout xmlns:android="http://schemas.android.com/apk/res/android"
    android:layout_width="fill_parent"
    android:layout_height="fill_parent"
    android:orientation="vertical" >

    <Button
        android:id="@+id/btnAdd"
        android:layout_width="match_parent"
```

```xml
        android:layout_height="wrap_content"
        android:onClick="addStudent"
        android:text="Add" />

    <Button
        android:id="@+id/btnShowAll"
        android:layout_width="match_parent"
        android:layout_height="wrap_content"
        android:onClick="showAll"
        android:text="Show All" />

    <Button
        android:id="@+id/btnUpdate"
        android:layout_width="match_parent"
        android:layout_height="wrap_content"
        android:onClick="updateStudent"
        android:text="Update" />

    <Button
        android:id="@+id/btnDelete"
        android:layout_width="match_parent"
        android:layout_height="wrap_content"
        android:onClick="deleteStudent"
        android:text="Delete" />

</LinearLayout>
```

2. Now, update the default activity class MainActivity.java with the following code
-

```java
package com.iducate.mycontentprovider;

import android.app.Activity;
import android.content.ContentResolver;
import android.content.ContentValues;
import android.database.Cursor;
import android.net.Uri;
import android.os.Bundle;
import android.view.View;
import android.widget.Toast;

public class MainActivity extends Activity {
```

```java
@Override
protected void onCreate(Bundle savedInstanceState) {
        super.onCreate(savedInstanceState);
        setContentView(R.layout.activity_main);
}

public void addStudent(View v) {
        ContentValues values = new ContentValues();
        values.put(StudentsProvider.NAME, "Adam Smith");
        values.put(StudentsProvider.DEPARTMENT, "EECS");

        ContentResolver cr = getContentResolver();

        Uri uri = cr.insert(StudentsProvider.CONTENT_URI, values);
        Toast.makeText(getBaseContext(), uri.toString(),
                        Toast.LENGTH_SHORT) .show();
}

public void updateStudent(View v) {
        ContentValues values = new ContentValues();
        values.put(StudentsProvider.DEPARTMENT, "CS");

        ContentResolver cr = getContentResolver();

        int numRows = cr.update(StudentsProvider.CONTENT_URI, values,
StudentsProvider._ID + " = ?", new String[] { "1" });

        Toast.makeText(getBaseContext(), "# of rows affected: " +
numRows, Toast.LENGTH_SHORT).show();
}

public void deleteStudent(View v) {
        ContentResolver cr = getContentResolver();
        int numRows = cr.delete(StudentsProvider.CONTENT_URI,
                        StudentsProvider._ID + " = ?", new String[] { "1" });

        Toast.makeText(getBaseContext(), "# of rows affected: " +
numRows, Toast.LENGTH_SHORT).show();
}

public void showAll(View v) {
        ContentResolver cr = getContentResolver();
        Cursor cursor = cr.query(StudentsProvider.CONTENT_URI,
```

356

```
                    null, null, null, null);

            if (cursor != null andand cursor.getCount() > 0) {
                    cursor.moveToFirst();

                    do {
                            String name = cursor.getString(
                                cursor.getColumnIndex(StudentsProvider.NAME));
                            String department = cursor.getString(cursor
                                .getColumnIndex(StudentsProvider.DEPARTMENT));

                            Toast.makeText(getBaseContext(),
                                        "Name: " + name + ", Dept: " +
                                                department,
Toast.LENGTH_SHORT).show();
                    } while (cursor.moveToNext());
            }

            cursor.close();
        }

}
```

3. Now run the application. You will see a screen with four buttons. We have added four buttons to perform four operations – insert, update, query and delete.

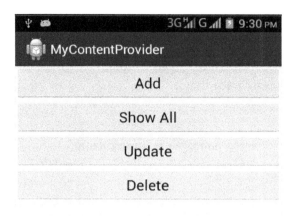

Figure 7.2: Using the content provider

4. Click the add button and a new student record will be added to the content provider. You will see a Toast message with the Uri of that record. The addStudent() method of MainActivity class handles the click of "Add" button -

```
public void addStudent(View v) {
        ContentValues values = new ContentValues();
        values.put(StudentsProvider.NAME, "Adam Smith");
        values.put(StudentsProvider.DEPARTMENT, "EECS");

        ContentResolver cr = getContentResolver();

        Uri uri = cr.insert(StudentsProvider.CONTENT_URI, values);

        Toast.makeText(getBaseContext(), uri.toString(),
                        Toast.LENGTH_SHORT) .show();
}
```

Within this addStudent() method, we have created a new ContentValues object and populated that with a student record. Next, we call the insert() method of ContentResolver instance to insert that record.

You will notice that we have used the *CONTENT_URI* constant to access the Uri of content provider and also used constants like *NAME* and *DEPARTMENT* to access the fields. This works because we are working within the same package. If we were using our content provider from other packages, then we will need to provide those values instead of constants -

```
public void addStudent(View v) {
        ContentValues values = new ContentValues();
        values.put("name", "Adam Smith");
        values.put("department", "EECS");

        ContentResolver cr = getContentResolver();

        Uri uri = cr.insert(
                "content://com.iducate.provider.Students/students",
values);

        Toast.makeText(getBaseContext(), uri.toString(),
                        Toast.LENGTH_SHORT) .show();
}
```

The above addStudent() method shows how you will likely use the field names and Uri from external packages. This holds true for other operations. So if you want to use the content provider from external packages, make necessary adjustment to the following methods as well.

The "Show All" button click is handled by showAll() method -

```
public void showAll(View v) {
        ContentResolver cr = getContentResolver();
        Cursor cursor = cr.query(StudentsProvider.CONTENT_URI,
                null, null, null, null);

        if (cursor != null andand cursor.getCount() > 0) {
                cursor.moveToFirst();

                do {
                        String name = cursor.getString(
```

```
                    cursor.getColumnIndex(StudentsProvider.NAME));
                    String department = cursor.getString(cursor
                    .getColumnIndex(StudentsProvider.DEPARTMENT));

                    Toast.makeText(getBaseContext(),
                            "Name: " + name + ", Dept: " +
                                    department,
Toast.LENGTH_SHORT).show();
                } while (cursor.moveToNext());
        }

        cursor.close();
    }
```

This code should look familiar to you because we have already seen how to access a built-in content provider in the previous section of the chapter. The process is exactly the same.

To update a record, we call the update() method of ContentResolver class which takes Uri, updated ContentValues, selection string and selectionArgs arguments -

```
public void updateStudent(View v) {
        ContentValues values = new ContentValues();
        values.put(StudentsProvider.DEPARTMENT, "CS");

        ContentResolver cr = getContentResolver();

        int numRows = cr.update(StudentsProvider.CONTENT_URI,          values,
StudentsProvider._ID + " = ?", new String[] { "1" });

        Toast.makeText(getBaseContext(), "# of rows affected: " +
        numRows, Toast.LENGTH_SHORT).show();
    }
```

Finally, this is how we delete a record from our content provider -

```
public void deleteStudent(View v) {
        ContentResolver cr = getContentResolver();
        int numRows = cr.delete(StudentsProvider.CONTENT_URI,
            StudentsProvider._ID + " = ?", new String[] { "1" });

        Toast.makeText(getBaseContext(), "# of rows affected: " +
```

```
numRows, Toast.LENGTH_SHORT).show();
}
```

We call the delete() method of ContentResolver instance with the Uri, selection string and selectionArgs arguments. However, if you want to delete all records, just pass null into the last two arguments.

Summary

In this chapter, we have learned about content providers which are Android's way of data sharing. We have started with some background information about content providers and then learned how to use built-in content providers. Finally, we implemented our own content provider class and also seen how to access that content provider programmatically.

Chapter 8: SMS and Email Messaging

In this chapter, we will learn how we can integrate messaging capabilities to our Android applications. Given proper permission, our application can intercept incoming SMS messages, as well as can send messages programatically. We will learn how to do both these operations in this chapter. We will also learn how we can invoke email application from our Android application to send email messages to other users.

SMS Messaging

SMS messaging is a popular form of communication among mobile phone users. A built-in messaging application is shipped with Android phones, which enables you to send and receive SMS messages. But as an Android application developer, you can also integrate messaging capabilities into your own application. Using broadcast receiver, you can intercept incoming messages. Also, you can send SMS messages programmatically from your Android application. These capabilities of intercepting and sending messages offer us the opportunity to develop a wide variety of interesting applications. For example, you can remotely control your home appliances by sending SMS commands to your Android phone (given proper interface between your phone and other devices exist), or you can build a location tracker application that sends location information by SMS message. (Obviously, sending SMS from your application will incur standard SMS charge applicable by your operator)

Using an Emulator for Testing SMS Messaging

The Android emulator provides you the facility to test SMS messages using an AVD. The emulator let's you simulate telephony actions like, sending SMS message or making voice call to your AVD. You will need to switch to DDMS perspective from Eclipse and then choose the tab "Emulator Control". You will see options to perform telephony actions there (figure 8.1) -

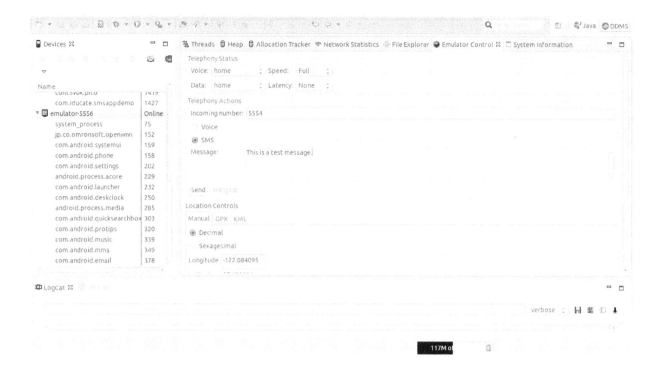

Figure 8.1: Using emulator control to send SMS

In order to send SMS to an AVD, first you need to select an AVD from the left panel (Devices panel). Then in the right panel, under the telephony actions, select SMS option. Your SMS message text should go into the text input area (beside the label "Message"). You will also notice a field named "Incoming number" (just below the Telephony Actions). You put a phone number there and this number will be appeared as sender number of this SMS. Now, if you click the "Send" button, the SMS message will be sent to the AVD selected at left panel. Your AVD should receive the SMS immediately and you can check the SMS by going to the messaging application (figure 8.2) -

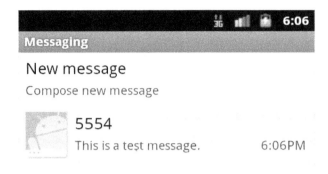

Figure 8.2: Messaging application of AVD

Receiving SMS Messages

You can intercept any incoming SMS message from your Android application. Using a BroadcastReceiver component, your application can get notified whenever an incoming SMS message arrives. By intercepting incoming messages, your application can perform certain actions. For example, you can build a location tracker application in which case, you will send a SMS to the phone with some secret code and by intercepting that SMS, your application can send that phone's current location coordinates back to the sender number.

In this section, we will see an example application project which can intercept incoming SMS messages.

1. Create a new project named SMSAppDemo.

2. Create new BroadcastReceiver class named SMSReceiver.java under the default

package of src/ directory with following code -

```java
package com.iducate.smsappdemo;

import android.content.BroadcastReceiver;
import android.content.Context;
import android.content.Intent;
import android.os.Bundle;
import android.telephony.SmsMessage;
import android.widget.Toast;

public class SMSReceiver extends BroadcastReceiver {

    @Override
    public void onReceive(Context context, Intent intent) {
        // get extras from Intent
        Bundle extras = intent.getExtras();
        SmsMessage[] messages = null;
        String senderNumber = "";
        String msgBody = "";

        if (extras != null) {

            // retrieve the SMS message chunks
            Object[] pdus = (Object[]) extras.get("pdus");
            messages = new SmsMessage[pdus.length];

            for (int i = 0; i < messages.length; i++) {
                messages[i] = SmsMessage.createFromPdu(
                                        (byte[]) pdus[i]);

                if (i == 0) {
                    // get the sender number
                    senderNumber =
messages[i].getOriginatingAddress();
                }

                // get message body
                msgBody += messages[i].getMessageBody();
            }

            Toast.makeText(
```

```
                    context, "SMS received from: "
                    + senderNumber + "\nSMS content: "
                    + msgBody, Toast.LENGTH_LONG).show();
            }
        }

}
```

3. We need to register the BroadcastReceiver class and also need to add a permission to receive SMS. Update your AndroidManifest.xml file with the following code -

```xml
<?xml version="1.0" encoding="utf-8"?>
<manifest xmlns:android="http://schemas.android.com/apk/res/android"
    package="com.iducate.smsappdemo"
    android:versionCode="1"
    android:versionName="1.0" >

    <uses-sdk
        android:minSdkVersion="8"
        android:targetSdkVersion="19" />

    <uses-permission android:name="android.permission.RECEIVE_SMS" />

    <application
        android:allowBackup="true"
        android:icon="@drawable/ic_launcher"
        android:label="@string/app_name"
        android:theme="@style/AppTheme" >
        <activity
            android:name="com.iducate.smsappdemo.MainActivity"
            android:label="@string/app_name" >
            <intent-filter>
                <action android:name="android.intent.action.MAIN" />

                <category android:name="android.intent.category.LAUNCHER" />
            </intent-filter>
        </activity>

        <receiver android:name="com.iducate.smsappdemo.SMSReceiver" >
            <intent-filter>
                <action
```

```
android:name="android.provider.Telephony.SMS_RECEIVED" />
        </intent-filter>
    </receiver>
  </application>

</manifest>
```

4. Run the application. You will see a screen with a hello world message which is our default activity screen. That is generated while we created our project. We don't need any user interface for this application. We will show the incoming message as a Toast notification. So just close the activity by pressing the back button.

5. Next, from the DDMS perspective of Eclipse, go to emulator control tab, select the running AVD and send a SMS message (review previous section if you need help regarding how to send SMS to AVD).

6. As soon as you send the SMS from emulator control, our SMSAppDemo application will intercept that message and you will see a Toast notification with that message's content and sender number (figure 8.3) -

Figure 8.3: SMS received from SMSAppDemo application

How It Works?

In order to intercept incoming SMS from our application, we need a BroadcastReceiver class. You can think of the broadcast receiver class as a component that listens for certain broadcast events. Android system or applications can send broadcast messages, like battery level is low, a new SMS received, phone is connected to WIFI network etc. Your application might be interested to listen for some of these broadcast events and do some actions in response to that event. You use BroadcastReceiver components to register for any of the broadcast events. If any application registers a broadcast receiver for an SMS receive event, when an incoming message arrives, the corresponding callback method of that broadcast receiver class will be fired.

In our demo application, we are interested in intercepting incoming SMS messages. So we create a new broadcast receiver class named SMSReceiver.java and register the SMS_RECEIVED event via AndroidManifest.xml file -

```xml
<receiver android:name="com.iducate.smsappdemo.SMSReceiver" >
  <intent-filter>
    <action

android:name="android.provider.Telephony.SMS_RECEIVED"/>
  </intent-filter>
</receiver>
```

Thus, whenever a new SMS message will be received, the SMSReceiver class's onReceive() method will be fired -

```java
public void onReceive(Context context, Intent intent) {
```

Two arguments are passed to the onReceive() method - a Context object and a Intent object that fired the broadcast receiver. This Intent object will have all the data associated with the SMS message. Each SMS message is stored as an array of PDU chunks (as separate messages of 160 characters), so we need to loop through that array to retrieve the full message -

```java
// retrieve the SMS message chunks
Object[] pdus = (Object[]) extras.get("pdus");
messages = new SmsMessage[pdus.length];

for (int i = 0; i < messages.length; i++) {
    messages[i] = SmsMessage.createFromPdu((byte[]) pdus[i]);

    if (i == 0) {
        // get the sender number
        senderNumber = messages[i].getOriginatingAddress();
    }

    // get message body
    msgBody += messages[i].getMessageBody();
}
```

You will notice that we get the message body of SMS by calling getMessageBody() method and get the sender phone number by calling getOriginatingAddress() method.

Receiving SMS message from our application is a security issue, so we need to declare a uses-permission in AndroidManifest.xml file -

```
<uses-permission android:name="android.permission.RECEIVE_SMS" />
```

To receive incoming SMS from our application, we don't need to leave our application running. Whenever any incoming SMS will arrive, our application will be automatically notified and the onReceive() method of our broadcast receiver class will be invoked.

Preventing a Messaging Application from Receiving SMS

In the previous section, we have seen how we can register a broadcast receiver component to receive incoming SMS messages. You might have noticed that when we send SMS from the emulator control to our AVD, our SMSAppDemo application received the SMS. But at the same time, the default messaging application of Android also received that SMS. This is the default behavior. Any application that is registered for the action android.provider.Telephony.SMS_RECEIVED will get notified whenever an incoming SMS is received. But what if your application requires that only your application should receive incoming SMS? (for example, if you are developing some sort of SMS filtering application that can block spam messages)

You can accomplish that pretty easily. In that case, your application will need to handle the incoming message before any other application. This can be done by adding the android:priority attribute to the <intent-filter> element -

```
    <receiver android:name="com.iducate.smsappdemo.SMSReceiver" >
    <intent-filter android:priority= "1000">
      <action

android:name="android.provider.Telephony.SMS_RECEIVED"/>
    </intent-filter>
    </receiver>
```

You need to set a higher priority so that your application can intercept the message before other applications. The higher the number, the earlier your application will intercept that message.

Now, to prevent other applications from being notified about this broadcast event, we need to call abortBroadcast() method from onReceive() method of our broadcast receiver class -

```
@Override
public void onReceive(Context context, Intent intent) {
    // stop the broadcast event
    abortBroadcast();

    // get extras from Intent
    Bundle extras = intent.getExtras();
    SmsMessage[] messages = null;
    String senderNumber = "";
    String msgBody = "";

    if (extras != null) {

        // retrieve the SMS message chunks
        Object[] pdus = (Object[]) extras.get("pdus");
        messages = new SmsMessage[pdus.length];

        for (int i = 0; i < messages.length; i++) {
            messages[i] = SmsMessage.createFromPdu(
                                    (byte[]) pdus[i]);

            if (i == 0) {
                // get the sender number
                senderNumber =

messages[i].getOriginatingAddress();
            }

            // get message body
            msgBody += messages[i].getMessageBody();
        }

        Toast.makeText(
            context, "SMS received from: "
            + senderNumber + "\nSMS content: "
            + msgBody, Toast.LENGTH_LONG).show();
    }
}
```

As soon as the SMS message will arrive, your application will intercept that message and stop the broadcast event, so no other application will be notified about that incoming SMS (even the default messaging application will not be able to receive any incoming SMS).

Sending SMS Messages Programmatically

We can send SMS messages from our application programmatically without any user intervention. Using this approach, let's extend our SMSAppDemo application, so that it can send an automatic reply to incoming SMS messages.

1. Update the SMSReceiver.java file with the highlighted code -

```
package com.iducate.smsappdemo;

import android.content.BroadcastReceiver;
import android.content.Context;
import android.content.Intent;
import android.os.Bundle;
import android.telephony.SmsManager;
import android.telephony.SmsMessage;
import android.widget.Toast;

public class SMSReceiver extends BroadcastReceiver {

    @Override
    public void onReceive(Context context, Intent intent) {
        // stop broadcast event
        abortBroadcast();

        // get extras from Intent
        Bundle extras = intent.getExtras();
        SmsMessage[] messages = null;
        String senderNumber = "";
        String msgBody = "";

        if (extras != null) {

            // retrieve the SMS message chunks
            Object[] pdus = (Object[]) extras.get("pdus");
            messages = new SmsMessage[pdus.length];
```

```
for (int i = 0; i < messages.length; i++) {
        messages[i] = SmsMessage.createFromPdu(
                        (byte[]) pdus[i]);

        if (i == 0) {
                // get the sender number
                senderNumber =

messages[i].getOriginatingAddress();
        }

        // get message body
        msgBody += messages[i].getMessageBody();
    }

    SmsManager smsManager = SmsManager.getDefault();
    smsManager.sendTextMessage(senderNumber, null,
            "This is an auto reply sms.", null, null);

    Toast.makeText(context, "SMS received from: "
            + senderNumber + "\nSMS content: "
            + msgBody, Toast.LENGTH_LONG).show();
        }
    }

}
```

2. To send SMS from our application, we need to add a new permission. Add the highlighted code to AndroidManifest.xml file -

```xml
<?xml version="1.0" encoding="utf-8"?>
<manifest xmlns:android="http://schemas.android.com/apk/res/android"
    package="com.iducate.smsappdemo"
    android:versionCode="1"
    android:versionName="1.0" >

    <uses-sdk
        android:minSdkVersion="8"
        android:targetSdkVersion="19" />

    <uses-permission android:name="android.permission.RECEIVE_SMS" />
```

373

```xml
<uses-permission android:name="android.permission.SEND_SMS" />

<application
    android:allowBackup="true"
    android:icon="@drawable/ic_launcher"
    android:label="@string/app_name"
    android:theme="@style/AppTheme" >
    <activity
        android:name="com.iducate.smsappdemo.MainActivity"
        android:label="@string/app_name" >
        <intent-filter>
            <action android:name="android.intent.action.MAIN" />

            <category android:name="android.intent.category.LAUNCHER" />
        </intent-filter>
    </activity>

    <receiver android:name="com.iducate.smsappdemo.SMSReceiver" >
        <intent-filter android:priority="1000" >
            <action
android:name="android.provider.Telephony.SMS_RECEIVED" />
        </intent-filter>
    </receiver>
</application>

</manifest>
```

3. Now, we will test this application using the emulator. Since our application will send and reply SMS, we need two AVDs. Run two AVDs. The first AVD will have id of 5554, while the second AVD will be assigned to id 5556. Using those numbers, you can send SMS from one AVD to another. We will install our SMSAppDemo application to second AVD (with id 5556). After you install the app to second AVD, send a SMS from first AVD with recipient phone number of 5556. You will see, a Toast message will appear in the second AVD which indicates that it received the SMS (figure 8.4). At the same time, a reply SMS is automatically sent to the first AVD (figure 8.5).

Figure 8.4: SMS received from 5554

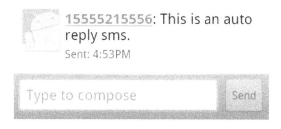

How It Works?

You will notice that our SMSReceiver broadcast receiver class just a couple of new lines of code -

```
SmsManager smsManager = SmsManager.getDefault();
smsManager.sendTextMessage(senderNumber, null,
                    "This is an auto reply sms.", null, null);
```

After we intercept the incoming message from the SMSReceiver class, we use SmsManager class's sendTextMessage() method to programmatically send a reply SMS to the sender's number. The sendTextMessage() method takes a number of arguments -

- destinationAddress – the phone number where the SMS will be sent
- scAddress – service center address, we pass null as scAdress
- smsBody – the message content
- sentIntent – a pending intent, which is invoked when message is sent
- deliveryIntent – a pending intent, which is invoked when the message is delivered

We get destinationAddress from the incoming SMS and using that number, we call the sendTextMessage() method to programmatically send a SMS message.

Sending SMS from your application requires a permission -

```
<uses-permission android:name="android.permission.SEND_SMS" />
```

This is how we can send SMS programmatically from our application.

Invoking Activity from BroadcastReceiver

In some cases, it might be useful to invoke an activity from BroadcastReceiver class. We can easily do that. Let's modify our previous example so that, whenever a new incoming SMS is received, the SMSReceiver class will automatically invoke our MainActivity class. We will also display message sender and message content to the activity.

1. Update SMSReceiver.java file with following highlighted code -

```java
package com.iducate.smsappdemo;

import android.content.BroadcastReceiver;
import android.content.Context;
import android.content.Intent;
import android.os.Bundle;
import android.telephony.SmsMessage;

public class SMSReceiver extends BroadcastReceiver {

    @Override
    public void onReceive(Context context, Intent intent) {
        // stop broadcast event
        abortBroadcast();

        // get extras from Intent
        Bundle extras = intent.getExtras();
        SmsMessage[] messages = null;
        String senderNumber = "";
        String msgBody = "";

        if (extras != null) {

            // retrieve the SMS message chunks
            Object[] pdus = (Object[]) extras.get("pdus");
            messages = new SmsMessage[pdus.length];

            for (int i = 0; i < messages.length; i++) {
                messages[i] = SmsMessage.createFromPdu(
                                            (byte[]) pdus[i]);

                if (i == 0) {
                    // get the sender number
                    senderNumber =

messages[i].getOriginatingAddress();
                }

                // get message body
                msgBody += messages[i].getMessageBody();
            }
```

```
                    Intent i = new Intent(context, MainActivity.class);
                    i.putExtra("senderNumber", senderNumber);
                    i.putExtra("smsBody", msgBody);
                    i.setFlags(Intent.FLAG_ACTIVITY_NEW_TASK);
                    context.startActivity(i);
            }
        }

}
```

2. Update the activity_main.xml layout file with the following code -

```
<LinearLayout xmlns:android="http://schemas.android.com/apk/res/android"
    android:layout_width="fill_parent"
    android:layout_height="fill_parent"
    android:orientation="vertical" >

    <TextView
        android:id="@+id/textView1"
        android:layout_width="wrap_content"
        android:layout_height="wrap_content" />

</LinearLayout>
```

3. Finally, put the following code to MainActivity.java file -

```
package com.iducate.smsappdemo;

import android.os.Bundle;
import android.widget.TextView;
import android.app.Activity;

public class MainActivity extends Activity {

    @Override
    protected void onCreate(Bundle savedInstanceState) {
        super.onCreate(savedInstanceState);
        setContentView(R.layout.activity_main);

        TextView textView = (TextView)
```

```
findViewById(R.id.textView1);

        Bundle extras = getIntent().getExtras();

        if (extras != null) {
                String senderNumber =

extras.getString("senderNumber");
                String smsBody = extras.getString("smsBody");

                textView.setText("SMS sender: " + senderNumber +
                        "\nMessage Body: " + smsBody);
        }
    }

}
```

4. Run the application and close the activity by pressing the back button. Now, from emulator control, send a message. You will notice that, the MainActivity is automatically invoked and the TextView is populated with message received (figure 8.6).

379

How It Works?

From the SMSReceiver class, after we intercept incoming SMS, we use an Intent object to start MainActivity class -

```
Intent i = new Intent(context, MainActivity.class);
i.putExtra("senderNumber", senderNumber);
i.putExtra("smsBody", msgBody);
i.setFlags(Intent.FLAG_ACTIVITY_NEW_TASK);
context.startActivity(i);
```

We pass the sender number and message body as extra values with the Intent object. To start activity, we call the startActivity() method of context object. We also need to set a flag FLAG_ACTIVITY_NEW_TASK .

Now, from MainActivity.java class's onCreate() method, we simply extract the extra values and set them to the TextView widget -

```
@Override
protected void onCreate(Bundle savedInstanceState) {
        super.onCreate(savedInstanceState);
        setContentView(R.layout.activity_main);

        TextView textView = (TextView)

findViewById(R.id.textView1);

        Bundle extras = getIntent().getExtras();

        if (extras != null) {
                String senderNumber =

extras.getString("senderNumber");
                String smsBody = extras.getString("smsBody");

                textView.setText("SMS sender: " + senderNumber +
                        "\nMessage Body: " + smsBody);
        }
}
```

Invoking a Messaging Application

We have previously seen how we can send SMS messages programmatically from our application. Sometimes however, it might be a good idea to simply invoke built-in messaging application and let the user send messages. This can be done by using an implicit intent.

```
Intent i = new Intent(android.content.Intent.ACTION_VIEW);
i.putExtra("address", "5556");
i.putExtra("sms_body", "Hi there! How are you?");
i.setType("vnd.android-dir/mms-sms");
startActivity(i);
```

You can see, we are creating a new Intent object with an action of ACTION_VIEW and also setting MIME type as vnd.android-dir/mms-sms. We then pass recipients number and message content as extra values, so that when the messaging application is invoked, these values will fill the corresponding fields (figure 8.7) -

Figure 8.7: Invoking messaging application

Caveats and Warnings

While messaging capabilities from our application gives the opportunity to make some cool applications, there are risks involved too. Any malicious application developer with bad intention can misuse this feature. By sending SMS messages from their application programmatically, they can send messages behind the scene without the user knowing. In the same way, they can also intercept incoming messages. By combining other capabilities with messaging, they can track a user's location, steal useful information or do other bad things.

Though a user is asked to explicitly give permission for these operations when they install the application, the truth is that most users aren't concerned about that. So it is a good idea to install applications from authentic sources only and also be aware of permissions requested by the application. Because once you approve the permissions when installing an app, it will never again ask for your permission.

Sending Email

Like SMS messaging, email communication is one of the most frequently used task of smart phone users. All Android phones come with an email application (even some devices are shipped with a separate Gmail application). In this section, we will see how we can invoke built-in email application from within our own application.

1. Create a new project named EmailsDemo.

2. Update the activity_main.xml layout file with the following code -

```xml
<LinearLayout xmlns:android="http://schemas.android.com/apk/res/android"
    android:layout_width="fill_parent"
    android:layout_height="fill_parent"
    android:orientation="vertical" >

    <Button
        android:id="@+id/btnSendEmail"
        android:layout_width="wrap_content"
        android:layout_height="wrap_content"
        android:onClick="sendEmail"
```

android:text="Send Email" />

</LinearLayout>

3. Update the MainActivity.java file with the following code -

```java
package com.iducate.emailsdemo;

import android.app.Activity;
import android.content.Intent;
import android.net.Uri;
import android.os.Bundle;
import android.view.View;

public class MainActivity extends Activity {

    @Override
    protected void onCreate(Bundle savedInstanceState) {
        super.onCreate(savedInstanceState);
        setContentView(R.layout.activity_main);
    }

    public void sendEmail(View v) {
        Intent intent = new Intent(Intent.ACTION_SEND);
        intent.setData(Uri.parse("mailto:"));
        intent.putExtra(Intent.EXTRA_EMAIL,
                        new String[]{"mail@example.com"});
        intent.putExtra(Intent.EXTRA_SUBJECT, "Test email");
        intent.putExtra(Intent.EXTRA_TEXT, "This is a test email");
        intent.setType("message/rfc822");
        startActivity(Intent.createChooser(intent, "Email"));
    }
}
```

4. Run the application and you will see a layout with a single button. Click that button widget. You will see the email application being invoked as shown in figure 8.8 -

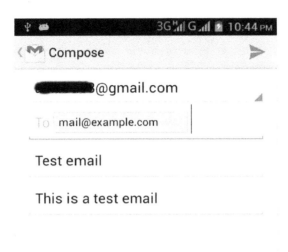

Figure 8.8: Invoking email application

If your device has more than one email application, you will see an application chooser dialog where you will need to pick one of the applications from the available application list.

How It Works?

Here, we have used implicit intent to invoke the built-in email application.

```
Intent intent = new Intent(Intent.ACTION_SEND);
intent.setData(Uri.parse("mailto:"));
intent.putExtra(Intent.EXTRA_EMAIL,
                        new String[]{"mail@example.com"});
intent.putExtra(Intent.EXTRA_SUBJECT, "Test email");
intent.putExtra(Intent.EXTRA_TEXT, "This is a test email");
intent.setType("message/rfc822");
startActivity(Intent.createChooser(intent, "Email"));
```

Using the setType() method of the Intent object, we set MIME type as `message/rfc822`, we also passed the recipient email address and other information as extra values.

Summary

In this chapter, we have discussed two key ways of communication from our application. By incorporating SMS message or email capabilities from our application, we can build useful and interesting real world applications.

Chapter 9: Location-Based Services

In this chapter, we will learn how to incorporate location-based services in our Android applications. In particular, we will learn how to make use of Google Maps in our application and also programmatically manipulate it. We will also learn about LocationManager class, which gives us the ability to obtain geographical location of users. We will finish this chapter by building a location tracker application that can track location of someone and send their current location as a SMS message.

Displaying Maps

Google Maps is one of the most popular services of Google, which let's you find everything from nearest restaurants to driving directions from one place to another. Android has had mapping capability from the very beginning, which over time improved. The current mapping solution (at this time of writing) provided by Google is known as Maps V2, we will learn how to use Maps V2 in our Android applications.

The previous mapping solution known as Maps V1, is no longer an option for new developers. Google no longer let's you create a Maps V1 API key.

Obtaining a Maps API Key

Before we can integrate maps to our application, we need to get a Google Maps API key. In order to get a free Google Maps API key, we need fingerprints of our application signing keys. The Maps V2 requires SHA1 hash of a certificate fingerprint.

First, we need to know the location of keystore which is used for signing our application. Though we haven't explicitly signed our application so far, behind the scene, Eclipse used a debug keystore to sign our applications. For now, we will get fingerprint for this debug keystore. The default location of this debug keystore depends on the operating system used-

- Windows OS: C:\Users\$USER\.android\debug.keystore
- OSX and Linux: ~/.android/debug.keystore

(where $USER indicates user name for Windows OS users).

You can also check location of your debug keystore from Eclipse –

Window → Preferences → Android → Build

and check for the field "Default debug keystore".

Chapter 12 will show how to use our own keystore for signing a application. We will also use that keystore to generate SHA1 hash of a production certificate fingerprint.

Once we have the location of debug keystore (or production keystore), we will use keytool command to dump information related to that keystore. Open your terminal (for Windows users, open Command Prompt) and run the following command -

keytool -list -v -keystore <keystore-location> -alias androiddebugkey -storepass android -keypass android

Replace the <keystore-location> with the actual location of your app signing keystore.

This will result in a similar output as figure 9.1 -

```
Alias name: androiddebugkey
Creation date: Feb 5, 2014
Entry type: PrivateKeyEntry
Certificate chain length: 1
Certificate[1]:
Owner: CN=Android Debug, O=Android, C=US
Issuer: CN=Android Debug, O=Android, C=US
Serial number: 413b0537
Valid from: Wed Feb 05 21:29:10 BDT 2014 until: Fri Jan 29 21:29:10 BDT 2044
Certificate fingerprints:
        MD5:   D5:FB:D1:C6:A0:93:A1:12:AD:AA:D4:40:BA:20:83:CB
        SHA1: 3D:DA:EF:32:3B:06:8A:17:4D:C4:05:A9:6F:49:EA:C2:0A:7E:E3:E6
        SHA256: 89:EC:5C:F6:9D:34:DA:1A:9E:1D:F8:D5:97:72:54:4F:F3:FB:81:4F:6A:DD
:0F:21:D6:7C:50:1E:52:C5:BF:F6
        Signature algorithm name: SHA256withRSA
        Version: 3

Extensions:

#1: ObjectId: 2.5.29.14 Criticality=false
SubjectKeyIdentifier [
```

Figure 9.1: Obtaining SHA1 hash for debug certificate fingerprint

Take note of the SHA1 fingerprint, we will need that while getting the Maps API key.

Now, let's see how we can obtain Maps API key. Follow the steps below -

* Login to Google Developers Console with your Google account -

    https://console.developers.google.com

* After you login, create a project via **CREATE PROJECT** option.

* Select the project you just created. From the left navigation menu, select **APIs and auth** option.

* From the available APIs, look for **Google Maps Android API v2**. Initially that API will be in OFF state. You will need to toggle that to ON. Attempting to toggle that to ON will launch the Terms of Services. Agree to that Terms of Services to enable the Maps API.

* Next, from the left navigation menu, under **APIs and auth**, select **Credentials** option.

- Under the **Public API access**, you will see an option named **CREATE NEW KEY**. Once you click **CREATE NEW KEY**, it will present you few other options. Select **Android key**.

- Once you select **Android key** option, you will be presented with a screen which has an input area for entering SHA1 fingerprint of your developer certificate and Android application package name. Fill in your SHA1 fingerprint, a semicolon and the package name of the app. With the SHA1 fingerprint obtained for our debug keystore and with application package name of com.iducate.mapsexample, it will look as follows -

3D:DA:EF:32:3B:06:8A:17:4D:C4:05:A9:6F:49:EA:C2:0A:7E:E3:E6;
com.iducate.mapsexample

(note: put the above in a single line)

- Finally, click the **Create** button to generate API key. Take note of that API key, we will use that in our application.

The Google Play Services Library

In order to use Maps V2 in our application, we also need to setup the Google Play Services library.

First, you will need to download the **Google Play Services** package from your SDK manager. Open the SDK manager by clicking **Window → Android SDK Manager** and under the Extras, you will find Google Play Services package (figure 9.2) -

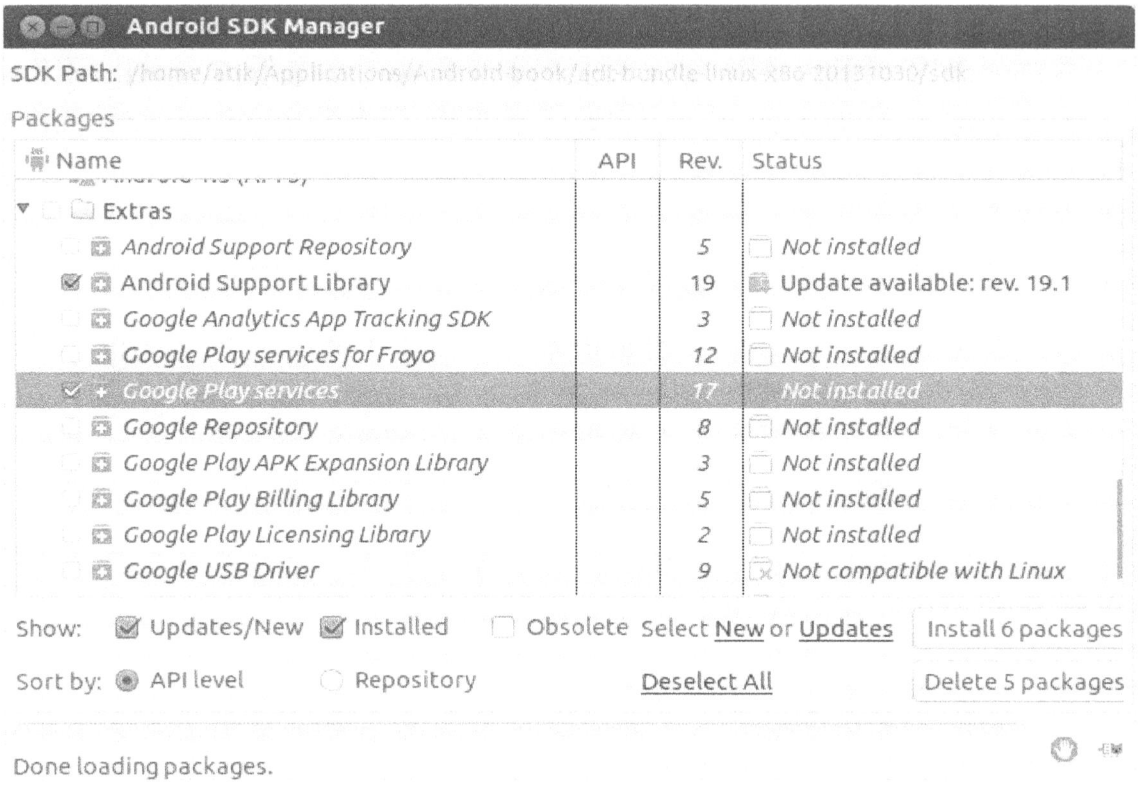

Name	API	Rev.	Status
▼ ☐ Extras			
☐ Android Support Repository		5	Not installed
☑ Android Support Library		19	Update available: rev. 19.1
☐ Google Analytics App Tracking SDK		3	Not installed
☐ Google Play services for Froyo		12	Not installed
☑ Google Play services		17	Not installed
☐ Google Repository		8	Not installed
☐ Google Play APK Expansion Library		3	Not installed
☐ Google Play Billing Library		5	Not installed
☐ Google Play Licensing Library		2	Not installed
☐ Google USB Driver		9	Not compatible with Linux

Show: ☑ Updates/New ☑ Installed ☐ Obsolete Select New or Updates Install 6 packages

Sort by: ◉ API level ○ Repository   Deselect All   Delete 5 packages

Done loading packages.

Figure 9.2: Downloading Google Play Services

Install the package and from within Eclipse, add the Play Services library project to your current workspace. You can do that by selecting **File → Import → General → Existing Project into Workspace** and then browsing the location where Play Services is installed. The Play Services will be installed under the directory extras/google/google_play_services/libproject/google-play-services_lib/ under the root directory of your Android SDK installation.

After you import the Play Services library project to your workspace, when you will create a project that uses Maps V2, you will need to add a reference to that library project. We will see how to do that when we create a sample project in the next section.

Using a Basic Map

In this section, we will create a new project and see how we can add a simple map to our activity powered by Maps V2 API.

1. Create a new project named MapsExample.

2. As I have mentioned in the previous section, you will need to add a reference to the Google Play Services library project. From the package explorer window of Eclipse, select the MapsExample project and right click. Then select **Properties → Android** and you will see a screen similar to figure 9.3 -

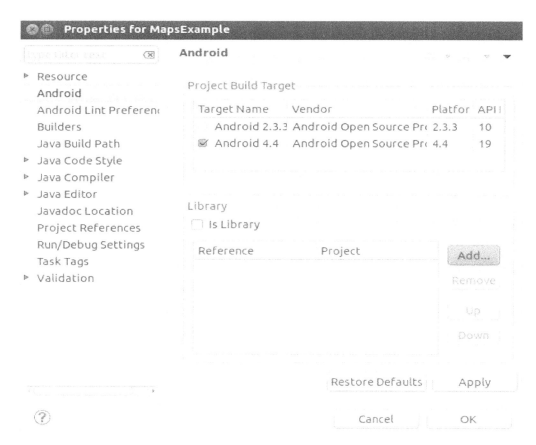

Figure 9.3: Adding reference to play services library

Click "Add..." button under the Library section and from the available libraries, select the Google Play Services library.

3. Now, update the activity_main.xml layout file with the following code -

```
<LinearLayout xmlns:android="http://schemas.android.com/apk/res/android"
    android:layout_width="fill_parent"
    android:layout_height="fill_parent"
    android:orientation="vertical" >

    <fragment
```

```
    android:id="@+id/map"
    android:name="com.google.android.gms.maps.MapFragment"
    android:layout_width="match_parent"
    android:layout_height="wrap_content" />
```

```
</LinearLayout>
```

4. You do not need to do anything with MainActivity.java file right now, but you need to update the AndroidManifest.xml file as follows -

```xml
<?xml version="1.0" encoding="utf-8"?>
<manifest xmlns:android="http://schemas.android.com/apk/res/android"
    package="com.iducate.mapsexample"
    android:versionCode="1"
    android:versionName="1.0" >

    <uses-sdk
        android:minSdkVersion="11"
        android:targetSdkVersion="19" />

    <uses-permission android:name="android.permission.INTERNET" />
    <uses-permission
android:name="android.permission.ACCESS_NETWORK_STATE" />
    <uses-permission
android:name="android.permission.WRITE_EXTERNAL_STORAGE" />

    <application
        android:allowBackup="true"
        android:icon="@drawable/ic_launcher"
        android:label="@string/app_name"
        android:theme="@style/AppTheme" >
        <activity
            android:name="com.iducate.mapsexample.MainActivity"
            android:label="@string/app_name" >
            <intent-filter>
                <action android:name="android.intent.action.MAIN" />

                <category android:name="android.intent.category.LAUNCHER" />
            </intent-filter>
        </activity>

        <meta-data
```

```
            android:name="com.google.android.maps.v2.API_KEY"
            android:value="AIzaSyD0eACumk7EK0-5D90EbWIDb5LfDz1JngY" /
>

        <meta-data
            android:name="com.google.android.gms.version"
            android:value="@integer/google_play_services_version" />
    </application>

</manifest>
```

5. Run the application and you will see a screen with a map (figure 9.4) -

Figure 9.4: Running MapsExample application

How It Works?

Since we are going to use Maps V2 API, we have made a reference to the Google Play Services library from our application.

The activity_main.xml layout file has a single `<fragment>` element, which points to a fragment class com.google.android.gms.maps.MapFragment which is part of the Google Play Services library. This fragment class knows how to display a map using Maps V2 API.

```
<fragment
android:id="@+id/map"
android:name="com.google.android.gms.maps.MapFragment"
android:layout_width="match_parent"
android:layout_height="wrap_content" />
```

In the AndroidManifest.xml file, we have added two <meta-data> elements under the <application> element -

```
<meta-data
android:name="com.google.android.maps.v2.API_KEY"
android:value="AIzaSyD0eACumk7EK0-5D90EbWlDb5LfDz1JngY" />
<meta-data
android:name="com.google.android.gms.version"
android:value="@integer/google_play_services_version" />
```

The first <meta-data> element com.google.android.maps.v2.API_KEY value is the API key that we obtained from Google APIs console. The second <meta-data> element com.google.android.maps.v2.API_KEY value is the version of play services library we are using.

Finally, we also need to add few <uses-permission> in our AndroidManifest.xml file -

```
<uses-permission android:name="android.permission.INTERNET" />
<uses-permission

android:name="android.permission.ACCESS_NETWORK_STATE" />
<uses-permission

android:name="android.permission.WRITE_EXTERNAL_STORAGE" />
```

Navigating to a Specific Location

In this section, we will update our sample project to demonstrate how we can show the map of a specific location and also add a marker to that location.

1. Update the MainActivity.java file with the following code -

```java
package com.iducate.mapsexample;

import android.app.Activity;
import android.os.Bundle;

import com.google.android.gms.maps.CameraUpdateFactory;
import com.google.android.gms.maps.GoogleMap;
import com.google.android.gms.maps.MapFragment;
import com.google.android.gms.maps.model.LatLng;
import com.google.android.gms.maps.model.MarkerOptions;

public class MainActivity extends Activity {

    private GoogleMap map;
    private static final LatLng LONDON =
                        new LatLng(+51.50000, -0.11670);

    @Override
    protected void onCreate(Bundle savedInstanceState) {
        super.onCreate(savedInstanceState);
        setContentView(R.layout.activity_main);

        map = ((MapFragment) getFragmentManager()
                .findFragmentById(R.id.map))
                .getMap();

        map.moveCamera(CameraUpdateFactory
                            .newLatLngZoom(LONDON, 15));
        map.addMarker(new MarkerOptions().position(LONDON));
    }

}
```

2. Run the application, you will see a screen similar to figure 9.5 -

395

Figure 9.5: Showing map of specific location

How It Works?

In order to work with our map programmatically, we first need to get a reference of it from our activity class -

```
map = ((MapFragment) getFragmentManager()
            .findFragmentById(R.id.map)).getMap();
```

Here, we first get reference of our fragment and then call the getMap() method to get reference of our Map instance.

Now, we want to show the map of London. Using the longitude and latitude information, we construct a LatLng object -

```
        private static final LatLng LONDON =
                                    new LatLng(+51.50000, –0.11670);
```

Next, to show the map of that particular location, we call the moveCamera() method of map instance -

```
    map.moveCamera(CameraUpdateFactory.newLatLngZoom(LONDON, 15));
```

The moveCamera() method expects a CameraUpdate object instance. We call the newLatLngZoom() static method of CameraUpdateFactory class with the LatLng object instance and zoom level as argument which returns a CameraUpdate object. That CameraUpdate object is passed as an argument to the moveCamera() method which simply shows the map of the specified location with the specified zoom level.

Finally, we want to add a marker to our specified location -

```
    map.addMarker(new MarkerOptions().position(LONDON));
```

the addMarker() method of the map instance is used to add marker to a specified location.

Showing a Satellite View

We can easily show a satellite view of our map by specifying the map type -

```
package com.iducate.mapsexample;

import android.app.Activity;
import android.os.Bundle;

import com.google.android.gms.maps.CameraUpdateFactory;
import com.google.android.gms.maps.GoogleMap;
import com.google.android.gms.maps.MapFragment;
import com.google.android.gms.maps.model.LatLng;
import com.google.android.gms.maps.model.MarkerOptions;

public class MainActivity extends Activity {

    private GoogleMap map;
    private static final LatLng LONDON =
                        new LatLng(+51.50000, –0.11670);
```

```java
@Override
protected void onCreate(Bundle savedInstanceState) {
        super.onCreate(savedInstanceState);
        setContentView(R.layout.activity_main);

        map = ((MapFragment) getFragmentManager()
                    .findFragmentById(R.id.map))
                    .getMap();

        map.moveCamera(CameraUpdateFactory
                                .newLatLngZoom(LONDON, 15));
        map.addMarker(new MarkerOptions().position(LONDON));

        map.setMapType(GoogleMap.MAP_TYPE_SATELLITE);

    }

}
```

The highlighted line calls the setMapType() method of map instance and pass the map type as GoogleMap.MAP_TYPE_SATELLITE, which sets the satellite view of the map (figure 9.6) -

Figure 9.6: Satellite view of map

Getting a Touched Location

We can touch any location on the map and get longitude and latitude of that location. This longitude and latitude information can be useful to get the address of that location. The highlighted lines show the code needed in order to handle touch events on a map -

```java
package com.iducate.mapsexample;

import android.app.Activity;
import android.os.Bundle;
import android.widget.Toast;

import com.google.android.gms.maps.CameraUpdateFactory;
```

```java
import com.google.android.gms.maps.GoogleMap;
import com.google.android.gms.maps.GoogleMap.OnMapClickListener;
import com.google.android.gms.maps.MapFragment;
import com.google.android.gms.maps.model.LatLng;
import com.google.android.gms.maps.model.MarkerOptions;

public class MainActivity extends Activity {

    private GoogleMap map;
    private static final LatLng LONDON =
                        new LatLng(+51.50000, -0.11670);

    @Override
    protected void onCreate(Bundle savedInstanceState) {
        super.onCreate(savedInstanceState);
        setContentView(R.layout.activity_main);

        map = ((MapFragment) getFragmentManager()
                    .findFragmentById(R.id.map))
                    .getMap();

        map.moveCamera(CameraUpdateFactory
                        .newLatLngZoom(LONDON, 15));
        map.addMarker(new MarkerOptions().position(LONDON));

        map.setOnMapClickListener(new OnMapClickListener() {

            @Override
            public void onMapClick(LatLng point) {
                Toast.makeText(MainActivity.this, "Location: " +
                    point, Toast.LENGTH_LONG).show();
            }
        });
    }
}
```

As you can see, we have set an OnMapClickListener to our map instance by calling setOnMapClickListener() method. Because SetOnMapClickListener() expects a listener to handle touch on map, we pass an anonymous inner class as listener. So whenever user touch the map, the corresponding callback method onMapClick() will be called -

```
@Override
public void onMapClick(LatLng point) {
        Toast.makeText(MainActivity.this, "Location: " +
                        point, Toast.LENGTH_LONG).show();
}
```

The onMapClick() method has a LatLng object as argument, which is the position of touched location. In our case, we simply show that location as a Toast message (figure 9.7) -

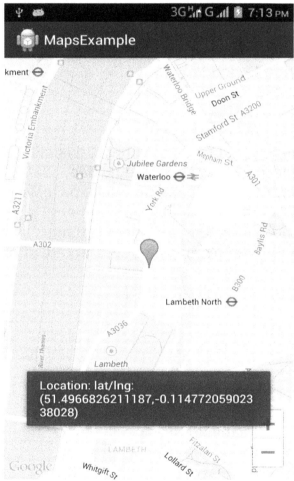

Figure 9.7: Getting touched location

Geocoding and Reverse Geocoding

Suppose you know the longitude and latitude of a location, you now want to find the address of that location. This can be done using the Geocoder class. This process of finding location address for longitude and latitude is known as reverse geocoding. Let's see how we can update our ongoing example and get the address

401

of the location that is touched on the map.

Update MainActivity.java file with the highlighted code -

```java
package com.iducate.mapsexample;

import java.io.IOException;
import java.util.List;
import java.util.Locale;

import android.app.Activity;
import android.location.Address;
import android.location.Geocoder;
import android.os.Bundle;
import android.widget.Toast;

import com.google.android.gms.maps.CameraUpdateFactory;
import com.google.android.gms.maps.GoogleMap;
import com.google.android.gms.maps.GoogleMap.OnMapClickListener;
import com.google.android.gms.maps.MapFragment;
import com.google.android.gms.maps.model.LatLng;
import com.google.android.gms.maps.model.MarkerOptions;

public class MainActivity extends Activity {

    private GoogleMap map;
    private static final LatLng LONDON = new LatLng(+51.50000,
-0.11670);

    @Override
    protected void onCreate(Bundle savedInstanceState) {
        super.onCreate(savedInstanceState);
        setContentView(R.layout.activity_main);

        map = ((MapFragment) getFragmentManager()
                        .findFragmentById(R.id.map)).getMap();

        map.moveCamera(CameraUpdateFactory
                            .newLatLngZoom(LONDON, 15));
        map.addMarker(new MarkerOptions().position(LONDON));
        map.setOnMapClickListener(new OnMapClickListener() {
```

```java
@Override
public void onMapClick(LatLng point) {
    /*
    Toast.makeText(MainActivity.this, "Location: " + point,
            Toast.LENGTH_LONG).show();
    */

    Geocoder geocoder = new
Geocoder(getBaseContext(), Locale.getDefault());
    try {
        List<Address> addresses =
geocoder.getFromLocation(point.latitude, point.longitude, 1);

        String addStr = "";
        if(addresses.size() > 0) {
            for (int i = 0; i <
addresses.get(0).getMaxAddressLineIndex(); i++) {
                addStr +=
addresses.get(0).getAddressLine(i) + "\n";
            }
        }
        Toast.makeText(getBaseContext(), addStr,
                Toast.LENGTH_LONG).show();
    } catch (IOException e) {
        e.printStackTrace();
    }
    }
});
    }

}
```

Here, we have used Geocoder object's getFromLocation() method to get address from the longitude and latitude information. The longitude and latitude is obtained from the LatLng object instance which is passed to the onMapClick() callback method as an argument. Once we obtain the address, we show that as a Toast message. Figure 9.8 shows an example of getting address of a touched location -

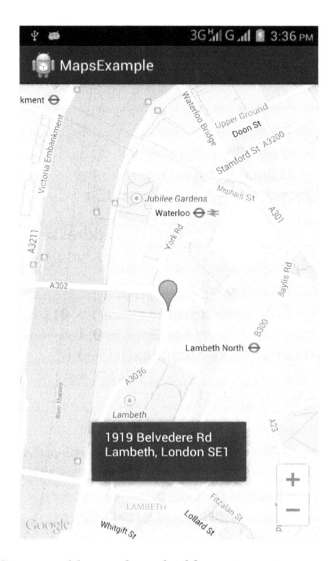

Figure 9.8: Getting address of touched location using reverse geocoding

Now, let's see how we can get the longitude and latitude of a location from it's address. This process is known as geocoding.

Again, we use Geocoder object and this time, we call getFromLocationName() method to get the location of the Taj Mahal Building (figure 9.9) -

```
@Override
protected void onCreate(Bundle savedInstanceState) {
        super.onCreate(savedInstanceState);
        setContentView(R.layout.activity_main);

        map = ((MapFragment) getFragmentManager()
                .findFragmentById(R.id.map)).getMap();
```

```java
        Geocoder geocoder = new Geocoder(this,
Locale.getDefault());
            try {
                List<Address> addrs = geocoder
                        .getFromLocationName("taj mahal", 5);

                if(addrs.size() > 0) {
                    LatLng tajmahal = new
LatLng(addrs.get(0).getLatitude(), addrs.get(0).getLongitude());

        map.moveCamera(CameraUpdateFactory.newLatLngZoom(tajmahal,
15));
                    map.addMarker(new
MarkerOptions().position(tajmahal));
                }
            } catch (IOException e1) {
                e1.printStackTrace();
            }
        }
```

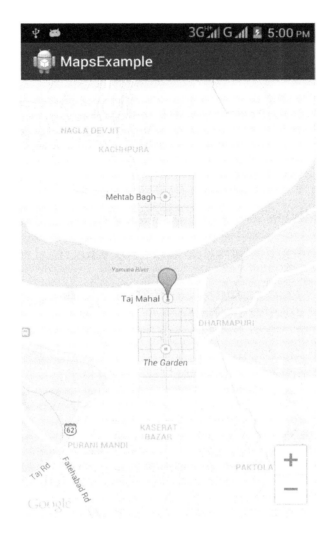

Figure 9.9: Using geocoding

Getting Location Data

Almost all Android mobile devices have a built-in GPS receiver which can be used to find the device's current location. Using the GPS receiver, it is possible to get high accuracy location data. GPS receiver work best when the user is located outdoor and the sky is clear. But it doesn't work well indoors or in locations where satellites can't penetrate.

In addition to the GPS receiver, there exist other location-sensing techniques, such as cell tower triangulation and Wi-Fi triangulation. Cell tower triangulation works by locating the identity of cell towers. It has a bit less accuracy than GPS receiver, but is works wherever a cellphone network is available. Wi-Fi triangulation has the least accuracy among all three.

The LocationManager class let's us use the above mentioned location-sensing techniques to determine the current location of a user. We will see how this works by updating our ongoing example project.

1. Update the MainActivity.java file with the highlighted code as shown below -

```java
package com.iducate.mapsexample;

import android.app.Activity;
import android.content.Context;
import android.location.Location;
import android.location.LocationListener;
import android.location.LocationManager;
import android.os.Bundle;
import android.widget.Toast;


import com.google.android.gms.maps.CameraUpdateFactory;
import com.google.android.gms.maps.GoogleMap;
import com.google.android.gms.maps.MapFragment;
import com.google.android.gms.maps.model.LatLng;
import com.google.android.gms.maps.model.MarkerOptions;

public class MainActivity extends Activity {

        private GoogleMap map;
        private static final LatLng LONDON =
                        new LatLng(+51.50000, -0.11670);

        private LocationManager lm;
        private LocationListener locationListener;

        @Override
        protected void onCreate(Bundle savedInstanceState) {
                super.onCreate(savedInstanceState);
                setContentView(R.layout.activity_main);

                map = ((MapFragment) getFragmentManager()
                        .findFragmentById(R.id.map))
                        .getMap();

                map.moveCamera(CameraUpdateFactory
                        .newLatLngZoom(LONDON, 15));
```

```java
        map.addMarker(new MarkerOptions().position(LONDON));

        lm = (LocationManager)

getSystemService(Context.LOCATION_SERVICE);
        locationListener = new MyLocationListener();
    }

    @Override
    protected void onResume() {
        super.onResume();

        lm.requestLocationUpdates(LocationManager.GPS_PROVIDER, 0,
                    0, locationListener);
    }

    @Override
    protected void onPause() {
        super.onPause();

        lm.removeUpdates(locationListener);
    }

    private class MyLocationListener implements LocationListener {

        @Override
        public void onLocationChanged(Location location) {
            if (location != null) {
                Toast.makeText(getBaseContext(),
                "Location changed: " + location.toString(),
                    Toast.LENGTH_LONG).show();

                LatLng latLng = new

LatLng(location.getLatitude(),
                            location.getLongitude());
                map.animateCamera(CameraUpdateFactory
                    .newLatLngZoom(latLng, 15));

                map.addMarker(new MarkerOptions()
                    .position(latLng));
            }
        }
```

```
        @Override
        public void onProviderDisabled(String provider) {

        }

        @Override
        public void onProviderEnabled(String provider) {
            // TODO Auto-generated method stub

        }

        @Override
        public void onStatusChanged(String provider, int status,
        Bundle extras) {
            // TODO Auto-generated method stub

        }

    }

}
```

2. Add a new uses-permission to the AndroidManifest.xml file -

```xml
<?xml version="1.0" encoding="utf-8"?>
<manifest xmlns:android="http://schemas.android.com/apk/res/android"
    package="com.iducate.mapsexample"
    android:versionCode="1"
    android:versionName="1.0" >

    <uses-sdk
        android:minSdkVersion="11"
        android:targetSdkVersion="19" />

    <uses-permission android:name="android.permission.INTERNET" />
    <uses-permission
android:name="android.permission.ACCESS_NETWORK_STATE" />
    <uses-permission
android:name="android.permission.WRITE_EXTERNAL_STORAGE" />
    <uses-permission
android:name="android.permission.ACCESS_FINE_LOCATION" />
```

```xml
<application
   android:allowBackup="true"
   android:icon="@drawable/ic_launcher"
   android:label="@string/app_name"
   android:theme="@style/AppTheme" >
   <activity
      android:name="com.iducate.mapsexample.MainActivity"
      android:label="@string/app_name" >
      <intent-filter>
         <action android:name="android.intent.action.MAIN" />

         <category android:name="android.intent.category.LAUNCHER" />
      </intent-filter>
   </activity>

   <meta-data
      android:name="com.google.android.maps.v2.API_KEY"
      android:value="AIzaSyD0eACumk7EK0-5D90EbWlDb5LfDz1JngY" />
   <meta-data
      android:name="com.google.android.gms.version"
      android:value="@integer/google_play_services_version" />
</application>

</manifest>
```

3. If you want to run this application on a AVD, you can use Emulator Control option to send mock location to AVD. To do this, first run the application to the AVD. Then, select DDMS perspective of Eclipse and choose "Emulator Control" option. From the left panel (Devices panel), make sure you select the AVD which is running the application and then under the Location Controls, you will find option to manually send Longitude and Latitude information (figure 9.10). You can either send a single location manually or use GPX or KML file to send a sequence of location.

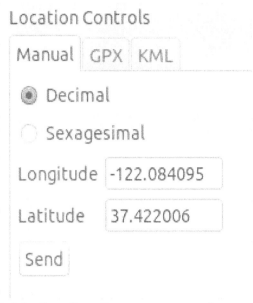

Figure 9.10: Sending Location coordinates to AVD

4. As you send a new location, you will see that the Map location is updated with new location and a Toast message is shown with current location information (figure 9.11) -

Figure 9.11: Running MapsExample application

How It Works?

The LocationManager class is used to provide location-based services like providing current location information, as well as firing an intent when the current location is changed.

We first get a reference of LocationManager class within the onCreate() method -

```
lm = (LocationManager)

getSystemService(Context.LOCATION_SERVICE);
```

We call the getSystemService() method and pass the **Context**.LOCATION_SERVICE as argument.

Within our MainActivity.java file, we have defined an private inner class named

412

MyLocationListener which implements the LocationListener abstract class.

```
private class MyLocationListener implements LocationListener {
```

We need to override four methods in our implementation of MyLocationListener class -

- onLocationChanged(Location location) – this method is called when the current location is changed.
- onProviderDisabled(String provider) – which is called when the particular provider is disabled by the user.
- onProviderEnabled(String provider) – this method is called when the provider is enabled by the user.
- onStatusChanged(String provider, int status, Bundle extras) – called when the provider status changes.

We are interested in the location change event, so we implement the onLocationChanged() method -

```
@Override
public void onLocationChanged(Location location) {
    if (location != null) {
        Toast.makeText(getBaseContext(),
        "Location changed: " + location.toString(),
            Toast.LENGTH_LONG).show();

        LatLng latLng = new LatLng(location.getLatitude(),

        location.getLongitude());
        map.animateCamera(CameraUpdateFactory
            .newLatLngZoom(latLng, 15));

        map.addMarker(new MarkerOptions()
            .position(latLng));
    }
}
```

The updated Location is passed to the onLocationChanged() method as an argument. Using this new Location instance, we navigate the map to that location and also show that location information as a Toast message.

Now, within the onCreate() method of our MainActivity class, we create an instance of the MyLocationListener class -

```
locationListener = new MyLocationListener();
```

We want to get notified when there is a change in location. So we register a request for a location update in onResume() method -

```
@Override
protected void onResume() {
        super.onResume();

        lm.requestLocationUpdates(LocationManager.GPS_PROVIDER, 0,
                                0, locationListener);
}
```

We call the requestLocationUpdates() method of LocationManager instance to register a request for location update. The requestLocationUpdates() method takes the following four arguments -

- provider – The name of the provider that we register. We have used GPS provider here, but we could also use network provider or Wi-Fi provider as well.
- minTime – the minimum time interval for notification in milliseconds.
- minDistance – the minimum distance interval for notifications in meters.
- listener – an object whose onLocationChanged() method will be called for each location update.

We want the location update as long as the activity is in the foreground because it doesn't make any sense to continuously get location updates when the user isn't looking at the screen. So, we remove the listener in onPause() method -

```
@Override
protected void onPause() {
        super.onPause();

        lm.removeUpdates(locationListener);
}
```

Finally, to access location data, we need to add an uses-permission to our manifest file -

```
<uses-permission

android:name="android.permission.ACCESS_FINE_LOCATION" />
```

Monitoring a Location

Using the LocationManager class, we can monitor a specific location. By monitoring location, I mean we can monitor if the user is within a specified radius of a particular location. The addProximityAltert() method of LocationManger instance is used to accomplish this.

The following code snippets shows how can we monitor a particular location, so that if the user is within fiver meter radius of that location, the app will fire an intent which will launch a web browser (you can do whatever is more appropriate, like sending an SMS or so) -

```
PendingIntent pendingIntent = PendingIntent.getActivity(
        this,
        0,
        new Intent(android.content.Intent.ACTION_VIEW,
                              Uri.parse("http://
www.google.com")), 0);

lm.addProximityAlert(31.32413, -132.180353, 5, -1,

pendingIntent);
```

The addProximityAlert() method takes five arguments – latitude, longitude, radius (in meters), expiration (duration for which the proximity alert is valid, we used -1 to indicate no expiration) and finally the pending intent.

Project – Building a Location Tracker

By combining the techniques we have learned in this chapter and SMS messaging capabilities, we will build a location tracker application. If the application is installed in a device, you will be able to send an SMS message with a specific code and it will automatically return the device's current location as a reply SMS message. Let's see how to do that.

1. Create a new project named LocationTracker.

2. We will need a broadcast receiver class in order to intercept the incoming SMS message. Create a new class named SMSReceiver.java under the src directory with the following code -

```java
package com.iducate.locationtracker;

import android.content.BroadcastReceiver;
import android.content.Context;
import android.content.Intent;
import android.location.Location;
import android.location.LocationListener;
import android.location.LocationManager;
import android.os.Bundle;
import android.telephony.SmsManager;
import android.telephony.SmsMessage;

public class SMSReceiver extends BroadcastReceiver {

    private LocationManager lm;
    private LocationListener locationListener;

    private String senderNumber;

    @Override
    public void onReceive(Context context, Intent intent) {
        Bundle extras = intent.getExtras();
        SmsMessage[] messages = null;
        String msgBody = "";

        if (extras != null) {
            Object[] pdus = (Object[]) extras.get("pdus");
            messages = new SmsMessage[pdus.length];

            for (int i = 0; i < messages.length; i++) {
                messages[i] = SmsMessage.createFromPdu((byte[])
                                    pdus[i]);
                if (i == 0) {
                    senderNumber =
messages[i].getOriginatingAddress();
```

```
            }

            msgBody += messages[i].getMessageBody().toString();
        }

        if (msgBody.equals("LT SEND LOCATION")) {
            lm = (LocationManager) context
                    .getSystemService(
                            Context.LOCATION_SERVICE);

            locationListener = new MyLocationListener();
            lm.requestLocationUpdates(
                    LocationManager.NETWORK_PROVIDER,
                    60000, 1000, locationListener);

            abortBroadcast();
        }
    }
}

private class MyLocationListener implements LocationListener {

    @Override
    public void onLocationChanged(Location location) {
        if (location != null) {
            SmsManager manager = SmsManager.getDefault();
            manager.sendTextMessage(
                    senderNumber,
                    null,
                    "http://maps.google.com/maps?q="
                    + location.getLatitude() +
                    "," + location.getLongitude(), null, null);

            lm.removeUpdates(locationListener);
        }
    }

    @Override
    public void onProviderDisabled(String provider) {
        // TODO Auto-generated method stub

    }
```

```java
        @Override
        public void onProviderEnabled(String provider) {
            // TODO Auto-generated method stub

        }

        @Override
        public void onStatusChanged(String provider, int status,
                Bundle extras) {
            // TODO Auto-generated method stub

        }

    }

}
```

3. Update the AndroidManifest.xml file with the following code -

```xml
<?xml version="1.0" encoding="utf-8"?>
<manifest xmlns:android="http://schemas.android.com/apk/res/android"
    package="com.iducate.locationtracker"
    android:versionCode="1"
    android:versionName="1.0" >

    <uses-sdk
        android:minSdkVersion="8"
        android:targetSdkVersion="19" />

    <uses-permission
android:name="android.permission.ACCESS_FINE_LOCATION" />
    <uses-permission android:name="android.permission.RECEIVE_SMS" />
    <uses-permission android:name="android.permission.SEND_SMS" />

    <application
        android:allowBackup="true"
        android:icon="@drawable/ic_launcher"
        android:label="@string/app_name"
        android:theme="@style/AppTheme" >
        <activity
            android:name="com.iducate.locationtracker.MainActivity"
            android:label="@string/app_name" >
            <intent-filter>
```

```xml
            <action android:name="android.intent.action.MAIN" />

            <category android:name="android.intent.category.LAUNCHER" />
        </intent-filter>
    </activity>

    <receiver android:name="com.iducate.locationtracker.SMSReceiver" >
        <intent-filter android:priority="1000" >
            <action
android:name="android.provider.Telephony.SMS_RECEIVED" />
        </intent-filter>
    </receiver>
</application>

</manifest>
```

4. In order to test the application, you need to install the application in a real Android device. Then from another device, you will need to send an SMS message with keyword "LT SEND LOCATION".

5. After the SMS message is received by other device, you will get a reply SMS message with that device's current location as a URL (figure 9.12) -

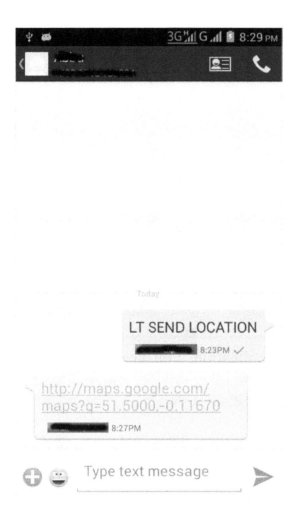

Figure 9.12: Getting location by sending SMS message

6. If you click the URL, you will see an app chooser dialog with a number of apps that can handle this URL. Choose Google Maps application and you will see the location through Google Maps (figure 9.13) -

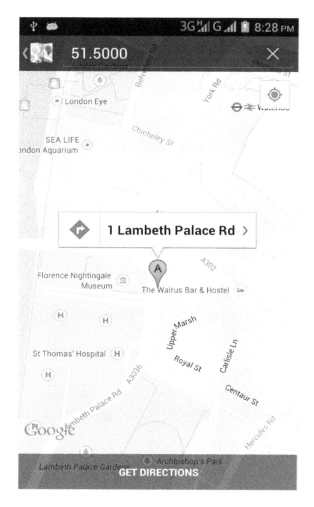

Figure 9.13: Showing location in Google Maps

How It Works?

Using a BroadcastReceiver class, we intercept any incoming message and retrieve the sender number and message body -

```
Bundle extras = intent.getExtras();
SmsMessage[] messages = null;
String msgBody = "";

if (extras != null) {
        Object[] pdus = (Object[]) extras.get("pdus");
        messages = new SmsMessage[pdus.length];

        for (int i = 0; i < messages.length; i++) {
                messages[i] = SmsMessage.createFromPdu((byte[])
                                    pdus[i]);
```

```
            if (i == 0) {
                    senderNumber =

messages[i].getOriginatingAddress();
                    }

                    msgBody += messages[i].getMessageBody().toString();
            }
```

This is exactly the same as we did in the previous chapter. Next, we check if the message body contains our desired keyword -

```
if (msgBody.equals("LT SEND LOCATION")) {
        lm = (LocationManager) context
                    .getSystemService(Context.LOCATION_SERVICE);

        locationListener = new MyLocationListener();
        lm.requestLocationUpdates(
                LocationManager.NETWORK_PROVIDER,
                60000, 1000, locationListener);

        abortBroadcast();
}
```

In our case, we are checking if the message body equals to the keyword "LT SEND LOCATION". When a match is found, we request for a location update using the LocationManager class. We also stop broadcasting the incoming message intent.

Once we get the location, we programmatically send a reply SMS message using the URL that points to Google Maps -

```
if (location != null) {
        SmsManager manager = SmsManager.getDefault();
        manager.sendTextMessage(senderNumber,
                null, "http://maps.google.com/maps?q="
                + location.getLatitude() + ","
                + location.getLongitude(), null, null);

        lm.removeUpdates(locationListener);
}
```

After the reply SMS message is sent, we remove the location update so that we do not listen for location changes anymore.

Notice the minTime and minDistance arguments of requestLocationUpdates() method. Unlike the previous example, we have set those values as 60,000 ms and 1,000 meters respectively. This is done to avoid sending SMS messages continuously. By the time we stop listening for location updates, the Location Manager would have called onLocationChanged() method several times if those argument values were set to 0.

Summary

We have learned how to use Maps V2 in our Android applications and see various configuration options for customizing maps. We have also learned about location-based services using LocationManager class which let us get the current location information as well as let us notify when the location changes. Finally, we have combined the power of location-based services with SMS messaging and built a location tracker application.

Chapter 10: Networking

In this chapter, we will learn how to use HTTP protocol to communicate with web servers. Along the way, we will see how to download binary data (like images) and text data. We will also learn how to consume both XML and JSON web services. Finally, we will learn how to connect to a Socket server.

Consuming Web Services Using HTTP

HTTP which stands for Hyper Text Transfer Protocol, is the most commonly used protocol to communicate over the Internet. In our Android application, we can use HTTP protocol to perform a wide range of tasks, like downloading web pages, downloading binary data (like images or documents) and more.

In this section, we will create a new project to demonstrate how we can use HTTP protocol from our Android application and download content.

1. Create a new project named NetworkingDemo.

2. Add the following code to activity_main.xml layout file -

```xml
<LinearLayout xmlns:android="http://schemas.android.com/apk/res/android"
    android:layout_width="fill_parent"
    android:layout_height="fill_parent"
    android:orientation="vertical" >

    <Button
        android:layout_width="wrap_content"
        android:layout_height="wrap_content"
        android:onClick="startDownload"
        android:text="Download Image" />

    <ImageView
        android:id="@+id/imageView1"
        android:layout_width="wrap_content"
        android:layout_height="wrap_content" />

</LinearLayout>
```

3. Update the MainActivity.java file with the following code -

```java
package com.iducate.networkingdemo;

import java.io.IOException;
import java.io.InputStream;
import java.net.HttpURLConnection;
import java.net.URL;

import android.app.Activity;
import android.content.Context;
import android.graphics.Bitmap;
import android.graphics.BitmapFactory;
import android.net.ConnectivityManager;
import android.net.NetworkInfo;
import android.os.AsyncTask;
import android.os.Bundle;
import android.util.Log;
import android.view.View;
import android.widget.ImageView;
import android.widget.Toast;

public class MainActivity extends Activity {

    private ImageView imageView;
    private static final String IMAGE_URL =
                                    "http://www.google.com/
images/srpr/logo11w.png";

    @Override
    protected void onCreate(Bundle savedInstanceState) {
        super.onCreate(savedInstanceState);
        setContentView(R.layout.activity_main);

        imageView = (ImageView) findViewById(R.id.imageView1);
    }

    public void startDownload(View v) {
        if (isNetworkAvailable()) {
            new DownloadTask().execute(IMAGE_URL);
        } else {
            Toast.makeText(this, "Network is not available",
```

```java
                            Toast.LENGTH_LONG).show();
        }
}

private boolean isNetworkAvailable() {
        boolean available = false;

        ConnectivityManager manager = (ConnectivityManager)
                    getSystemService(Context.CONNECTIVITY_SERVICE);

        NetworkInfo networkInfo = manager.getActiveNetworkInfo();
        if (networkInfo != null andand networkInfo.isAvailable()) {
              available = true;
        }

        return available;
}

private Bitmap downloadImage(String urlStr) throws IOException {
        Bitmap bitmap = null;
        InputStream inputStream = null;

        try {
                URL url = new URL(urlStr);
                HttpURLConnection urlConnection = (HttpURLConnection)
                      url.openConnection();
                urlConnection.connect();
                inputStream = urlConnection.getInputStream();
                bitmap = BitmapFactory.decodeStream(inputStream);
        } catch (Exception e) {
                Log.d("NetworkingDemo", e.toString());
        } finally {
                inputStream.close();
        }

        return bitmap;
}

private class DownloadTask extends AsyncTask<String, Void,
  Bitmap> {

        Bitmap bitmap = null;
```

```java
    @Override
    protected Bitmap doInBackground(String... params) {
        try {
            bitmap = downloadImage(params[0]);
        } catch (Exception e) {
            Log.d("NetworkingDemo", e.toString());
        }
        return bitmap;
    }

    @Override
    protected void onPostExecute(Bitmap result) {
        imageView.setImageBitmap(result);
    }
    }

}
```

4. Add the following uses-permission to the AndroidManifest.xml file -

```xml
<?xml version="1.0" encoding="utf-8"?>
<manifest xmlns:android="http://schemas.android.com/apk/res/android"
    package="com.iducate.networkingdemo"
    android:versionCode="1"
    android:versionName="1.0" >

    <uses-sdk
        android:minSdkVersion="9"
        android:targetSdkVersion="19" />

    <uses-permission android:name="android.permission.INTERNET" />
    <uses-permission
android:name="android.permission.ACCESS_NETWORK_STATE" />

    <application
        android:allowBackup="true"
        android:icon="@drawable/ic_launcher"
        android:label="@string/app_name"
        android:theme="@style/AppTheme" >
        <activity
            android:name="com.iducate.networkingdemo.MainActivity"
            android:label="@string/app_name" >
            <intent-filter>
```

427

```
            <action android:name="android.intent.action.MAIN" />

            <category android:name="android.intent.category.LAUNCHER" />
        </intent-filter>
      </activity>
    </application>

</manifest>
```

5. Run the application. You will see a simple UI with a button. Click the button and you will see an image downloaded and shown below the button (figure 10.1) -

Figure 10.1: Downloading image

How It Works?

The downloadImage() method is responsible for downloading our image -

```
private Bitmap downloadImage(String urlStr) throws IOException {
    Bitmap bitmap = null;
```

```
        InputStream inputStream = null;

        try {
                URL url = new URL(urlStr);
                HttpURLConnection urlConnection = (HttpURLConnection)
                        url.openConnection();
                urlConnection.connect();
                inputStream = urlConnection.getInputStream();
                bitmap = BitmapFactory.decodeStream(inputStream);
        } catch (Exception e) {
                Log.d("NetworkingDemo", e.toString());
        } finally {
                inputStream.close();
        }
        return bitmap;
    }
```

This downloadImage() method takes a string argument (URL of image) and returns a Bitmap instance. In this case, we have used HttpURLConnection class to communicate between our application and web server.

We start by creating a new instance of URL class by passing a url string as argument to the constructor of URL class. We then create an instance of HttpURLConnection class by calling openConnection() method of the URL object instance. The connect() method of HttpURLConnection instance is used to connect to the target url. The getInputStream() method which returns a InputStream instance is used to read data. We pass that InputStream instance as an argument to decodeStream() static method of the BitmapFactory class which returns a Bitmap instance.

To perform download, we create a new subclass of AsyncTask class because we are not allowed to perform network operations in a UI thread -

```
    private class DownloadTask extends AsyncTask<String, Void,
    Bitmap> {

        Bitmap bitmap = null;

        @Override
        protected Bitmap doInBackground(String... params) {
                try {
                        bitmap = downloadImage(params[0]);
```

```
        } catch (Exception e) {
                Log.d("NetworkingDemo", e.toString());
        }
        return bitmap;
    }


    @Override
    protected void onPostExecute(Bitmap result) {
            imageView.setImageBitmap(result);
    }
  }
```

The AsyncTask class's doInBackground() runs in a new thread. Within that method, we call the downloadImage() method to download the image from web server. Once the download is complete, onPostExecute() method is called. This onPostExecute() method runs in a UI thread, so we can set the downloaded image to the ImageView widget.

To start downloading the image, we need to create a new instance of DownloadTask class and call its execute method. Before that however, we need to make sure the Android phone's connectivity is active (either packet data or wifi connectivity). We check for that using a helper method as follows -

```
    private boolean isNetworkAvailable() {
          boolean available = false;

          ConnectivityManager manager = (ConnectivityManager)
                  getSystemService(Context.CONNECTIVITY_SERVICE);

          NetworkInfo networkInfo = manager.getActiveNetworkInfo();
          if (networkInfo != null andand networkInfo.isAvailable()) {
                available = true;
          }

          return available;
    }
```

We are now done with the setup steps. On button click and after checking network availability, we create a new instance of DownloadTask class and call execute method -

```
    public void startDownload(View v) {
```

```
        if (isNetworkAvailable()) {
                new DownloadTask().execute(IMAGE_URL);
        } else {
                Toast.makeText(this, "Network is not available",
                                Toast.LENGTH_LONG).show();
        }
    }
```

We pass the image url as argument to the execute method.

Since we are accessing network state and Internet connectivity, we need to add couple of uses-permission in AndroidManifest.xml file -

```
<uses-permission
        android:name="android.permission.INTERNET" />
<uses-permission

android:name="android.permission.ACCESS_NETWORK_STATE" />
```

Downloading Text Content

Besides downloading binary data, we can also download text content. Let's see how we can extend our previous example project to enable downloading web page content using HTTP protocol.

1. In our layout file, we need to add another button. Update activity_main.xml layout file with the highlighted code -

```
<LinearLayout xmlns:android="http://schemas.android.com/apk/res/android"
    android:layout_width="fill_parent"
    android:layout_height="fill_parent"
    android:orientation="vertical" >

  <Button
    android:layout_width="wrap_content"
    android:layout_height="wrap_content"
    android:onClick="startDownload"
    android:text="Download Image" />

  <Button
    android:layout_width="wrap_content"
    android:layout_height="wrap_content"
```

```
        android:onClick="downloadText"
        android:text="Download Text" />

    <ImageView
        android:id="@+id/imageView1"
        android:layout_width="wrap_content"
        android:layout_height="wrap_content" />

</LinearLayout>
```

2. Update MainActivity.java file with the following highlighted code -

```
package com.iducate.networkingdemo;

import java.io.BufferedReader;
import java.io.IOException;
import java.io.InputStream;
import java.io.InputStreamReader;
import java.net.HttpURLConnection;
import java.net.URL;

import android.app.Activity;
import android.content.Context;
import android.graphics.Bitmap;
import android.graphics.BitmapFactory;
import android.net.ConnectivityManager;
import android.net.NetworkInfo;
import android.os.AsyncTask;
import android.os.Bundle;
import android.util.Log;
import android.view.View;
import android.widget.ImageView;
import android.widget.Toast;

public class MainActivity extends Activity {

    private ImageView imageView;
    private static final String IMAGE_URL =
                        "http://www.google.com/images/srpr/
logo11w.png";

    @Override
    protected void onCreate(Bundle savedInstanceState) {
```

432

```java
        super.onCreate(savedInstanceState);
        setContentView(R.layout.activity_main);

        imageView = (ImageView) findViewById(R.id.imageView1);
    }

    // download image
    public void startDownload(View v) {
        ...
    }

    // download text
    public void downloadText(View v) {
        if (isNetworkAvailable()) {
            new ReadStreamTask()
                    .execute("http://www.i-ducate.com");
        } else {
            Toast.makeText(this, "Network is not available",
                    Toast.LENGTH_LONG).show();
        }
    }

    private boolean isNetworkAvailable() {
        boolean available = false;

        ConnectivityManager manager = (ConnectivityManager)
                getSystemService(Context.CONNECTIVITY_SERVICE);

        NetworkInfo networkInfo = manager.getActiveNetworkInfo();

        if (networkInfo != null andand networkInfo.isAvailable()) {
            available = true;
        }

        return available;
    }

    private String readStream(String urlStr) throws IOException {
        String str = "";
        InputStream inputStream = null;
        BufferedReader reader = null;

        try {
```

433

```
            URL url = new URL(urlStr);
            HttpURLConnection urlConnection = (HttpURLConnection)
                  url.openConnection();
            inputStream = urlConnection.getInputStream();

            reader = new BufferedReader(new

InputStreamReader(inputStream));
            String line = "";

            while ((line = reader.readLine()) != null) {
                  str += line;
            }

      } catch (Exception e) {
            Log.d("NetworkingDemo", e.toString());
      } finally {
            inputStream.close();
            reader.close();
      }

      return str;
}

private class ReadStreamTask extends AsyncTask<String, Void,
      String> {

      String str = "";

      @Override
      protected String doInBackground(String... params) {
            try {
                  str = readStream(params[0]);
            } catch (Exception e) {
                  Log.d("NetworkingDemo", e.toString());
            }
            return str;
      }

      @Override
      protected void onPostExecute(String result) {
            Toast.makeText(getBaseContext(), result,
                              Toast.LENGTH_LONG).show();
```

```java
        }

    }

    private Bitmap downloadImage(String urlStr) throws IOException {
        ...
    }

    private class DownloadTask extends AsyncTask<String, Void,
            Bitmap> {
        ...
    }

}
```

3. If you run the application, you will see a new button called "Download Text". Click that button and you will see a Toast message with text content retrieved similar to figure 10.2 -

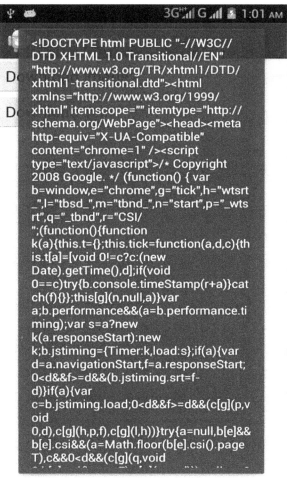

435

How It Works?

The readStream() method takes an URL as argument and returns the text content -

```
private String readStream(String urlStr) throws IOException {
        String str = "";
        InputStream inputStream = null;
        BufferedReader reader = null;

        try {
                URL url = new URL(urlStr);
                HttpURLConnection urlConnection = (HttpURLConnection)
                        url.openConnection();
                inputStream = urlConnection.getInputStream();

                reader = new BufferedReader(new

InputStreamReader(inputStream));
                String line = "";

                while ((line = reader.readLine()) != null) {
                        str += line;
                }

        } catch (Exception e) {
                Log.d("NetworkingDemo", e.toString());
        } finally {
                inputStream.close();
                reader.close();
        }

        return str;
}
```

In this case, after we get an instance of HttpURLConnection class by calling openConnection() method, we call getInputStream() method to get an InputStream instance. This InputStream instance is passed as an argument to the InputStreamReader class's constructor, which returns a new InputStreamReader instance. We then extract the text content by looping through the InputStreamReader and calling readLine() method.

To execute the above mentioned readStream() method, we create a new AsyncTast subclass, named ReadStreamTask -

```
private class ReadStreamTask extends AsyncTask<String, Void,
    String> {

    String str = "";

    @Override
    protected String doInBackground(String... params) {
        try {
            str = readStream(params[0]);
        } catch (Exception e) {
            Log.d("NetworkingDemo", e.toString());
        }
        return str;
    }

    @Override
    protected void onPostExecute(String result) {
        Toast.makeText(getBaseContext(), result,
                        Toast.LENGTH_LONG).show();
    }

}
```

The doInBackground() method calls readStream() method to get text content as string and onPostExecute() method show a Toast message with that string.

Finally, we create a new instance of ReadStreamTask and call execute() method -

```
public void downloadText(View v) {
    if (isNetworkAvailable()) {
        new ReadStreamTask()
                .execute("http://www.i-ducate.com");
    } else {
        Toast.makeText(this, "Network is not available",
                        Toast.LENGTH_LONG).show();
    }
}
```

The execute() method passes the URL from which text content is downloaded. We pass the URL of i-ducate.com. As a result, we see the source code of the index page when we click the "Download Text" button.

Consuming XML Web Services

XML is a widely used data exchange format and you will often need to download XML files and parse the content from your Android application. In this section, we will see how to connect to a web service using HTTP, download the XML data and parse it using XML parser offered by Android. In particular, we will parse weather data from the Google Weather API. Figure 10.3 shows a sample XML file returned from Google Weather API when viewed in a browser -

```
▼<current>
    ▼<city id="2643743" name="London">
        <coord lon="-0.13" lat="51.51"/>
        <country>GB</country>
        <sun rise="2014-06-04T03:46:17" set="2014-06-04T20:11:32"/>
    </city>
    <temperature value="285.38" min="284.15" max="286.48" unit="kelvin"/>
    <humidity value="87" unit="%"/>
    <pressure value="1007" unit="hPa"/>
    ▼<wind>
        <speed value="4.36" name="Gentle Breeze"/>
        <direction value="237.002" code="WSW" name="West-southwest"/>
    </wind>
    <clouds value="56" name="broken clouds"/>
    <precipitation value="2.04" mode="rain" unit="3h"/>
    <weather number="500" value="light rain" icon="10d"/>
    <lastupdate value="2014-06-04T06:15:18"/>
</current>
```

Figure 10.3: Sample XML file

1. Create a new project named XMLParserDemo.

2. Update the activity_main.xml layout file with the following code -

```
<LinearLayout xmlns:android="http://schemas.android.com/apk/res/android"
    android:layout_width="fill_parent"
    android:layout_height="fill_parent"
    android:orientation="vertical" >

    <EditText
        android:id="@+id/etLocation"
        android:layout_width="match_parent"
```

```xml
        android:layout_height="wrap_content"
        android:hint="Enter location:" />

    <Button
        android:id="@+id/btnGetWeather"
        android:layout_width="wrap_content"
        android:layout_height="wrap_content"
        android:onClick="getWeather"
        android:text="Get Weather" />

    <TextView
        android:id="@+id/tvOutput"
        android:layout_width="wrap_content"
        android:layout_height="wrap_content" />

</LinearLayout>
```

3. Update the MainActivity.java file with the following code -

```java
package com.iducate.xmlparserdemo;

import java.io.InputStream;
import java.net.HttpURLConnection;
import java.net.URL;

import org.xmlpull.v1.XmlPullParser;
import org.xmlpull.v1.XmlPullParserFactory;

import android.app.Activity;
import android.os.AsyncTask;
import android.os.Bundle;
import android.view.View;
import android.widget.EditText;
import android.widget.TextView;

public class MainActivity extends Activity {

    private String baseUrl =
                                    "http://
api.openweathermap.org/data/2.5/weather?q=";
    private String parseMode = "andmode=xml";

    private EditText etLocation;
```

439

```java
private TextView tvOutput;

@Override
protected void onCreate(Bundle savedInstanceState) {
        super.onCreate(savedInstanceState);
        setContentView(R.layout.activity_main);

        etLocation = (EditText) findViewById(R.id.etLocation);
        tvOutput = (TextView) findViewById(R.id.tvOutput);
}

public void getWeather(View view) {
        String location = etLocation.getText().toString();
        String urlString = baseUrl + location + parseMode;

        new XMLParserTask().execute(urlString);
}

public String[] parseXML(XmlPullParser parser) {

        String[] data = { null, null, null };

        int event;

        try {
                event = parser.getEventType();

                while (event != XmlPullParser.END_DOCUMENT) {

                        String name = parser.getName();

                        switch (event) {
                        case XmlPullParser.END_TAG:
                                if (name.equals("humidity")) {
                                        data[0] = parser.getAttributeValue(null,
"value");
                                } else if (name.equals("pressure")) {
                                        data[1] = parser.getAttributeValue(null,
"value");
                                } else if (name.equals("temperature")) {
                                        data[2] = parser.getAttributeValue(null,
"value");
                                }
```

```java
                    break;
                }

                event = parser.next();
            }
        } catch (Exception e) {
            e.printStackTrace();
        }

        return data;
    }

    private String fetchWeatherData(String urlString) {
        String[] dataArr = { null, null, null };
        String weatherData = null;

        XmlPullParserFactory xmlFactory;

        try {
            URL url = new URL(urlString);
            HttpURLConnection conn = (HttpURLConnection)
                            url.openConnection();
            conn.setReadTimeout(10000);
            conn.setConnectTimeout(15000);
            conn.connect();

            InputStream stream = conn.getInputStream();
            xmlFactory = XmlPullParserFactory.newInstance();
            XmlPullParser myParser = xmlFactory.newPullParser();

            myParser.setFeature(
                XmlPullParser.FEATURE_PROCESS_NAMESPACES, false);
            myParser.setInput(stream, null);
            dataArr = parseXML(myParser);
            stream.close();

            if (dataArr[0] != null andand dataArr[1] != null andand
                    dataArr[2] != null) {
                weatherData = "Temperature: " + dataArr[2]
                + "\nHumidity: " + dataArr[0]
                + "\nPressure: " + dataArr[1];
            }
```

```
            } catch (Exception e) {
                    e.printStackTrace();
            }
            return weatherData;
    }

    private class XMLParserTask extends AsyncTask<String, Void,
            String> {

            @Override
            protected String doInBackground(String... params) {

                    String weatherData = fetchWeatherData(params[0]);

                    return weatherData;
            }

            @Override
            protected void onPostExecute(String result) {
                    if (result != null) {
                            tvOutput.setText(result);
                    } else {
                            tvOutput.setText("Can't fetch weather data!");
                    }
            }

    }
}
```

4. We need to add an uses-permission in AndroidMainifest.xml file -

```
<?xml version="1.0" encoding="utf-8"?>
<manifest xmlns:android="http://schemas.android.com/apk/res/android"
  package="com.iducate.xmlparserdemo"
  android:versionCode="1"
  android:versionName="1.0" >

  <uses-sdk
    android:minSdkVersion="8"
    android:targetSdkVersion="19" />

  <uses-permission android:name="android.permission.INTERNET" />
```

```xml
<application
    android:allowBackup="true"
    android:icon="@drawable/ic_launcher"
    android:label="@string/app_name"
    android:theme="@style/AppTheme" >
    <activity
        android:name="com.iducate.xmlparserdemo.MainActivity"
        android:label="@string/app_name" >
        <intent-filter>
            <action android:name="android.intent.action.MAIN" />

            <category android:name="android.intent.category.LAUNCHER" />
        </intent-filter>
    </activity>
</application>

</manifest>
```

5. Run the application, you will see a layout with a EditText and a button. Enter a location name and press the button. You will see weather data similar to figure 10.4 -

Figure 10.4: Getting weather data by parsing XML

How It Works?

Android provides three types of XML parsers – DOM, SAX and XmlPullParser. Here, we have used XmlPullParser, which is the recommended way as it is efficient and easy to use.

We have defined a helper method called parseXML(), which takes an XmlPullParser as argument and return an array of string containing humidity, pressure and temperature values -

```
public String[] parseXML(XmlPullParser parser) {
```

```
            String[] data = { null, null, null };

            int event;

            try {
                event = parser.getEventType();

                while (event != XmlPullParser.END_DOCUMENT) {

                    String name = parser.getName();

                    switch (event) {
                    case XmlPullParser.END_TAG:
                        if (name.equals("humidity")) {
                            data[0] =
parser.getAttributeValue(null, "value");
                        } else if (name.equals("pressure")) {
                            data[1] =
parser.getAttributeValue(null, "value");
                        } else if (name.equals("temperature")) {
                            data[2] =
parser.getAttributeValue(null, "value");
                        }
                        break;
                    }

                    event = parser.next();
                }
            } catch (Exception e) {
                e.printStackTrace();
            }

            return data;
        }
```

The getEventType() mtethod of XmlPullParser instance is used to get the type of event (like start of tag, end of tag, end of document etc). We loop through the entire XML document until we encounter the end of the document.

The getName() method of parser instance returns the name of the tag. We match

445

the tag name to see if it is one of the tags we are interested in. We then get the value of those tags using getArrtibuteValue() method call.

The fetchWeatherData() method connects to the web service, download the XML file and then parse it using the above discussed parseXML() method -

```java
private String fetchWeatherData(String urlString) {
        String[] dataArr = { null, null, null };
        String weatherData = null;

        XmlPullParserFactory xmlFactory;

        try {
                URL url = new URL(urlString);
                HttpURLConnection conn = (HttpURLConnection)
                                url.openConnection();
                conn.setReadTimeout(10000);
                conn.setConnectTimeout(15000);
                conn.connect();

                InputStream stream = conn.getInputStream();
                xmlFactory = XmlPullParserFactory.newInstance();
                XmlPullParser myParser = xmlFactory.newPullParser();

                myParser.setFeature(
                        XmlPullParser.FEATURE_PROCESS_NAMESPACES, false);
                myParser.setInput(stream, null);
                dataArr = parseXML(myParser);
                stream.close();

                if (dataArr[0] != null andand dataArr[1] != null andand
                        dataArr[2] != null) {
                        weatherData = "Temperature: " + dataArr[2]
                        + "\nHumidity: " + dataArr[0]
                        + "\nPressure: " + dataArr[1];
                }

        } catch (Exception e) {
                e.printStackTrace();
        }
        return weatherData;
    }
```

446

Similar to the previous two examples, we again define a new subclass of AsyncTask class to run the network operations -

```
private class XMLParserTask extends AsyncTask<String, Void,
    String> {

    @Override
    protected String doInBackground(String... params) {

        String weatherData = fetchWeatherData(params[0]);

        return weatherData;
    }

    @Override
    protected void onPostExecute(String result) {
        if (result != null) {
            tvOutput.setText(result);
        } else {
            tvOutput.setText("Can't fetch weather data!");
        }
    }

}
```

The doInBackground() method calls fetchWeatherData() method, which returns a string with weather information (or null in case something bad happens). Notice the params[0] argument passed to featchWeatherData() method, this is how we are passing location name.

Once the doInBackground() method's tasks finishes in another thread, the onPostExecute() method is executed with the string argument returned from doInBackground() method. This method runs in the UI thread and updates the UI with weather data (or error message).

Now, none of the above mentioned steps can occur unless we create a new instance of XMLParserTask class and call it's execute method -

```
public void getWeather(View view) {
    String location = etLocation.getText().toString();
    String urlString = baseUrl + location + parseMode;
```

447

```
    new XMLParserTask().execute(urlString);
}
```

The execute() method takes a URL as argument. We construct the URL by appending a base url with the location name returned from UI.

Since we are connecting to web services, we need to have Internet uses-permission -

```
<uses-permission android:name="android.permission.INTERNET" />
```

Consuming JSON Web Services

In the previous section, we have learned how to consume XML web services. In this section, we will learn how to consume JSON services, another popular data exchange format. JSON (Javascript Object Notation) is a lightweight data-interchange format, which is readable to human and also convenient to access using programming languages.

JSON syntax is much like a subset of Javascript object notation syntax, where data is represented in name-value pairs. Each set of name-value pair is separated by commas. Curly braces hold a group of objects and square brackets hold items of an array. There could be multiple level of nesting of items. If you aren't familiar with JSON yet, have a quick look at this online tutorial

http://www.w3schools.com/json/

We will use the same Google Weather API that we have used in previous section. The Google Weather API provides data in both XML and JSON format. Figure 10.5 shows a sample weather data in JSON format -

```json
{
    "coord": {
        "lon": -0.13,
        "lat": 51.51
    },
    "sys": {
        "message": 0.0685,
        "country": "GB",
        "sunrise": 1401853577,
        "sunset": 1401912691
    },
    "weather": [
        {
            "id": 500,
            "main": "Rain",
            "description": "light rain",
            "icon": "10d"
        }
    ],
    "base": "cmc stations",
    "main": {
        "temp": 286.14,
        "humidity": 53,
        "pressure": 1004,
        "temp_min": 284.82,
        "temp_max": 288.71
    },
    "dt": 1401872278,
    "id": 2643743,
    "name": "London",
    "cod": 200
}
```

Figure 10.5: Sample Weather Data in JSON Format

Let's create a new project and see how to parse JSON from our Android applications.

449

1. Create a new project named JSONParserDemo.

2. The layout file, activity_main.xml is exactly the same as we did for XMLParserDemo project -

```xml
<LinearLayout xmlns:android="http://schemas.android.com/apk/res/android"
    android:layout_width="fill_parent"
    android:layout_height="fill_parent"
    android:orientation="vertical" >

    <EditText
        android:id="@+id/etLocation"
        android:layout_width="match_parent"
        android:layout_height="wrap_content"
        android:hint="Enter location:" />

    <Button
        android:layout_width="wrap_content"
        android:layout_height="wrap_content"
        android:onClick="getWeather"
        android:text="Get Weather" />

    <TextView
        android:id="@+id/tvOutput"
        android:layout_width="wrap_content"
        android:layout_height="wrap_content" />

</LinearLayout>
```

3. Update the MainActivity.java file with the following code -

```java
package com.iducate.jsonparserdemo;

import java.io.IOException;
import java.io.InputStream;
import java.net.HttpURLConnection;
import java.net.MalformedURLException;
import java.net.URL;

import org.json.JSONObject;

import android.app.Activity;
```

```java
import android.os.AsyncTask;
import android.os.Bundle;
import android.view.View;
import android.widget.EditText;
import android.widget.TextView;

public class MainActivity extends Activity {

    private EditText etLocation;
    private TextView tvOutput;

    private String base_url =
                                    "http://
api.openweathermap.org/data/2.5/weather?q=";

    @Override
    protected void onCreate(Bundle savedInstanceState) {
        super.onCreate(savedInstanceState);
        setContentView(R.layout.activity_main);

        etLocation = (EditText) findViewById(R.id.etLocation);
        tvOutput = (TextView) findViewById(R.id.tvOutput);
    }

    public void getWeather(View v) {
        String location = etLocation.getText().toString();
        String urlString = base_url + location;

        new JSONParserTask().execute(urlString);
    }

    private String[] parseJSON(String in) {
        String[] dataArr = { null, null, null };

        try {
            JSONObject reader = new JSONObject(in);

            JSONObject main = reader.getJSONObject("main");

            dataArr[0] = main.getString("temp");
            dataArr[1] = main.getString("pressure");
            dataArr[2] = main.getString("humidity");
        } catch (Exception e) {
```

```java
            e.printStackTrace();
        }

        return dataArr;
    }


    private String fetchWeatherData(String urlString) {
        String weatherData = null;

        try {
            URL url = new URL(urlString);
            HttpURLConnection conn = (HttpURLConnection)
                    url.openConnection();
            conn.setReadTimeout(10000);
            conn.setConnectTimeout(15000);
            conn.connect();

            InputStream stream = conn.getInputStream();

            String data = convertStreamToString(stream);


            String[] dataArr = parseJSON(data);

            if (dataArr[0] != null andand dataArr[1] != null andand
                    dataArr[2] != null) {
                weatherData = "Temperature: " + dataArr[0]
                        + "\nPressure: " + dataArr[1]
                        + "\nHumidity: " + dataArr[2];
            }

        } catch (MalformedURLException e) {
            e.printStackTrace();
        } catch (IOException e) {
            e.printStackTrace();
        }

        return weatherData;
    }

    static String convertStreamToString(java.io.InputStream is) {
        java.util.Scanner scanner = new java.util.Scanner(is)
                .useDelimiter("\\A");
```

```java
            return scanner.hasNext() ? scanner.next() : "";
        }

        private class JSONParserTask extends AsyncTask<String, Void,
String> {

            @Override
            protected String doInBackground(String... params) {
                String result = fetchWeatherData(params[0]);
                return result;
            }

            @Override
            protected void onPostExecute(String result) {
                if (result != null) {
                    tvOutput.setText(result);
                } else {
                    tvOutput.setText("Can't fetch weather data!");
                }
            }
        }
    }
}
```

4. Add a new uses-permission to the AndroidManifest.xml file -

```xml
<?xml version="1.0" encoding="utf-8"?>
<manifest xmlns:android="http://schemas.android.com/apk/res/android"
  package="com.iducate.jsonparserdemo"
  android:versionCode="1"
  android:versionName="1.0" >

  <uses-sdk
     android:minSdkVersion="8"
     android:targetSdkVersion="19" />

  <uses-permission android:name="android.permission.INTERNET" />

  <application
     android:allowBackup="true"
     android:icon="@drawable/ic_launcher"
     android:label="@string/app_name"
     android:theme="@style/AppTheme" >
```

```
<activity
    android:name="com.iducate.jsonparserdemo.MainActivity"
    android:label="@string/app_name" >
    <intent-filter>
        <action android:name="android.intent.action.MAIN" />

        <category android:name="android.intent.category.LAUNCHER" />
    </intent-filter>
</activity>
</application>

</manifest>
```

5. Run the application, enter a location and click the button. You will get weather information similar to figure 10.6 -

Figure 10.6: Getting weather data by parsing JSON

How It Works?

The parseJSON() method takes a string argument formatted as JSON and returns an array of weather information -

```
private String[] parseJSON(String in) {
    String[] dataArr = { null, null, null };

    try {
        JSONObject reader = new JSONObject(in);

        JSONObject main = reader.getJSONObject("main");

        dataArr[0] = main.getString("temp");
        dataArr[1] = main.getString("pressure");
        dataArr[2] = main.getString("humidity");
    } catch (Exception e) {
        e.printStackTrace();
    }

    return dataArr;
}
```

Within this method, we create a new instance of JSONObject by passing the json string as argument to the constructor retrieved from the web service. By analyzing the JSON string (figure 10.5), we can see that the weather information we are interested in (temperature, pressure, humidity) are under the key "main". That's why we create a new JSONObject by passing "main" as argument to the constructor. Then, we retrieve temperature, pressure and humidity by calling getString() method with the corresponding keys.

Similar to the previous project with XML web service, we define a fetchWeatherData() method, which takes URL as argument and returns a string with weather information -

```
private String fetchWeatherData(String urlString) {
    String weatherData = null;

    try {
        URL url = new URL(urlString);
        HttpURLConnection conn = (HttpURLConnection)
                url.openConnection();
        conn.setReadTimeout(10000);
        conn.setConnectTimeout(15000);
```

```
            conn.connect();

            InputStream stream = conn.getInputStream();

            String data = convertStreamToString(stream);

            String[] dataArr = parseJSON(data);

            if (dataArr[0] != null andand dataArr[1] != null andand
                    dataArr[2] != null) {
                weatherData = "Temperature: " + dataArr[0]
                        + "\nPressure: " + dataArr[1]
                        + "\nHumidity: " + dataArr[2];
            }

        } catch (MalformedURLException e) {
            e.printStackTrace();
        } catch (IOException e) {
            e.printStackTrace();
        }

        return weatherData;
    }
```

Within this method, we connect to the web service and retrieve JSON data. In order to convert stream to string, we defined a helper method -

```
    static String convertStreamToString(java.io.InputStream is) {
        java.util.Scanner scanner = new java.util.Scanner(is)
                    .useDelimiter("\\A");
        return scanner.hasNext() ? scanner.next() : "";
    }
```

We next have a subclass of AsyncTask named JSONParserTask -

```
    private class JSONParserTask extends AsyncTask<String, Void,
String> {

        @Override
        protected String doInBackground(String... params) {
            String result = fetchWeatherData(params[0]);
            return result;
```

```
        }

        @Override
        protected void onPostExecute(String result) {
            if (result != null) {
                tvOutput.setText(result);
            } else {
                tvOutput.setText("Can't fetch weather data!");
            }
        }
    }
```

The doInBackground() method of JSONParserTask which runs on a separate thread, calls the fetchWeatherData() method and return weather information retrieved (or null, in case an error occurred).

Once the doInBackground() method finishes running, onPostExecute() method runs in the UI thread, where we update the UI with fetched weather data (or show error message).

Having done all the setup steps, we create a new instance of JSONParserTask class and call the execute() method with url -

```
    public void getWeather(View v) {
        String location = etLocation.getText().toString();
        String urlString = base_url + location;

        new JSONParserTask().execute(urlString);
    }
```

As usual, we need to add uses-permission in AndroidManifest.xml file for accessing the Internet -

```
    <uses-permission android:name="android.permission.INTERNET" />
```

Socket Programming

We have seen how we can consume XML and JSON web services from our Android application by using HTTP protocol. While HTTP protocol serves the purpose very well, it has a disadvantage of being a stateless protocol. If your application requires to maintain a persistent connection to the server, you are likely

457

to use socket programming. Socket programming is a technique through which you can establish a connection between a client and a server.

In this section, we will create a chat client application that can connect to a socket server and send message. Other clients can also connect to the server at the same time.

1. Create a new application named SocketsDemo.

2. Update the layout file, activity_main.xml with the following code -

```xml
<?xml version="1.0" encoding="utf-8"?>
<LinearLayout xmlns:android="http://schemas.android.com/apk/res/android"
    android:layout_width="fill_parent"
    android:layout_height="fill_parent"
    android:orientation="vertical" >

    <ListView
        android:id="@+id/listView"
        android:layout_width="match_parent"
        android:layout_weight="1"
        android:layout_height="wrap_content" />

    <LinearLayout
        android:layout_width="match_parent"
        android:layout_height="wrap_content"
        android:gravity="bottom"
        android:orientation="horizontal" >

        <EditText
            android:id="@+id/etInput"
            android:layout_width="wrap_content"
            android:layout_height="wrap_content"
            android:layout_weight="0.8"
            android:hint="Enter your message:" />

        <Button
            android:id="@+id/btnSend"
            android:layout_width="wrap_content"
            android:layout_height="wrap_content"
            android:layout_weight="0.2"
            android:text="Send" />
```

```
    </LinearLayout>

</LinearLayout>
```

3. Update the MainActivity.java file with the following code -

```java
package com.iducate.socketsdemo;

import java.io.BufferedReader;
import java.io.IOException;
import java.io.InputStreamReader;
import java.io.PrintWriter;
import java.net.Socket;
import java.net.UnknownHostException;

import android.app.Activity;
import android.os.Bundle;
import android.os.Handler;
import android.view.View;
import android.widget.ArrayAdapter;
import android.widget.Button;
import android.widget.EditText;
import android.widget.ListView;

public class MainActivity extends Activity {

    private Handler handler = new Handler();
    public ListView msgList;
    public ArrayAdapter<String> adapter;

    private static final String HOST_ADDR = "10.0.2.2";
    private static final int PORT_NUMBER = 8013;

    @Override
    public void onCreate(Bundle savedInstanceState) {
        super.onCreate(savedInstanceState);
        setContentView(R.layout.activity_main);

        msgList = (ListView) findViewById(R.id.listView);

        adapter = new ArrayAdapter<String>(this,
                    android.R.layout.simple_list_item_1);
        msgList.setAdapter(adapter);
```

```java
        Button btnSend = (Button) findViewById(R.id.btnSend);

        receiveMsg();
        btnSend.setOnClickListener(new View.OnClickListener() {

            @Override
            public void onClick(View v) {
                final EditText etMessage = (EditText)
                                    findViewById(R.id.etInput);
                sendMessageToServer(
                    etMessage.getText().toString());
                msgList.smoothScrollToPosition(
                    adapter.getCount() - 1);


            }
        });
    }

    public void sendMessageToServer(String str) {

        final String msg = str;
        new Thread(new Runnable() {

            @Override
            public void run() {
                PrintWriter out;
                try {
                    Socket socket = new Socket(
                                HOST_ADDR, PORT_NUMBER);

                    out = new PrintWriter(
                        socket.getOutputStream());
                    out.println(msg);
                    out.flush();
                } catch (UnknownHostException e) {
                    e.printStackTrace();
                } catch (IOException e) {
                    e.printStackTrace();
                }


            }
        }).start();
```

460

```java
        }

        public void receiveMsg() {
                new Thread(new Runnable() {
                        @Override
                        public void run() {
                                Socket socket = null;
                                BufferedReader in = null;
                                try {
                                        socket = new Socket(HOST_ADDR,
PORT_NUMBER);
                                } catch (UnknownHostException e) {
                                        e.printStackTrace();
                                } catch (IOException e) {
                                        e.printStackTrace();
                                }

                                try {
                                        in = new BufferedReader(
                                                        new InputStreamReader(
                                                                socket.getInputStream()));
                                } catch (IOException e) {
                                        e.printStackTrace();
                                }

                                while (true) {
                                        String msg = null;
                                        try {
                                                msg = in.readLine();
                                        } catch (IOException e) {
                                                e.printStackTrace();
                                        }
                                        if (msg == null) {
                                                break;
                                        } else {
                                                displayMsg(msg);
                                        }
                                }
                        }
                }).start();

        }
```

```java
public void displayMsg(String msg) {
    final String msgText = msg;
    handler.post(new Runnable() {

        @Override
        public void run() {
            adapter.add(msgText);
            msgList.setAdapter(adapter);
            msgList.smoothScrollToPosition(
                adapter.getCount() - 1);
        }
    });

}

}
```

4. Add a new uses-permission to the AndroidManifest.xml file -

```xml
<?xml version="1.0" encoding="utf-8"?>
<manifest xmlns:android="http://schemas.android.com/apk/res/android"
  package="com.iducate.socketsdemo"
  android:versionCode="1"
  android:versionName="1.0" >

  <uses-sdk
    android:minSdkVersion="8"
    android:targetSdkVersion="19" />

  <uses-permission android:name="android.permission.INTERNET" />

  <application
    android:allowBackup="true"
    android:icon="@drawable/ic_launcher"
    android:label="@string/app_name"
    android:theme="@style/AppTheme" >
    <activity
      android:name="com.iducate.socketsdemo.MainActivity"
      android:label="@string/app_name" >
      <intent-filter>
        <action android:name="android.intent.action.MAIN" />

        <category android:name="android.intent.category.LAUNCHER" />
```

```
    </intent-filter>
  </activity>
  </application>
```

```
</manifest>
```

5. Now, in order to run the application, we will need a socket server. The source code in the current chapter contains a directory named "chat_server" which contains a java class named ChatServer.java. All you need to do is, compile that class file from terminal (or Command Prompt in windows) and then run it. Here are the instructions -

- Open Terminal (or Command Prompt in Windows)
- Change into the chat_server directory, replace directory/path with actual directory path -

  cd directory/path/chat_server

- Compile the class using following command -

  javac ChatServer.java

- Run the file using following command -

  java ChatServer

6. Once you run the ChatServer.java from terminal, it will act as a socket server and will listen to localhost at port 8013.

7. Now, keep the socket server running and launch your application to an AVD. You will notice a message "Connected to server..." appearing on your application's UI (figure 10.7). From your application, if you send a message using "Send" button, it will appear in the terminal window where the socket server is running (figure 10.8).

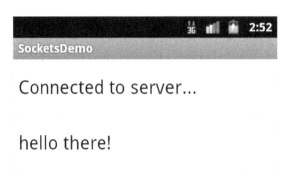

Figure 10.7: Running SocketsDemo application

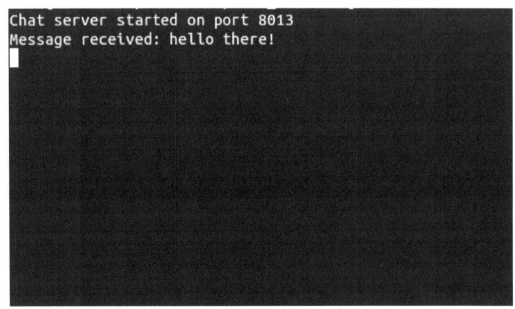

Figure 10.8: Terminal view of ChatServer

How It Works?

The sendMessageToServer() method sends a text message to the socket server -

```java
public void sendMessageToServer(String str) {

    final String msg = str;
    new Thread(new Runnable() {

        @Override
        public void run() {
            PrintWriter out;
            try {
                Socket socket = new Socket(
                        HOST_ADDR, PORT_NUMBER);

                out = new PrintWriter(
                    socket.getOutputStream());
                out.println(msg);
                out.flush();
            } catch (UnknownHostException e) {
                e.printStackTrace();
            } catch (IOException e) {
                e.printStackTrace();
            }

        }
    }).start();
}
```

Within this method, we start a new thread to perform it's tasks. We create a new socket instance by passing the host address and port number. Then, we create a new instance of PrintWriter class by passing the output stream obtained from socket. Finally, we display the message to the console window by calling println() method.

The receiveMsg() method is responsible for getting messages from the socket server -

```java
public void receiveMsg() {
    new Thread(new Runnable() {
        @Override
```

```java
            public void run() {
                Socket socket = null;
                BufferedReader in = null;
                try {
                    socket = new Socket(HOST_ADDR,
PORT_NUMBER);
                } catch (UnknownHostException e) {
                    e.printStackTrace();
                } catch (IOException e) {
                    e.printStackTrace();
                }

                try {
                    in = new BufferedReader(
                            new InputStreamReader(
                                socket.getInputStream()));
                } catch (IOException e) {
                    e.printStackTrace();
                }

                while (true) {
                    String msg = null;
                    try {
                        msg = in.readLine();
                    } catch (IOException e) {
                        e.printStackTrace();
                    }
                    if (msg == null) {
                        break;
                    } else {
                        displayMsg(msg);
                    }
                }
            }
        }).start();

    }
```

We get the messages from socket server by using a BufferedReader object instance and then display them using a helper method displayMsg() -

```java
    public void displayMsg(String msg) {
```

```
        final String msgText = msg;
        handler.post(new Runnable() {

                @Override
                public void run() {
                        adapter.add(msgText);
                        msgList.setAdapter(adapter);
                        msgList.smoothScrollToPosition(
                                adapter.getCount() – 1);
                }
        });


    }
```

Since we can't update UI thread from a separate thread, we use the Handler class for updating our application's UI with the content retrieved from socket server.

In this example, we are connecting to a socket server which is running on a local server. However, instead of using IP address of 127.0.0.1, we need to use the IP address 10.0.2.2. Else, the emulator will not recognize the local server.

Summary

This chapter provides us information about how to connect with the outside world from our Android application. We have seen how to use HTTP protocol to consume XML and JSON services which are popular ways to consume data from web servers. Finally, we have also shown another way to connect to outside world – by using socket programming, which provides us a way to maintain connection between client and server.

Chapter 11: Developing Android Services

In this chapter, we will learn about 'Service' – which is another building block of Android applications. We will learn how to create a service that runs in the background and how to perform long-running background tasks in a separate thread. We will also see how to communicate with an activity from a service.

Creating Your Own Services

A service is an application component that runs in the background without needing to interact with the user. For example, a music player application uses a service to keep playing music while the user might browse the web. Services are typically useful for scenarios where your application don't need to present a UI to the user. In this section, we will create a new project to demonstrate how to start and stop a service.

1. Create a new project named ServicesDemo.

2. Add a new Java class file named MyService.java under the default project package of the src directory. Populate MyService.java class with the following code -

```java
package com.iducate.servicesdemo;

import android.app.Service;
import android.content.Intent;
import android.os.IBinder;
import android.widget.Toast;

public class MyService extends Service {

    @Override
    public IBinder onBind(Intent arg0) {
        // TODO Auto-generated method stub
```

```
        return null;
    }


    @Override
    public int onStartCommand(Intent intent, int flags, int startId)        {
        Toast.makeText(this, "Service Started",
                                    Toast.LENGTH_LONG).show();
        return START_STICKY;
    }



    @Override
    public void onDestroy() {
        super.onDestroy();
        Toast.makeText(this, "Service Destroyed",
                                    Toast.LENGTH_LONG).show();

    }
}
```

3. Since Service a building block of Android, like activity, we need to register them to AndroidManifest.xml file -

```xml
<?xml version="1.0" encoding="utf-8"?>
<manifest xmlns:android="http://schemas.android.com/apk/res/android"
    package="com.iducate.servicesdemo"
    android:versionCode="1"
    android:versionName="1.0" >

    <uses-sdk
        android:minSdkVersion="8"
        android:targetSdkVersion="19" />

    <application
        android:allowBackup="true"
        android:icon="@drawable/ic_launcher"
        android:label="@string/app_name"
        android:theme="@style/AppTheme" >
        <activity
            android:name="com.iducate.servicesdemo.MainActivity"
            android:label="@string/app_name" >
            <intent-filter>
                <action android:name="android.intent.action.MAIN" />
```

469

```
        <category android:name="android.intent.category.LAUNCHER" />
      </intent-filter>
    </activity>

    <service android:name="MyService" />
  </application>

</manifest>
```

4. Now, update the activity_main.xml layout file to include couple of Button widgets -

```xml
<LinearLayout xmlns:android="http://schemas.android.com/apk/res/android"
   android:layout_width="fill_parent"
   android:layout_height="fill_parent"
   android:orientation="vertical" >

   <Button
      android:id="@+id/btnStart"
      android:layout_width="match_parent"
      android:layout_height="wrap_content"
      android:onClick="startService"
      android:text="Start Service" />

   <Button
      android:id="@+id/btnStop"
      android:layout_width="match_parent"
      android:layout_height="wrap_content"
      android:onClick="stopService"
      android:text="Stop Service" />

</LinearLayout>
```

5. Update the MainActivity.java file with the following code -

```java
package com.iducate.servicesdemo;
```

```java
import android.app.Activity;
import android.content.Intent;
import android.os.Bundle;
import android.view.View;

public class MainActivity extends Activity {

    @Override
    protected void onCreate(Bundle savedInstanceState) {
        super.onCreate(savedInstanceState);
        setContentView(R.layout.activity_main);
    }

    public void startService(View v) {
        Intent intent = new Intent(this, MyService.class);
        startService(intent);
    }

    public void stopService(View v) {
        Intent intent = new Intent(this, MyService.class);
        stopService(intent);
    }

}
```

6. Run the application and you will see a layout with two buttons – one for starting the service and another for stopping the service (figure 11.1) -

Figure 11.1: Starting service

How It Works?

The above example shows how to create a very simple Android service. All our service classes should extend the base Service class -

```
public class MyService extends Service {
```

Within MyService class, we have implemented three methods -

```
@Override
public IBinder onBind(Intent arg0) { ... }

@Override
public int onStartCommand(Intent intent, int flags, int startId)        { ... }


@Override
```

```
public void onDestroy() { ... }
```

The onBind() method let us bind an activity (or even another service) to a service. This enables us to access members and methods of a service from an activity class. In our simple example, the onBind() method is just returning null. Later, we will see how to do binding.

The onStartCommand() method is called when we start the service explicitly by calling startService() method. In our example, we have returned the constant START_STICKY, so the service will continue to run until it is explicitly stopped.

The onDestroy() method is called when the service is stopped by calling stopService() method. We generally use this method to clean up the resources used by our service.

Our implementation of onStartCommand() and onDestroy() method simply show a Toast message.

Like activity, we need to register the service class to AndroidManifest.xml file -

```
<service android:name="MyService" />
```

To start a service, we call the startService() method -

```
Intent intent = new Intent(this, MyService.class);
startService(intent);
```

The startService() method takes an Intent object, which defines the context and the service class we are going to start.

To stop a service, we call the stopService() method -

```
Intent intent = new Intent(this, MyService.class);
stopService(intent);
```


Performing Long-Running Tasks in a Service

Though services run in the background, that doesn't mean it runs on a separate thread. It is important to remember that, like activity, services run on the same UI thread (with the exception of IntentService, which will be introduced later in this chapter). So, if our service need to execute a long running task, we should run that on a separate thread. We can use either standard Java Thread class or AsyncTask class for executing long-running tasks. We will update the previous project to simulate a file download task.

1. Update the MyService.java file with the highlighted code -

```java
package com.iducate.servicesdemo;

import java.net.MalformedURLException;
import java.net.URL;

import android.app.Service;
import android.content.Intent;
import android.os.AsyncTask;
import android.os.IBinder;
import android.util.Log;
import android.widget.Toast;

public class MyService extends Service {

    @Override
    public IBinder onBind(Intent arg0) {
        // TODO Auto-generated method stub
        return null;
    }

    @Override
    public int onStartCommand(Intent intent, int flags, int startId)     {

        try {
            new DownloadTask().execute(new URL(
                "http://www.example.com/downloads/file.pdf"));
        } catch (MalformedURLException e) {
            // TODO Auto-generated catch block
            e.printStackTrace();
        }

        return START_STICKY;
    }
```

```java
@Override
public void onDestroy() {
        super.onDestroy();
        Toast.makeText(this, "Service Destroyed",
                                Toast.LENGTH_LONG).show();
}

private class DownloadTask extends AsyncTask<URL, Integer,
String> {

        @Override
        protected String doInBackground(URL... params) {
                for (int i = 1; i <= 10; i++) {
                        try {
                                Thread.sleep(1000);
                        } catch (InterruptedException e) {
                                // TODO Auto-generated catch block
                                e.printStackTrace();
                        }
                        publishProgress(i * 10);
                }

                return null;
        }

        @Override
        protected void onProgressUpdate(Integer... values) {
                super.onProgressUpdate(values);
                Log.d("DownloadTask", values[0] + "% downloaded");
        }

        @Override
        protected void onPostExecute(String result) {
                super.onPostExecute(result);
                Toast.makeText(getBaseContext(), "Download Complete",
                                Toast.LENGTH_LONG).show();
                stopSelf();
        }

}
}
```

2. Run the project again with the above modifications. Once you click the "Start Service" button, you will notice the LogCat view outputs download progress periodically (figure 11.2) and once the AsyncTask class's execution is finished, a Toast message will be shown.

How It Works?

Here you will notice that we have added a new AsyncTask subclass named DownloadTask as a private inner class of our MyService class.

The doInBackground() method of DownloadTask class simulates a file download -

```
@Override
protected String doInBackground(URL... params) {
    for (int i = 1; i <= 10; i++) {
        try {
            Thread.sleep(1000);
        } catch (InterruptedException e) {
            // TODO Auto-generated catch block
            e.printStackTrace();
        }
        publishProgress(i * 10);
    }

    return null;
}
```

This method runs on a separate background thread. Within this method, we simply loop through from 1 to 10 and make a delay of 1000 milliseconds. We also periodically publish updates by calling publishProgress() method -

```
@Override
protected void onProgressUpdate(Integer... values) {
    super.onProgressUpdate(values);
    Log.d("DownloadTask", values[0] + "% downloaded");
}
```

The onProgressUpdate() method show a log message with progress (figure 11.2) -

L	Time	PID	TID	Application	Tag	Text
D	06-11 12:28:06.665	14303	14303	com.iducate.servicesdemo	DownloadTask	10% downloaded
D	06-11 12:28:07.665	14303	14303	com.iducate.servicesdemo	DownloadTask	20% downloaded
D	06-11 12:28:08.666	14303	14303	com.iducate.servicesdemo	DownloadTask	30% downloaded
D	06-11 12:28:09.666	14303	14303	com.iducate.servicesdemo	DownloadTask	40% downloaded
D	06-11 12:28:10.667	14303	14303	com.iducate.servicesdemo	DownloadTask	50% downloaded
D	06-11 12:28:11.667	14303	14303	com.iducate.servicesdemo	DownloadTask	60% downloaded
D	06-11 12:28:12.668	14303	14303	com.iducate.servicesdemo	DownloadTask	70% downloaded
D	06-11 12:28:13.668	14303	14303	com.iducate.servicesdemo	DownloadTask	80% downloaded
D	06-11 12:28:14.669	14303	14303	com.iducate.servicesdemo	DownloadTask	90% downloaded
D	06-11 12:28:15.669	14303	14303	com.iducate.servicesdemo	DownloadTask	100% downloaded

Figure 11.2: LogCat view with progress messages

Once the doInBackground() method has finished execution, the onPostExecute() method is called -

```
@Override
protected void onPostExecute(String result) {
        super.onPostExecute(result);
        Toast.makeText(getBaseContext(), "Download Complete",
                Toast.LENGTH_LONG).show();
        stopSelf();
}
```

Within this method, we show a Toast message indicating download is completed and also stop the service by calling stopSelf() method.

We update the onStartCommand() method to create a new instance of DownloadTask class and call it's execute method -

```
@Override
public int onStartCommand(Intent intent, int flags, int startId)        {

        try {
                new DownloadTask().execute(new URL(
                        "http://www.example.com/downloads/file.pdf"));
        } catch (MalformedURLException e) {
                // TODO Auto-generated catch block
                e.printStackTrace();
        }

        return START_STICKY;
}
```

Performing Repeated Tasks in a Service

In addition to executing long-running tasks in a service, we can also perform repeated tasks in a service. We can use the Timer class within our service to execute a block of code at regular time intervals. In this section, we will update our ongoing example project to perform a repeated task in our MyService class.

1. Update MyService.java class file with the highlighted lines -

```java
package com.iducate.servicesdemo;

import java.net.MalformedURLException;
import java.net.URL;
import java.util.Timer;
import java.util.TimerTask;

import android.app.Service;
import android.content.Intent;
import android.os.AsyncTask;
import android.os.IBinder;
import android.util.Log;
import android.widget.Toast;

public class MyService extends Service {

    private int counter = 0;
    private static final int UPDATE_INTERVAL = 1000;
    private Timer timer = new Timer();

    @Override
    public IBinder onBind(Intent arg0) {
        // TODO Auto-generated method stub
        return null;
    }

    @Override
    public int onStartCommand(Intent intent, int flags, int startId)     {

        doRepeatedly();

        return START_STICKY;
```

```java
}

private void doRepeatedly() {
        TimerTask task = new TimerTask() {

                @Override
                public void run() {
                        Log.d("TimerTask", "Counter: "+counter);
                        counter++;
                }
        };

        timer.scheduleAtFixedRate(task, 0, UPDATE_INTERVAL);
}

@Override
public void onDestroy() {
        super.onDestroy();

        if(timer != null) {
                timer.cancel();
        }

        Toast.makeText(this, "Service Destroyed",
                                Toast.LENGTH_LONG).show();
}

private class DownloadTask extends AsyncTask<URL, Integer,
        String> {

        @Override
        protected String doInBackground(URL... params) {
                for (int i = 1; i <= 10; i++) {
                        try {
                                Thread.sleep(1000);
                        } catch (InterruptedException e) {
                                // TODO Auto-generated catch block
                                e.printStackTrace();
                        }
                        publishProgress(i * 10);
                }

                return null;
```

```
        }

        @Override
        protected void onProgressUpdate(Integer... values) {
            super.onProgressUpdate(values);
            Log.d("DownloadTask", values[0] + "% downloaded");
        }

        @Override
        protected void onPostExecute(String result) {
            super.onPostExecute(result);
            Toast.makeText(getBaseContext(), "Download Complete",
                    Toast.LENGTH_LONG).show();
            stopSelf();
        }

    }
}
```

2. Now run the application and click the "Start Service" button. If you check the LogCat view, you will find that in every 1000 milliseconds, it outputs a new count (figure 11.3) -

Le	Time	PID	TID	Application	Tag	Text
D	06-11 20:14:14.099	19660	19677	com.iducate.servicesdemo	TimerTask	Counter: 0
D	06-11 20:14:15.098	19660	19677	com.iducate.servicesdemo	TimerTask	Counter: 1
D	06-11 20:14:16.098	19660	19677	com.iducate.servicesdemo	TimerTask	Counter: 2
D	06-11 20:14:17.098	19660	19677	com.iducate.servicesdemo	TimerTask	Counter: 3
D	06-11 20:14:18.099	19660	19677	com.iducate.servicesdemo	TimerTask	Counter: 4
D	06-11 20:14:19.098	19660	19677	com.iducate.servicesdemo	TimerTask	Counter: 5
D	06-11 20:14:20.098	19660	19677	com.iducate.servicesdemo	TimerTask	Counter: 6
D	06-11 20:14:21.098	19660	19677	com.iducate.servicesdemo	TimerTask	Counter: 7
D	06-11 20:14:22.099	19660	19677	com.iducate.servicesdemo	TimerTask	Counter: 8
D	06-11 20:14:23.098	19660	19677	com.iducate.servicesdemo	TimerTask	Counter: 9
D	06-11 20:14:24.099	19660	19677	com.iducate.servicesdemo	TimerTask	Counter: 10

Figure 11.3: LogCat view of running repeated task

How It Works?

Here, we have created a new instance of Timer object and called scheduleAtFixedRate() method -

```
private void doRepeatedly() {
    TimerTask task = new TimerTask() {
```

480

```
                    @Override
                    public void run() {
                            Log.d("TimerTask", "Counter: "+counter);
                            counter++;
                    }
            };

            timer.scheduleAtFixedRate(task, 0, UPDATE_INTERVAL);
    }
```

The scheduleAtFixedRate() method takes three arguments – the first one is an instance of TimerTask class. The second argument specifies the time in milliseconds before first execution. Finally, the third argument specifies a time interval between subsequent executions. The code inside run() method of TimerTask instance runs at the specified time interval, within which we simply show a Log message.

Once you will start the service via "Start Service" button, it will call the onStartCommand() life cycle method of MyService, which simply calls doRepeatedly() method -

```
    @Override
    public int onStartCommand(Intent intent, int flags, int startId)        {

        doRepeatedly();

        return START_STICKY;
    }
```

As long as the service will keeps running, the code inside run() method of TimerTask will keep executing.

If however, user stops the service, the onDestroy() method of MyService will be called, which will cancel the timer by calling cancel() method -

```
    if(timer != null) {
        timer.cancel();
    }
```

Executing Asynchronous Tasks on Separate Threads Using

IntentService

Now, we know how to use services to run background tasks. Since the code inside the onStartCommand() method executes on the main UI thread, we use a separate thread or AsyncTask subclass to schedule long-running operations. This ensures that the tasks executes in a separate worker thread. Once the task has finished execution, we call the stopSelf() method to stop that service.

There is actually a better way to do these sort of operations by using an IntentService. An IntentService is a subclass of the Service class. It executes its task within a separate worker thread and terminates itself after the task is completed. In this section, we will see how to use IntentService class.

1. Using the ongoing example project, create a new Java class file named MyIntentService.java under the src directory.

2. Populate the MyIntentService.java with following code -

```java
package com.iducate.servicesdemo;

import java.net.MalformedURLException;
import java.net.URL;

import android.app.IntentService;
import android.content.Intent;
import android.util.Log;

public class MyIntentService extends IntentService {

    public MyIntentService() {
        super("MyIntentService");
    }

    @Override
    protected void onHandleIntent(Intent intent) {
        try {
            downloadFile(new URL(
                "http://www.example.com/downloads/somefile.pdf"));
            Log.d("MyIntentService", "Download completed");
        } catch (MalformedURLException e) {
            e.printStackTrace();
```

```
            }
        }

        private void downloadFile(URL url) {
            try {
                    // simulate download file task
                    Thread.sleep(3000);
            } catch (InterruptedException e) {
                    e.printStackTrace();
            }
        }

}
```

3. We need to register the MyIntentService.java class to AndroidManifest.xml file -

```xml
<?xml version="1.0" encoding="utf-8"?>
<manifest xmlns:android="http://schemas.android.com/apk/res/android"
    package="com.iducate.servicesdemo"
    android:versionCode="1"
    android:versionName="1.0" >

    <uses-sdk
        android:minSdkVersion="8"
        android:targetSdkVersion="19" />

    <application
        android:allowBackup="true"
        android:icon="@drawable/ic_launcher"
        android:label="@string/app_name"
        android:theme="@style/AppTheme" >
        <activity
            android:name="com.iducate.servicesdemo.MainActivity"
            android:label="@string/app_name" >
            <intent-filter>
                <action android:name="android.intent.action.MAIN" />

                <category android:name="android.intent.category.LAUNCHER" />
            </intent-filter>
        </activity>

        <service android:name="MyService" />
        <service android:name="MyIntentService" />
```

```
</application>

</manifest>
```

4. We want to start this IntentService when user clicks the "Start Service" button. Update the MainActivity.java file with the highlighted code -

```java
package com.iducate.servicesdemo;

import android.app.Activity;
import android.content.Intent;
import android.os.Bundle;
import android.view.View;

public class MainActivity extends Activity {

    @Override
    protected void onCreate(Bundle savedInstanceState) {
        super.onCreate(savedInstanceState);
        setContentView(R.layout.activity_main);
    }

    public void startService(View v) {
        //Intent intent = new Intent(getBaseContext(), MyService.class);
        //startService(intent);
        startService(new Intent(
                getBaseContext(), MyIntentService.class));
    }

    public void stopService(View v) {
        Intent intent = new Intent(this, MyService.class);
        stopService(intent);
    }

}
```

5. Now, run the application and click "Start Service" button. If you monitor the LogCat view, you will see a log message appear as shown in figure 11.4 -

L	Time	PID	TID	Application	Tag	Text
D	06-12 11:17:08.835	26842	26868	com.iducate.servicesdemo	MyIntentService	Download completed

How It Works?

The first thing to notice is that our MyIntentService class extends IntentService class instead of Service class -

```
public class MyIntentService extends IntentService {
```

We need to implement a constructor for our class and call it's superclass constructor with a string argument (the string argument could be anything, though it is more common to provide class name) -

```
public MyIntentService() {
        super("MyIntentService");
}
```

We then implement the onHandleIntent() method, which is executed on a separate worker thread -

```
@Override
protected void onHandleIntent(Intent intent) {
        try {
                downloadFile(new URL(
                    "http://www.example.com/downloads/somefile.pdf"));
                Log.d("MyIntentService", "Download completed");
        } catch (MalformedURLException e) {
                e.printStackTrace();
        }
}
```

This is the method where we put the code for long-running operations. In this case, we have simulated file download behavior by putting the thread to sleep for certain duration. When the code has finished execution, the thread is terminated and the service is stopped automatically.

Like a regular Service component, IntentService is also started by calling startService() method -

```
startService(new Intent(
                    getBaseContext(), MyIntentService.class));
```

Establishing Communication Between a Service and an Activity

Services often execute in it's own thread for background tasks, like updating a database asynchronously. In those cases, it is fine to run the service and do its task independently of the activity that started the service. In some scenarios however, you will need to communicate from a service to the activity that started the service. For example, if you want to download a file, you can start a service from your activity. This service will download the file and when the download will finish, you will need some way to communicate back to the activity to let the user know that the download is finished.

In this section, we will see how a service can communicate with an activity using the BroadcastReceiver.

1. We will use the same project that we created in the previous section. Update the MyIntentService.java file with the highlighted code -

```java
package com.iducate.servicesdemo;

import java.net.MalformedURLException;
import java.net.URL;

import android.app.IntentService;
import android.content.Intent;
import android.util.Log;

public class MyIntentService extends IntentService {

    public MyIntentService() {
        super("MyIntentService");
    }

    @Override
    protected void onHandleIntent(Intent intent) {
        try {
            downloadFile(new URL(
                "http://www.example.com/downloads/somefile.pdf"));
            Log.d("MyIntentService", "Download completed");
```

486

```java
                     // send a broadcast to notify the activity when the
                     // download is finished
            Intent broadcastIntent = new

Intent("FILE_DOWNLOAD_ACTION");
                        getBaseContext().sendBroadcast(broadcastIntent);


            } catch (MalformedURLException e) {
                e.printStackTrace();
            }
        }

        private void downloadFile(URL url) {
            try {
                     // simulate download file task
                Thread.sleep(3000);
            } catch (InterruptedException e) {
                e.printStackTrace();
            }
        }
    }

}
```

2. Update the MainActivity.java file with the highlighted code -

```java
package com.iducate.servicesdemo;

import android.app.Activity;
import android.content.BroadcastReceiver;
import android.content.Context;
import android.content.Intent;
import android.content.IntentFilter;
import android.os.Bundle;
import android.view.View;
import android.widget.Toast;

public class MainActivity extends Activity {
    IntentFilter intentFilter;

    @Override
    protected void onCreate(Bundle savedInstanceState) {
        super.onCreate(savedInstanceState);
```

```java
        setContentView(R.layout.activity_main);
    }

    @Override
    protected void onResume() {
        super.onResume();

        intentFilter = new IntentFilter();
        intentFilter.addAction("FILE_DOWNLOAD_ACTION");

        registerReceiver(receiver, intentFilter);
    }

    @Override
    protected void onPause() {
        super.onPause();

        unregisterReceiver(receiver);
    }

    private BroadcastReceiver receiver = new BroadcastReceiver() {

        @Override
        public void onReceive(Context context, Intent intent) {
            Toast.makeText(getBaseContext(), "File download
                        completed!", Toast.LENGTH_LONG).show();
        }
    };

    public void startService(View v) {
        startService(new Intent(getBaseContext(),

MyIntentService.class));
    }

    public void stopService(View v) {
        Intent intent = new Intent(this, MyService.class);
        stopService(intent);
    }

}
```

3. Run the application and click the "Start Service" button. After three seconds,

you will see a Toast message which indicates that the simulated file download is finished (figure 11.5) -

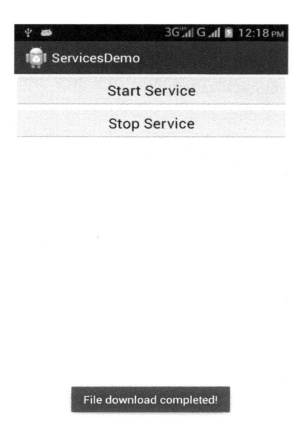

Figure 11.5: Running Application

How It Works?

In order to notify an activity when a service has finished execution, we broadcast an intent using the sendBroadcast() method call -

```
@Override
protected void onHandleIntent(Intent intent) {
    try {
        downloadFile(new URL(
            "http://www.example.com/downloads/somefile.pdf"));
        Log.d("MyIntentService", "Download completed");

        // send a broadcast to notify the activity when the
        // download is finished
```

```
                    Intent broadcastIntent = new

Intent("FILE_DOWNLOAD_ACTION");
            getBaseContext().sendBroadcast(broadcastIntent);

        } catch (MalformedURLException e) {
                e.printStackTrace();
        }
    }
```

We set the action string of the broadcast intent as FILE_DOWNLOAD_ACTION, which means that any activity listening for this intent will be invoked.

In our MainActivity.java file, we created a BroadcastReceiver class which will handles the broadcast intent from MyIntentService class -

```
    private BroadcastReceiver receiver = new BroadcastReceiver() {

        @Override
        public void onReceive(Context context, Intent intent) {
                Toast.makeText(getBaseContext(), "File download
                        completed!", Toast.LENGTH_LONG).show();
        }
    };
```

Within onResume() method of MainActivity.java class, we create an intent filter with the action string of FILE_DOWNLOAD_ACTION and register a broadcast receiver by calling registerReceiver() method -

```
    @Override
    protected void onResume() {
        super.onResume();

        intentFilter = new IntentFilter();
        intentFilter.addAction("FILE_DOWNLOAD_ACTION");

        registerReceiver(receiver, intentFilter);
    }
```

The registerReceiver() method takes two arguments – a broadcast receiver class that will handle broadcast event and an intent filter for which the receiver will listen for.

So, when the download task is completed, the service will broadcast the intent. Our broadcast receiver class will listen for that event and it's onReceive() method will be invoked. Within onReceive() method, we show a Toast message.

We are only interested in receiving broadcast notification as long as the activity is running. So we unregister our broadcast receiver within onPause() method by calling unRegisterReceiver() method -

```
@Override
protected void onPause() {
        super.onPause();

        unregisterReceiver(receiver);
}
```

Binding Activities to Services

In some cases, you will find that it is convenient if we could pass data from our activity to the service. We have seen an example in this chapter where we have simulated a file download service. If you revisit the example, you will notice we have used a hardcoded url within the service class. What if we want to pass urls from the activity? One approach might be to pass the data as extra values with Intent. This approach works for some cases, when you have relatively complex data to deal with, it becomes a problem. A better approach will be to bind an activity to a service, so that the activity can call any public members and methods on the service directly. This section will demonstrate this binding of activity with service.

1. Using the ServicesDemo project we created earlier, add the following highlighted code to MyService.java file -

```
package com.iducate.servicesdemo;

import java.net.URL;
import java.util.Timer;
import java.util.TimerTask;

import android.app.Service;
import android.content.Intent;
```

```java
import android.os.AsyncTask;
import android.os.Binder;
import android.os.IBinder;
import android.util.Log;
import android.widget.Toast;

public class MyService extends Service {

        private int counter = 0;
        private static final int UPDATE_INTERVAL = 1000;
        private Timer timer = new Timer();

        URL[] urls;
        private final IBinder binder = new MyBinder();

        public class MyBinder extends Binder {
            MyService getService() {
                    return MyService.this;
            }
        }

        @Override
        public IBinder onBind(Intent arg0) {
            return binder;
        }

        @Override
        public int onStartCommand(Intent intent, int flags, int startId)    {

            //doRepeatedly();

            new DownloadTask().execute(urls);

            return START_STICKY;
        }

        private void doRepeatedly() {
            ...
        }

        @Override
        public void onDestroy() {
            ...
```

```
        }

        private class DownloadTask extends AsyncTask<URL, Integer,
        String> {
                ...
        }
}
```

2. Add the highlighted code to MainActivity.java file -

```
package com.iducate.servicesdemo;

import java.net.MalformedURLException;
import java.net.URL;

import android.app.Activity;
import android.content.BroadcastReceiver;
import android.content.ComponentName;
import android.content.Context;
import android.content.Intent;
import android.content.IntentFilter;
import android.content.ServiceConnection;
import android.os.Bundle;
import android.os.IBinder;
import android.view.View;
import android.widget.Toast;

public class MainActivity extends Activity {
        IntentFilter intentFilter;

        MyService serviceBinder;
        Intent intent;

        private ServiceConnection connection = new ServiceConnection() {

                @Override
                public void onServiceDisconnected(ComponentName name) {
                        serviceBinder = null;
                }

                @Override
                public void onServiceConnected(ComponentName name, IBinder
                service) {
```

```java
            serviceBinder =

    ((MyService.MyBinder)service).getService();

                try {
                    URL[] urls = new URL[] {
                new URL("http://www.example.com/downloads/
file1.pdf"),

                new URL("http://www.example.com/downloads/
file2.pdf"),

                new URL("http://www.example.com/downloads/
file3.pdf"),

                    };
                    serviceBinder.urls = urls;
                } catch (MalformedURLException e) {
                    e.printStackTrace();
                }
                startService(intent);
            }
    };

    @Override
    protected void onCreate(Bundle savedInstanceState) {
        super.onCreate(savedInstanceState);
        setContentView(R.layout.activity_main);
    }

    @Override
    protected void onResume() {
        super.onResume();

        intentFilter = new IntentFilter();
        intentFilter.addAction("FILE_DOWNLOAD_ACTION");

        registerReceiver(receiver, intentFilter);
    }

    @Override
    protected void onPause() {
        super.onPause();

        unregisterReceiver(receiver);
    }
```

```java
    private BroadcastReceiver receiver = new BroadcastReceiver() {

        @Override
        public void onReceive(Context context, Intent intent) {
            Toast.makeText(getBaseContext(), "File download
                          completed!", Toast.LENGTH_LONG).show();
        }
    };

    public void startService(View v) {
        intent = new Intent(this, MyService.class);
        bindService(intent, connection, Context.BIND_AUTO_CREATE);
    }

    public void stopService(View v) {
        Intent intent = new Intent(this, MyService.class);
        stopService(intent);
    }

}
```

3. Run the application. When you click the "Start Service" button, it will start the service as usual.

How It Works?

In order to bind an activity to a service, we first need to declare a subclass of Binder class -

```java
    public class MyBinder extends Binder {
        MyService getService() {
            return MyService.this;
        }
    }
```

The MyBinder class implements a single method named getService(), which simply returns an instance of the service.

We have created an instance of the MyBinder class -

495

```
private final IBinder binder = new MyBinder();
```

The onBind() method of our MyService class returns the MyBinder instance -

```
@Override
public IBinder onBind(Intent arg0) {
        return binder;
}
```

Within onStartCommand() method, we called execute() method of DownloadTask class, with urls array as argument -

```
@Override
public int onStartCommand(Intent intent, int flags, int startId)          {
        new DownloadTask().execute(urls);

        return START_STICKY;
}
```

We defined urls array as a public member in our service class. This urls array will be set from our activity class directly.

Within MainActivity.java class, we declare an instance of our service class -

```
MyService serviceBinder;
```

We will use the serviceBinder object as a reference to the service and access it directly. In particular, we populate urls array which is a member variable of service class.

We create an instance of ServiceConnection class which will be used to monitor the state of the service -

```
private ServiceConnection connection = new ServiceConnection() {

        @Override
        public void onServiceDisconnected(ComponentName name) {
                serviceBinder = null;
        }

        @Override
```

```
public void onServiceConnected(ComponentName name, IBinder
service) {
        serviceBinder =

((MyService.MyBinder)service).getService();

        try {
            URL[] urls = new URL[] {
        new URL("http://www.example.com/downloads/file1.pdf"),
        new URL("http://www.example.com/downloads/file2.pdf"),
        new URL("http://www.example.com/downloads/file3.pdf"),
            };
            serviceBinder.urls = urls;
        } catch (MalformedURLException e) {
            e.printStackTrace();
        }
        startService(intent);
    }
};
```

Within the subclass of ServiceConnection class, we need to implement two methods – onServiceConnected() and onServiceDisconnected(). The onServiceConnected() method is called when our activity is connected to the service and onServiceDisconnected() is called when the service is disconnected from the activity.

Within onServiceConnected() method, we obtain an instance of the service by calling getService() method of the service argument and assign it to serviceBinder object. Through the serviceBinder object which has a reference to the service, we can access all the members and methods of the service class. That's how we set urls array from our activity class -

```
URL[] urls = new URL[] {
        new URL("http://www.example.com/downloads/file1.pdf"),
        new URL("http://www.example.com/downloads/file2.pdf"),
        new URL("http://www.example.com/downloads/file3.pdf"),
};

serviceBinder.urls = urls;
```

Then we start the service using an Intent object –

```
startService(intent);
```

Before we could start the service however, we need to bind the activity to the service -

```
public void startService(View v) {
        intent = new Intent(this, MyService.class);
        bindService(intent, connection, Context.BIND_AUTO_CREATE);
}
```

We call the bindService() method to bind activity to the service, which takes three arguments – an Intent object, a ServiceConnection object and a flag to indicate how the service should be bound.

Understanding Threading

At this point, you are well familiar with the fact that if you have a long-running task, you should run it on a separate thread. The code you execute from your activity classes or from service classes (except IntentService), run on UI threads (also known as main application thread). If you run any long-running task on a UI thread, your application's UI will freeze. It will not be responsive and users will have a bad experience. What's even worse is if it takes a bit longer (typically 3 to 5 seconds), Android will show a "Application Not Responding" dialog (also known as ANR dialog), which allows the user to forcefully close the application.

For the above mentioned reasons, if you do any task from your application that can potentially take longer to execute, you should run that on a separate thread. As a Java programmer, you can do this by using standard Java Threading mechanism (like creating instance of Thread class). One problem that is typically faced by new developers is to create a new instance of Thread class to execute some task and then updating UI from that thread. Android platform will not let you manipulate or update user interface from any thread other than the UI thread. Android provides the Handler class to update UI from a non-UI thread. Yet, you have a better option using the AsyncTask class, which lets you run the long-running task in a separate background thread and also lets you update the UI thread including periodically publishing the progress.

Though we have used both Thread and AsyncTask classes in many occasions throughout previous chapters and within this current chapter, for the sake of completeness, we will create a new project to demonstrate the usage of both

Thread and AsyncTask classes.

1. Create a new project named ThreadingDemo.

2. Update the activity_main.xml layout file with the following code -

```xml
<LinearLayout xmlns:android="http://schemas.android.com/apk/res/android"
    android:layout_width="fill_parent"
    android:layout_height="fill_parent"
    android:orientation="vertical" >

    <Button
        android:id="@+id/btnFetch"
        android:layout_width="wrap_content"
        android:layout_height="wrap_content"
        android:onClick="fetchData"
        android:text="Fetch Data" />

    <TextView
        android:id="@+id/tvOutput"
        android:layout_width="wrap_content"
        android:layout_height="wrap_content" />

</LinearLayout>
```

3. Update MainActivity.java class file with the following code -

```java
package com.iducate.threadingdemo;

import android.app.Activity;
import android.os.Bundle;
import android.os.Handler;
import android.view.View;
import android.widget.TextView;

public class MainActivity extends Activity {

    private TextView tvOutput;
    private static final int SUCCESS = 1;

    @Override
    protected void onCreate(Bundle savedInstanceState) {
```

```java
        super.onCreate(savedInstanceState);
        setContentView(R.layout.activity_main);

        tvOutput = (TextView) findViewById(R.id.tvOutput);
    }

    public void fetchData(View v) {
        tvOutput.setText("Fetching data from remote server...");
        thread.start();
    }

    Thread thread = new Thread(new Runnable() {

        @Override
        public void run() {
            for (int i = 0; i < 10; i++) {
                try {
                    Thread.sleep(1000);
                } catch (InterruptedException e) {
                    // TODO Auto-generated catch block
                    e.printStackTrace();
                }
            }
            handler.sendEmptyMessage(SUCCESS);
        }
    });

    Handler handler = new Handler() {
        public void handleMessage(android.os.Message msg) {
            if(msg.what == SUCCESS) {
                tvOutput.setText("Data fetched from remote server
                    successfully!");
            }
        }
    };

}
```

4. Run the application and click "Fetch Data" button. You will see the TextView below the button show a message saying "Fetching data from remote server...". After ten seconds, the TextView will be updated with text "Data fetched from remote server successfully!" (figure 11.6) -

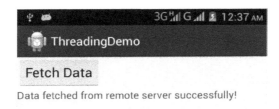

Figure 11.6: Running Application

How It Works?

In this example project, we have simulated fetching network data by putting our thread to sleep for certain period of time. To do that, we have created a new thread -

```
Thread thread = new Thread(new Runnable() {

    @Override
    public void run() {
        for (int i = 0; i < 10; i++) {
            try {
                Thread.sleep(1000);
            } catch (InterruptedException e) {
                // TODO Auto-generated catch block
                e.printStackTrace();
            }
        }
```

```
                    handler.sendEmptyMessage(SUCCESS);
        }
    });
```

Within the run() method, we simply loop through ten times and put the thread in sleep for 1000 milliseconds so it takes ten seconds to finish execution of the run() method.

When the thread execution finishes, we want to update the TextView. But we can not update UI from a separate thread. In order to update the UI, we have thus created a Handler class -

```
Handler handler = new Handler() {
    public void handleMessage(android.os.Message msg) {
        if(msg.what == SUCCESS) {
            tvOutput.setText("Data fetched from remote server
                successfully!");
        }
    }
};
```

The Handler class's handleMessage() method runs in the UI thread, so we can update the UI from the handleMessage() method.

Once the thread's run() method execution is finished, we send a message to our Handler class -

```
handler.sendEmptyMessage(SUCCESS);
```

The sendEmptyMessage() method takes a single argument, an integer number. This number can be used within handleMessage() method of Handler class to identify different results. In this case, we have sent a single message. But in a real life situation, you will most likely send different messages by calling sendEmptyMessage() method multiple times with different number and then check that within handleMessage() method to provide different feedback to the user.

Now, we will see how we can use AysncTask class to do exactly same thing, but more conveniently.

Update the MainActivity.java file with highlighted code -

```java
package com.iducate.threadingdemo;

import android.app.Activity;
import android.os.AsyncTask;
import android.os.Bundle;
import android.os.Handler;
import android.view.View;
import android.widget.TextView;
public class MainActivity extends Activity {

    private TextView tvOutput;
    private static final int SUCCESS = 1;

    @Override
    protected void onCreate(Bundle savedInstanceState) {
        super.onCreate(savedInstanceState);
        setContentView(R.layout.activity_main);

        tvOutput = (TextView) findViewById(R.id.tvOutput);
    }

    public void fetchData(View v) {
        tvOutput.setText("Fetching data from remote server...");
        new FetchTask().execute();
        // thread.start();
    }

    Thread thread = new Thread(new Runnable() {

        @Override
        public void run() {
            for (int i = 0; i < 10; i++) {
                try {
                    Thread.sleep(1000);
                } catch (InterruptedException e) {
                    // TODO Auto-generated catch block
                    e.printStackTrace();
                }
            }
            handler.sendEmptyMessage(SUCCESS);
        }
    });
```

```java
Handler handler = new Handler() {
    public void handleMessage(android.os.Message msg) {
        if (msg.what == SUCCESS) {
            tvOutput.setText("Data fetched from remote server
                successfully!");
        }
    }
};

private class FetchTask extends AsyncTask<Void, Void, String> {

    @Override
    protected String doInBackground(Void... params) {
        for (int i = 0; i < 10; i++) {
            try {
                Thread.sleep(1000);
            } catch (InterruptedException e) {
                // TODO Auto-generated catch block
                e.printStackTrace();
            }
        }

        return null;
    }

    @Override
    protected void onPostExecute(String result) {
        tvOutput.setText("Data fetched from remote server
            successfully!");
    }

}

}
```

The doInBackground() method has exactly the same code we previously had in run() method of our new thread -

```java
@Override
protected String doInBackground(Void... params) {
    for (int i = 0; i < 10; i++) {
```

```
        try {
                Thread.sleep(1000);
        } catch (InterruptedException e) {
                // TODO Auto-generated catch block
                e.printStackTrace();
        }
    }
    return null;
}
```

This method will run in a background thread and once this method execution is finished, the onPostExecute() method runs in the UI thread so we can update the TextView from this method -

```
@Override
protected void onPostExecute(String result) {
        tvOutput.setText("Data fetched from remote server
                        successfully!");
}
```

Now, to execute the AysncTask subclass, we create a new instance and call execute() method -

```
new FetchTask().execute();
```

Summary

In this chapter, we learned how to create a service and run long-running tasks. We have discussed about different types of services and showed how to do background tasks in asynchronous fashion. We have also learned how to bind activity with service, so that it can access members and method of service directly. Finally, we finish the chapter by discussing threading and updating UI thread.

Chapter 12: Publishing Android Applications

In this chapter, we will learn about how to prepare our application for deployment. In order to deploy our application, we need to export our application as an APK file and sign it with a certificate. We will also learn about different strategies for distributing our application and finally show how to publish our application to Google Play, where we can sell the applications and make money.

Preparing for Publishing

Publishing our Android application is relatively easy, we just need to take care of the following steps -

- We need to export our application as an APK (Android Package) file.
- Generate our own self-signed certificate and digitally sign the application with it.
- Deploy the signed application.
- Finally, we need to list our application to Google Play for distributing and selling.

The following sections will discuss different steps we need to follow in order to prepare our application for signing and then deploy it.

We will use MapsExample application that we developed in Chapter 9 to demonstrate how to deploy an Android application. We choose MapsExample application for deployment because it involves the usage of Maps API key.

Versioning Your Application

The AndroidManifest.xml file contains attributes like `android:versionCode` and `android:versionName`, that are used for versioning our Android applications -

```
<?xml version="1.0" encoding="utf-8"?>
```

```xml
<manifest xmlns:android="http://schemas.android.com/apk/res/android"
    package="com.iducate.mapsexample"
    android:versionCode="1"
    android:versionName="1.0" >

    <uses-sdk
        android:minSdkVersion="11"
        android:targetSdkVersion="19" />

    <uses-permission android:name="android.permission.INTERNET" />
    <uses-permission
android:name="android.permission.ACCESS_NETWORK_STATE" />
    <uses-permission
android:name="android.permission.WRITE_EXTERNAL_STORAGE" />
    <uses-permission
android:name="android.permission.ACCESS_FINE_LOCATION" />

    <application
        android:allowBackup="true"
        android:icon="@drawable/ic_launcher"
        android:label="@string/app_name"
        android:theme="@style/AppTheme" >
        <activity
            android:name="com.iducate.mapsexample.MainActivity"
            android:label="@string/app_name" >
            <intent-filter>
                <action android:name="android.intent.action.MAIN" />

                <category android:name="android.intent.category.LAUNCHER" />
            </intent-filter>
        </activity>

        <meta-data
            android:name="com.google.android.maps.v2.API_KEY"
            android:value="AIzaSyD0eACumk7EK0-5D90EbWlDb5LfDz1JngY" />
        <meta-data
            android:name="com.google.android.gms.version"
            android:value="@integer/google_play_services_version" />
    </application>

</manifest>
```

The android:versionCode attribute represents the version number of our Android application. For every revision we make to our application, we should increment this value by 1. This value of android:versionCode attribute is used by Google Play store to determine whether a new version of application is available and thus notify the current users about the upgraded version of your application.

On the other hand, the android:versionName attribute contains the versioning information that is actually visible to users. The value of android:versionName attribute should be a string that represents version information in a more user friendly format. The general convention followed for setting format of android:versionName is as follows -

<major>.<minor>.<point>

Depending upon the type of upgrade, we increase the value of the corresponding part of the version name string. So, if our application undergoes a major upgrade, we increase the value of <major> by 1. For small incremental updates, we increase the value of either <minor> or <point> by 1. For example, when we publish a new application, we might have a version name of "1.0.0". For small incremental update, we might change it to "1.1.0" or "1.0.1". When we have our next major update, we might change the version name to "2.0.0".

So, we can update our AndroidMainifest.xml file as follows -

```xml
<?xml version="1.0" encoding="utf-8"?>
<manifest xmlns:android="http://schemas.android.com/apk/res/android"
    package="com.iducate.mapsexample"
    android:versionCode="1"
    android:versionName="1.0.0" >

    <uses-sdk
        android:minSdkVersion="11"
        android:targetSdkVersion="19" />

    <uses-permission android:name="android.permission.INTERNET" />
    <uses-permission
android:name="android.permission.ACCESS_NETWORK_STATE" />
    <uses-permission
android:name="android.permission.WRITE_EXTERNAL_STORAGE" />
    <uses-permission
android:name="android.permission.ACCESS_FINE_LOCATION" />
```

```
<application
    android:allowBackup="true"
    android:icon="@drawable/ic_launcher"
    android:label="@string/app_name"
    android:theme="@style/AppTheme" >
    <activity
        android:name="com.iducate.mapsexample.MainActivity"
        android:label="@string/app_name" >
        <intent-filter>
            <action android:name="android.intent.action.MAIN" />

            <category android:name="android.intent.category.LAUNCHER" />
        </intent-filter>
    </activity>

    <meta-data
        android:name="com.google.android.maps.v2.API_KEY"
        android:value="AIzaSyD0eACumk7EK0-5D90EbWlDb5LfDz1JngY" />
    <meta-data
        android:name="com.google.android.gms.version"
        android:value="@integer/google_play_services_version" />
</application>

</manifest>
```

At this point, our AndroidMainfest.xml file looks good except the value of Maps API key -

```
<meta-data
        android:name="com.google.android.maps.v2.API_KEY"

        android:value="AIzaSyD0eACumk7EK0-5D90EbWlDb5LfDz1JngY" />
```

Since we are using Maps V2 in our application, we need the Maps API key. We earlier (in Chapter 9) generated this Maps API key for our debug certificate. But, in order to publish the app to Play Store, we will need to sign our application with a production certificate (we will use a self-generated certificate) and update the value of Maps API key to reflect the new signing certificate.

Digitally Signing Your Android Application

All Android applications must be digitally signed before you can upload them to a device, to an emulator, to Google Play or to other app marketplaces. You need to use a digital certificate to sign the APK file for your application which identifies you as the author of the app. A digital certificate includes your name or company name, contact information etc. Unlike some other platform, you don't need to purchase a digital certificate from a certificate authority (CA) to sign your application. Instead, you can generate your own self-signed certificate and use it to sign your Android applications.

Throughout the book, we haven't explicitly signed our application before running them to an emulator or device. Eclipse did that for us automatically using a debug keystore. This was done to simplify the development and testing of application, so we don't need to go through the signing steps while we are developing the application.

However, if you are going to publish your Android application to Google Play, you will need to sign the application with your own certificate. In this section, I will show you how to generate your own application signing certificate and then export a signed APK with that certificate.

1. Select the MapsExample application project in Eclipse and select **File** → **Export.** You will see a new Export dialog window appears (figure 12.1) -

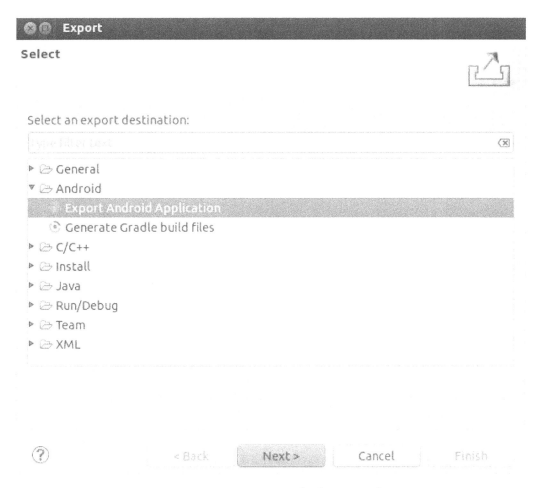

Figure 12.1: Export dialog window

2. In the Export dialog window, expand the Android item and select Export Android Application (as shown in above figure). Then click Next.

3. You will be taken to the Export Android Application window (figure 12.2), which will have MapsExample project automatically selected. If not, use the Browse... button to select MapsExample project and click Next.

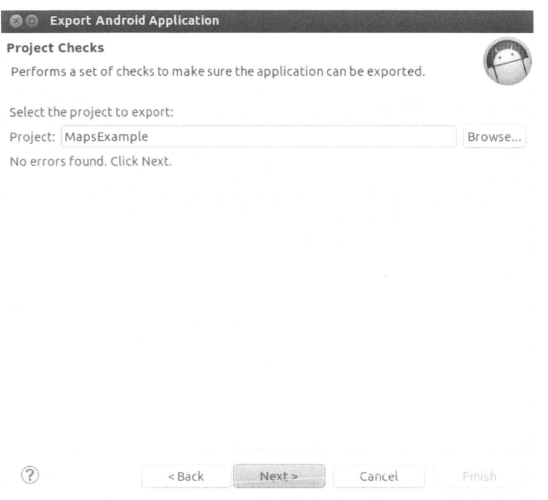

Figure 12.2: Export Android Application window

4. The next window will prompt you to either select an existing keystore or create a new keystore. We will create a new keystore. Select "Create new keystore" option to create a new certificate for signing your application (figure 12.3). Enter a path next to Location field and also enter password. Then click Next.

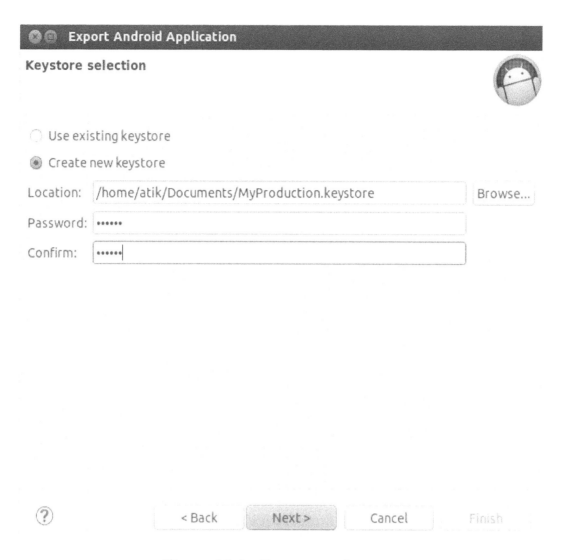

Figure 12.3: Create new keystore

5. The next step is the Key Creation step where you will need to provide information regarding your keystore (figure 12.4). You will need to provide an alias for your keystore, a password to protect the private key and a validity period for the certificate. Enter a number of years from now, so that validity period ends after 22 October 2033 (you can simply provide a validity period of 100 years). Finally, provide some information about yourself (provide value for at least First and Last Name field, other fields are optional). Click Next.

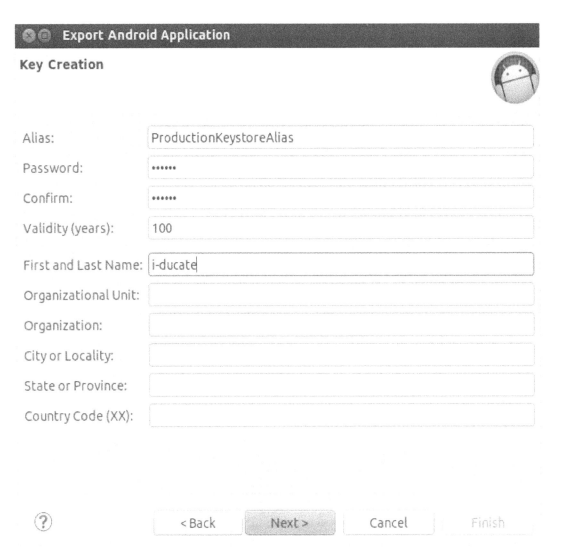

Figure 12.4: Key Creation step

6. Enter a path to store the destination APK file (figure 12.5) and click finish. Now, the APK file will be generated, signed with your own digital signing certificate.

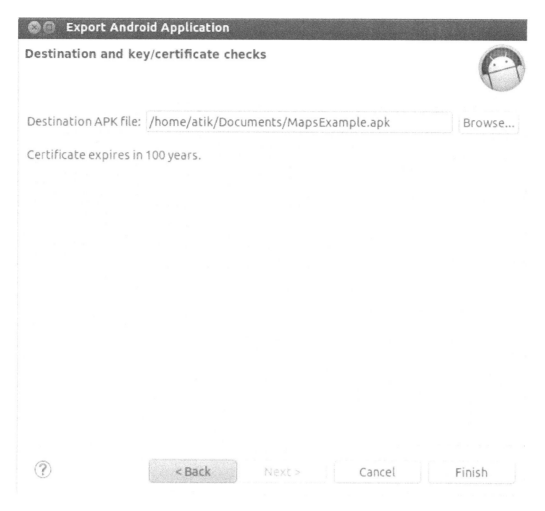

Figure 12.5: Export APK step

7. Now, if our application wasn't using Maps API, we could move to the next step to deploy our app to the Play Store. But since we are using the Google Maps API key, we need to get an updated Maps API key for our new production keystore because previously, we obtained an Maps API key for the debug keystore. If you recall the steps of obtaining Maps API key from Chapter 9, we need to generate a SHA1 hash of production certificate. We will use the keytool command as we did previously. We need to enter the following command from the terminal (or Command Prompt) –

keytool -list -v -keystore <keystore-location> -alias ProductionKeystoreAlias -storepass 123456 -keypass 123456

(make sure you replace <keystore-location> with the actual path of the production keystore that you created at step 4. Also we have used 123456 as password for both step 4 and 5. Replace those with your own passwords which you have used at those steps)

Figure 12.6: Generating certificate fingerprints

8. Take note of the SHA1 fingerprint and go to https://console.developers.google.com/ and sign up for a new Maps V2 API key. (If you don't recall how to do this, check Chapter 9 for step by step instructions)

9. Update the AndroidMinifest.xml file and replace the old Maps API key with the new Maps API key -

```xml
<?xml version="1.0" encoding="utf-8"?>
<manifest xmlns:android="http://schemas.android.com/apk/res/android"
    package="com.iducate.mapsexample"
    android:versionCode="1"
    android:versionName="1.0.0" >

    <uses-sdk
        android:minSdkVersion="11"
        android:targetSdkVersion="19" />

    <uses-permission android:name="android.permission.INTERNET" />
    <uses-permission
android:name="android.permission.ACCESS_NETWORK_STATE" />
    <uses-permission
android:name="android.permission.WRITE_EXTERNAL_STORAGE" />
    <uses-permission
android:name="android.permission.ACCESS_FINE_LOCATION" />

    <application
        android:allowBackup="true"
        android:icon="@drawable/ic_launcher"
        android:label="@string/app_name"
        android:theme="@style/AppTheme" >
        <activity
            android:name="com.iducate.mapsexample.MainActivity"
            android:label="@string/app_name" >
            <intent-filter>
                <action android:name="android.intent.action.MAIN" />
```

```
        <category android:name="android.intent.category.LAUNCHER" />
      </intent-filter>
    </activity>

    <meta-data
       android:name="com.google.android.maps.v2.API_KEY"
       android:value="new_maps_api_key_goes_here" />
    <meta-data
       android:name="com.google.android.gms.version"
       android:value="@integer/google_play_services_version" />
  </application>

</manifest>
```

10. Since we have made changes to the AndroidManifest.xml file, we need to export the application again. Repeat steps 1 to 3. When you are asked to select a keystore, instead of creating a new one, use the existing keystore (figure 12.7) which you have created earlier. You will need to enter the password and click Next.

Figure 12.7: Use existing keystore

11. Select "Use existing key" option (figure 12.8) and from the dropdown, select the Alias, then enter the password you set earlier. Click Next.

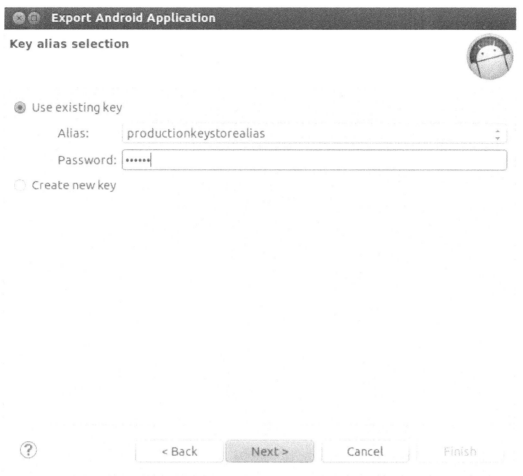

Figure 12.8: Select existing keystore

12. Click finish to generate the APK file again (figure 12.9) -

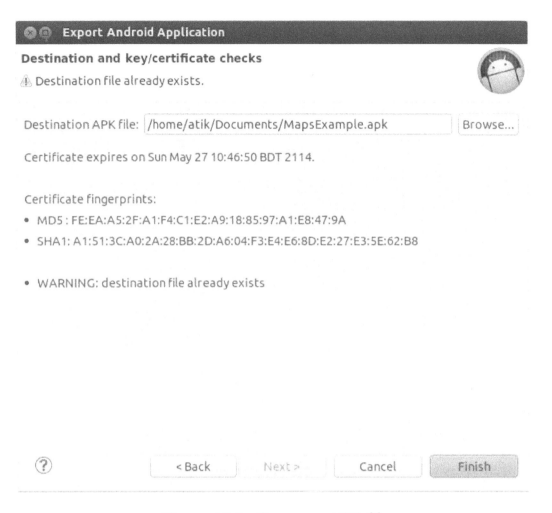

Figure 12.9: Generate APK file

Deploying APK Files

After we digitally sign our application with the production certificate, we are ready to distribute them to user devices. The following sections will describe various ways to deploy the application APK files. Publishing our application to Google Play store is the main distribution channel for Android application developers though there are other ways to distribute our applications.

Publishing on Google Play Store

Google Play Store (formerly known as Android Market) is the Google's official store and portal for digital distribution of Android applications. Applications submitted to Google Play Store are accessible by Android users through the Play Store application, which is pre-installed in most Android devices. This way, your application can reach millions of Android users all over the world. Google Play

520

Store offers you to distribute your apps as either free or paid application.

In this section, you will learn how to publish your Android application on the Google Play Store.

Creating a Developer Profile

To publish apps on Google Play, you must register for an account at -

http://play.google.com/apps/publish/signup/

Figure 12.10: Creating developer account

Once you sign-in with your Google account, you will need to accept the developer agreement. You will then need to pay a one-time registration fee of $25 and after making the payment, you will be able to complete your developer account registration.

Submitting Your Apps

After you have set up your developer account, you are ready to submit your application to Google Play. If you want to sell application, you will need to setup a Google Wallet Merchant Account which is available to Google Play developers in 32 countries. For more information regarding merchant account and to see if your country is in supported country list, visit the following link -

https://support.google.com/googleplay/android-developer/table/3539140?rd=1

Once you are logged in to the Google Play developer account, click "Add new application" option to submit a new application (figure 12.11), you will see a window similar to figure 12.12.

Figure 12.11: Add new application option

Figure 12.12: Upload new app

Fill in the Title field and then click "Upload APK" button. This will give you option to upload the APK file for your application (figure 12.13) -

Figure 12.13: Upload APK option

After you upload the APK for your application, from the left menu, click "Store Listing" option, which will let you add information about your application (figure 12.14) -

Figure 12.14: Store Listing

The store listing page requires you to fill informations like, app title, description, screenshots, app icons, app type, app category etc. You will need to provide at least two screenshots of your application. A high-resolution app icon (512 * 512 pixels) is also required. Optionally you could also add promotional graphics or promotional video.

You will also need to indicate whether your application employs copy protection and specify a content. You will need to provide your website URL and contact information (either email address or phone number, at least one is required).

Once you are done with the setup steps and have checked the two guidelines and agreements, click Publish to publish your application to Google Play.

Once that is done, your app will be available to the Play Store within a few hours. After your app is live, the developer console will provide some additional information regarding ratings and comments provided by the app users, any crash or bug reports, statistics about your app usage etc.

Good luck with your application!

Other Android App Marketplaces

Though Google Play is by far the most popular marketplace for Android application, still there are other marketplaces where you can submit your application -

Amazon Appstore – http://www.amazon.com/mobile-apps/b?node=2350149011
GetJar – http://www.getjar.com/
Moborobo – http://www.moborobo.com
SlideMe – http://www.slideme.org

Other App Distribution Methods

In addition to submitting your app to Google Play (or other marketplaces), you can alternatively distribute your app through other methods. Some of them are highlighted in this section. Methods listed in this section will expose your application to a minority of users, so you should consider Google Play and/or other app marketplaces as mentioned in previous sections.

Distribution Through Your Website

You can use your own website to distribute the application APK file by providing the application APK file as a downloadable item. A user can download the APK file and then copy that APK file to the SD card of their Android phone. Once the APK is copied to the SD card, user can install the application.

Distribution Through File Sharing Website

Instead of hosting the application APK file to your own website, you can use any file sharing website to host the APK file and share the link. User can download the APK file and copy that to the SD card of an Android phone and then install the application.

By default, installation of application from sources other than Google Play is disabled. You will need to go to application settings and find an option to accept installation of application from "Unknown sources". Simply check that item and you will be able to install an APK file from your SD card.

Summary

This chapter showed you what are the steps involved to prepare your application for distribution. We then learned how to create a developer account at Google Play and what are the steps to publish your application to Google Play. Finally, we have explored some other alternative methods for app distribution.

Author's Note

Hello and thank you for reading our book. We would love to get your feedback, learning what you liked and didn't for us to improve. Please feel free to email us at support@i-ducate.com

If you didn't like the book, please email us and let us know how we could improve it. This book can only get better thanks to readers like you.

If you like the book, I would appreciate if you could leave us a review too.

Thank you and all the best to your learning journey in Android programming.